OLD WINE
AND
FOOD STORIES

By

Daniel J. Demers

DEDICATION

This book is dedicated to my daughters

Shannon
Mary-Nora
Tara
Noelle

ACKNOWLEDGEMENTS

I want to acknowledge and thank Walter R. Thompson, Esq. for painstakingly proof reading this manuscript as it evolved. His detailed spelling, grammar and punctuation corrections are deeply appreciated. Likewise I'd like to thank Conway Burns and Joan Johnson who helped me format this book and handle the digital aspects of modern book publishing. Thanks are also due to Terry Milko, a good friend who supported and encouraged my writing efforts over the past decade. There are also a number of fellow writers who periodically took the time to listen, read and critique my stories as I developed them—Mike Tuggle, a recent Sonoma County Poet Laureate, journalist/writers Robert Feuer, Stephen Gross, Bob Jones, poet-writers Richard Fiorentino, Pat Nolan, Gregorio Pershon, Shashana Proctor, Oak Reinier, Dan Coshnear, and Scott Serkes. Sadly we lost our good friend Art Poulin just before publication. I also would like to acknowledge the assistance given me by the staff at the Library of Congress and the San Francisco Public Library, History Center. It goes without saying that this book would not have been possible without the loving support of my wife Christina Nichols.

INTRODUCTION

This book is comprised of ninety individual vignettes--the great majority of which have been gleaned from the Library of Congress' digital newspaper archives (ChroniclingAmerica. com). The site currently offers over eleven million American newspaper pages free on-line in digital format covering the period 1836 through 1922. The 1922 cut-off is due to current copyright laws.

All the stories have wine or food as a thematic nexus. Since wine and food are very popular subjects, I thought the stories I developed would be of interest to both audiences. In the vast majority of the stories presented, my work involved weaving several newspaper accounts on the same or similar subjects into the individual vignettes. Mine is a pioneering effort which chronicles the history of American social development as it was reported to the American public. Such an effort has become available because of modern digital technology.

The Library of Congress' digital archives offer a virtual treasure trove of original source material which mirrors America's cultural and economic growth and development. As is often said "fact is often stranger than fiction." Surfing the site reveals literally tens of millions of thought-provoking newspaper articles from yesteryear. It is helpful to remember that during the period covered America was primarily a rural-agrarian nation. The bulk of America's citizens lived on family owned farms. Chronologically one sees the gradual growth of our nation from a rural, farm-like civilization to the industrial revolution and growth of our cities.

During the period newspapers were the primary method by which information was transmitted to the American people. Radio, television and the internet simply were non-existent. By necessity local newspapers educated and informed the American public.

The vignettes presented run the gamut of human emotions. Some are humorous, some cute, some sad, some surprising, some ironic, some macabre and some evince the dark side of human nature. Many of the stories are simply amazing and long forgotten but...

Table of Contents

Napoleon and Patsy

Napoleon and Patsy, two bull snakes "fell from grace in a sad manner," claimed Petie Bigelow of the *San Francisco Examiner* in 1894. One era newspaper claimed Petie "was the best known newspaper man on the Pacific coast, and the most picturesque in five continents." Petie told the story about Napoleon and Patsy while "rusticating in New York." He was ducking a Fresno grand jury indictment for "accessory after the fact."

Petie had tracked down two train robbers in their mountain hideout and had "returned with a front page interview which was printed in the *Examiner*." The robbers were being chased by a posse with "Apache trailers, [who] could only get near enough to the robbers to get shot by them." When Petie refused to tell authorities the whereabouts of the hideout, he was indicted. The matter was dropped after the robbers were apprehended.

Napoleon and Patsy were owned by "an orchardist in the Sonoma Valley." They "had a wide reputation for the celerity [swiftness] and thoroughness with which they cleaned out the rats and mice of any ranch building they were put into." The snake's owner made "quite an income renting them out… to neighbors with vermin-infested barns."

Petie told a Napa County vintner about the snakes who had "an old wine cellar where mice and rats were so plentiful it was really discouraging, especially as his wines are very good and pleasant to sample." "Rats and mice" were not good company when wine tasting.

The vintner engaged the bull snakes, but ignoring the vermin, Napoleon and Patsy "took to drinking in a manner really shocking," claimed Petie.

The wines were transferred from one cask to another with siphoning hoses. This required "many open bungholes." The two six-foot long snakes created a dilemma for the winery. The "cellar men became nervous…[never knowing] whether the black thing hanging out of the bung was a section of hose or Patsy or Napoleon."

Unfortunately Petie gave it away when he claimed the curious thing about drunk snakes "instead of moving forward on its belly in a crooked line. It moves backward, on its back in a straight line." So the real question is—can snakes get drunk?

An 1888 article in the Abbeville, North Carolina *Press and Banner* recites a lecture by the Reverend Ben Deering who told an audience of a youthful experience working at a Kentucky distillery. Snakes were "often seen approach[ing] the premises [and] lapping up the liquor." Deering claimed the inebriated snakes, like their human counterparts, either sunned themselves to sleep it off or "sought the society of their companions." Suspecting the problem was bigger than a few snakes the employees "ripped up the [distillery's] floor and discovered a concentration of drunken moccasin snakes a foot or more thick." Would a man of God lie about such a thing?

Another era story claims British soldiers in India discovered a cobra in their camp. They placed out a pan of wine, which the cobra discovered. The snake, the article continued, became "mellow [and] sought out its mate…both were captured and sent to the British Museum in London."

The most bizarre story, though, was about James O'Grady of Syracuse, New York. The canal boat captain "complained of severe pains in his stomach and apparent writhing about of something with much life," a February 1891 article reported. O'Grady told reporters that he believed a snake was living in his stomach which "he swallowed while drinking from a brook" some years before. The snake he believed had bored its way into his lungs. He couldn't lie down to sleep because the snake "comes up and chokes him." Whenever O'Grady drank port wine the snake, "immediately appeared at his throat" and stuck its head out but had grown so big it couldn't be pulled out. Skeptical physicians experimented with wine to remove the snake "by means of O'Grady's throat." The physicians confirmed that O'Grady was close to death and planned a post mortem examination. The thirty-six year old O'Grady died in August of 1891. Mrs. O'Grady told the press "she would permit no post mortem examination." She claimed she saw the snake and had "tried to coax it out with some water and a glass of the wine." Jerome Clark in his book *Unexplained!* claims an autopsy was performed which found "nothing but intestinal gas." Clark also claims O'Grady died in November while era newspapers recorded his death three months earlier. Library of Congress archival research failed to find any newspaper mention of an autopsy.

A Risky Bisque or Gazpacho to Dispatch You

Jules Chanay, the head chef of Chicago's exclusive University Club became irritated when his assistant, Jean Crones failed to show for work. He called Crones' boarding house and was told that his assistant hadn't come home the previous evening.

Chanay was preparing a banquet for 300 of the city's social elite who were to converge that evening at the club to honor George Mundelein the newly appointed Catholic Archbishop. Chanay's dinner would be served to the presidents of three universities, "over forty executives of the nation's railroads and leaders of Chicago's great corporations" and scores of other dignitaries. The head table included the governor of Illinois and Chicago's mayor. Also in attendance were thirty Bishops from all over America who came to honor Mundelein.

Sunday, February 10, 1916 was a blustery Chicago winter day.

Unbeknownst to Chanay, the previous afternoon, before he disappeared, Crones surreptitiously poured several vials of arsenic into 50 gallons of chicken, spices and water in several copper pots, which he was reducing into 20 gallons of bouillon—the second course of the four-course dinner. The soup would follow *petit* appetizers of oysters and caviar.

Chicago authorities inspect poison vials

An agitated Chef Chanay directed another kitchen worker to mix Crones' bouillon with other ingredients into a gourmet soup.

Once finished, it was ladled into fine porcelain bowls. As busboys removed appetizer plates, uniformed waiters carefully placed the bowls of soup before the guests. Steward's re-filled wine glasses as the patrons started their second course.

As the guests finished their soup, busboys collected their bowls while waiters began serving the fish *entrée*. The result of the soup course, though, was predictable. Slowly the tuxedo-clad men and cassocked prelates began to rise and head to the bathrooms. The trickle turned to a mob as guest after guest-sought sanctuary in the nearest restroom. The first victim, Thomas O'Shaughnessy said: "I thought it was bad ventilation and went out on the fire escape. I became dizzy, went inside, and started downstairs. In one of the lower halls, I became deadly sick. An attendant found me and called a physician who administered an emetic and had me sent to the hospital." One hundred of the three hundred guests got violently sick.

Confronted with a public relations disaster of the worst sort, the University Club's manager, H. J. Doherty fearing food poisoning alleged that Crones had been solely responsible for rendering and preparing the chicken bouillon. Doherty "visited Crones' rented room and "was astounded at what he saw"—a virtual chemistry laboratory. "There were numerous bottles and many contained poisons," he said. He also discovered that Crones was taking mail-order chemistry courses. Additionally there were volumes of anarchist literature. Another surprise, Jean Crones was an alias—his real name was Nester Dondoglio—an anarchist.

The Chicago Police called in federal investigators. They found "rows of bottles and vials containing various poisons along with retorts and test tubes and gas plates for carrying out tests." One can of gun cotton was so saturated that it could blow up the whole house.

Fortunately the 30-year-old chemistry student had bollixed his brew. Investigators said "the plotter erred in his dose." According to chemists engaged by the police, "there was enough arsenic in the 20 gallons of rendered bouillon to end the lives of 296 persons; but, once diluted into a soup the poison was distributed throughout a [bigger volume] of soup." This lowered the dosage which "failed to result fatally for anybody, and some of those present undoubtedly were able to throw off the effects of the arsenic."

Fortunately no one died. "Archbishop Mundelein had not touched his soup (or much else of his dinner) and was unaffected." Nor was Illinois Governor Ed Dunne who was sitting next to the Archbishop. It was later suggested that another kitchen worker may have inadvertently saved the guests when he diluted the poisoned soup even further "when he detected an unpleasant taste in it."

Crones was traced to New York, where he began telephoning and writing taunting messages to the press correcting newspaper accounts. In response to the allegation of the saturated gun cotton, Crones wrote, "The stupid Chicago Police. The gun cotton is nothing more than asbestos sheets" used to surround several bottles of acid in a package. In another, he "defied the police to catch him." He was indicted *in absentia* but was never caught.

Mundelein downplayed the poison banquet, referring to the incident "as the work of a crank or mentally unbalanced man."

"Oh, What a Tangled Web
We Weave..."

"This is my spider school," said the young woman in a 1905 interview. She demonstrated by brushing a few webs from the wall. She had a dozen rows of wine bottles upon which she was training spiders to spin their webs. "I train the spiders to weave on bottles only—I tear down webs woven anywhere else—and it is amazing how quickly these well-schooled pupils of mine will cover a case of port or claret with cobwebs." She sold the spiders to unscrupulous wine merchants to aid them in aging cheap wine. "Six spiders a week will add two years to the aspect of a dozen bottles of wine," she reported. Besides selling her webs to crooked wine merchants she also had a lively trade with surgeons who used them to stop hemorrhages and "the makers of certain astronomical instruments—instruments so "delicate [that] a human hair would not take their place because a hair is neither fine enough nor durable enough."

Stories about wine swindlers using spider webs to give the appearance of age to wine bottles first started appearing in the nation's press in 1895. A *New York World* story first disclosed the practice which it claimed was being carried on by "a Frenchman" in New Jersey. He was reported to be selling his spiders for 50¢ apiece "to dealers in old wines and brandies…to give [their bottles] an ancient appearance." The merchants also affixed "old musty labels marked vintage of 1800, or 1820, or 1830." These bottles would then be sold to the unsuspecting buyer for $5 a bottle [$170 in current values]. One commentator called the practice "a novel enterprise."

The same year a *Philadelphia Times* article described Pierre Grantaire's Philadelphia "money making industry." His spider webs were sold "to the wine vaults of merchants and the *nouveaux riches*." His trade was chiefly with the wholesale wine merchants who were able to "stock a cellar with new, shining, freshly labeled bottles, and in three months see them veiled with filmy cobwebs , so that the effect of twenty years of storage is secured at a small cost." The swindler

18

delighted in showing his customers wines in bins covered with dust "with cobwebs spun from cork to cork, and that drape the neck like delicate lace, the seal of years of slow mellowing."

Grantaire's spider-growing facility was described as a house "covered with wire squares from six inches to a foot across and behind the screen the walls are covered with rough planking." The planking is dotted with knot holes and splintered crevices upon which crawled his spiders. The species used by the entrepreneur were Epeira Vulgaris [Gray Cross spider] and Nephila Plumipes [silk spider] which weaved "fine, large open lines and circles—they are the only lines that look artistic in the wine cellar or on the bottle," Grantaire claimed. The spiders were sold in mating pairs of two in small paper boxes "with many holes for the ingress of air" at ten dollars per hundred pairs. The *Times* concluded that for "forty or fifty dollars the spiders dressed" the wine merchant's bottles allowing the merchant to sell his stock "for a thousand or more dollars above what he could have obtained for it before the spiders."

An 1896 article in the *Washington Morning Times* society section described the wine cellars of some of America's richest men. The article disclosed that spider webs were being used by the wealthy as a kind of cosmetic brush-up. The financier George Gould had a claret vintage dating to 1791 while Comstock Lode magnate John Mackay "pressed" his own Chateau wines which were "put away to become famous wine twenty years later" which he sent as Christmas gifts. Railroad tycoon Collis P. Huntington had some 1801 brandies and twenty-five year old red Chateaus. "Good wine is like a diamond," the *Morning Times* reported. The reporter cautioned the reader that "the presence of cobwebs upon a bottle is not a guarantee of age." He noted that "at a pinch a host who wants to put on much assumption of style will set a wine bottle in a wooden arbor, where spiders are thick and allow them to spin a web over the bottle in a night." He continued "Spider webs are prized, but for another reason…the master of the house" picks up his bottles from the wine cellar "as gently as though they were eggs, and places them side by side, without removing the dust or the webs." At the table the butler "lifts the bottle tenderly, dusts it off gingerly, and pulls the cork" thus demonstrating to the guests the age authenticity of the wine or champagne being served.

A Glass of Wine With Daniel Webster

In the summer of 1851 Tom Booster was an inspector for the U. S. Custom House in Boston. He took a summer vacation to Cape Cod with a fishing rod and fowling piece [shotgun] to make "sorties upon fish and fowl, as his fancy dictated." About a mile from Daniel Webster's Marshfield estate, he "landed a beautiful trout." Farther along the brook widened and deepened. Looking for a convenient spot to ford, he spotted "a strongly built, heavy-framed man...[wearing] high topped rubber boots...[with] a fishing pole in his hand and a hook" in the water.

Booster shouted across the stream, proposing that the man carry him across in exchange for 25¢. The "light and nimble" Booster climbed upon the stranger's shoulders and was carried across the water. He paid the fee and got an added bonus when the man showed him a good spot to cast his hook.

Daniel Webster

Two nights later, Booster was invited to a local shindig with a "gathering of noble people," including renowned statesman and then Secretary of State Daniel Webster. When introduced to Webster he "gasped... [seeing] before him...the man he had hired." Webster laughed and the two enjoyed a glass of wine together.

Stories about Webster's affinity for drink are abundant. He loved to lavishly entertain friends with dinner parties and fishing excursions. Doing his own shopping "he always selected the best...and dinner at Webster's house meant good solid food...and the best wines," recalled "old" Judge Snell, a Washington D.C. police judge, in an 1887 interview.

Webster was what we would call today a functional drunk. James Kent, a contemporary of Webster's who had him to dinner in 1840 critically wrote: "He is 57 years old …he ate but little, and drank wine freely," recounts historian Robert Remini. Remini continues "Webster loved to imbibe…many observers commented on his drinking habits…he had acquired the rare ability to appear sober even after a long night of imbibing."

Professor Merrill Peterson recounts how Webster "fell into the arms of the mayor [of Rochester] after offering a toast… [and then] spoke superbly for two hours." Peterson concludes that "his drinking habits did not significantly impair his mental powers or his functioning in public office." He offers several examples, one being at Boston's Union Oyster House where "Webster was a constant customer. He drank a tall tumbler of brandy with each half dozen oysters and seldom had less than six plates." On another occasion, according to an 1868 *Sacramento Daily Union* article, Webster attended a concert by famed opera singer Jenny Lind, popularly dubbed the "Swedish Nightingale." He arrived after enjoying "a good dinner and choice wines." When Lind sang *Hail Columbia*, the inebriated Webster rose and "added his deep, sonorous voice to the chorus," —all the while "Mrs. Webster kept tugging at his coat-tail to make him sit down and stop singing." Regardless "Jenny Lind's tenor and Daniel Webster's bass received a thunderous applause." He bowed graciously to Lind and she "curtsied to the floor" and the house applauded again. The duo repeated their dramatic overtures to one another nine times.

A 1930 *Milwaukee Journal* article recites a local attorney who attempted to debunk the numerous stories about Webster's alcoholism. The attorney repeats many humorous allegations such as a story about Webster attending a temperance banquet "with two bottles of Madeira under his buff waistcoat [while] applauding every [temperance] reference by the clergy…"

As further clarification of his affection for liquor, in 1865 thirteen years after his death his wine collection was put up for auction. It consisted of "upwards of 500 bottles [and] were sold in packages by the bottle at high rates." They had been in the hands of the trustees of his will and the proceeds were "for the benefit of his son Ashburton Webster."

Webster died in 1852 from complications of cirrhosis of the liver after a fall from a horse. He was seventy years old. At the time the average life expectancy was 45.

Whether his drinking was exaggerated or not is moot. Webster is considered the greatest Senatorial orator of all time. Besides enjoying liquor Daniel Webster was a constitutional lawyer who argued over 220 cases before the Supreme Court—several of them precedent setting. Additionally he served twenty-seven years combined in the House of Representatives and U. S. Senate, as well as serving twice as U.S. Secretary of State under two different presidents (Tyler and Fillmore). He also ran three times for the presidency and was offered the Vice Presidency twice (William Henry Harrison and Zachary Taylor) which he declined. In a cruel irony both Harrison and Taylor died in office and Webster would have acceded to the presidency.

The Chicken and the Egg and a Good Yoke too!

Sometimes reality is much funnier than the greatest figments of our imagination.

In August of 1919 World War I had been over for less than a year. As part of American demobilization, numerous military bases were closed and vast numbers of pilots and support personnel of the Army Air Service were discharged. With ever-

Hap Arnold

shrinking military budgets, the competing branches within the Army successfully fought off increased expenditures for the military air service effectively shrinking it to near extinction.

The Army Air Service spread its meager personnel and resources around the country. Major Edward "Hap" Arnold was sent to San Francisco as the Commanding Officer of Crissy Field located at the Presidio. In this position he was in charge of "Army flying on the West Coast." His assistant was Major Carl "Tooey" Spaatz. The two "joined forces to keep military aviation in the public eye." They were assisted in their endeavors by General Hunter Liggett who had commanded the American First Army in France and was now Commanding General at the Presidio. Liggett was one of the Army's few ground officers who appreciated and understood the importance of military aviation.

At the time Petaluma, California boasted that it was the chicken and egg capitol of the world—producing 20,000,000 eggs a year and 400,000 fryer chickens per month. The city lay a mere thirty miles from San Francisco but was accessible only by boat since no bridges yet spanned San Francisco Bay. The small rural community provided San Francisco with the vast majority of its culinary fryer chickens and eggs.

As a part of their public relations campaign Arnold and Spaatz, in conjunction with the *San Francisco Bulletin,* decided to fly to Petaluma during that city's annual Butter and Egg Day Celebration. Spaatz talked a local celebrity chef, Victor Hirtzler, into flying with him to Petaluma to pick up a prize White Leghorn layer hen. The hen in turn was expected to lay an egg which would be cooked by the chef as

After graduating from West Point, Spaatz served with the Infantry in Hawaii. Then he reported for flight training at San Diego, where he posed with this Martin trainer aircraft.

the plane winged its way back across San Francisco Bay.

The *Bulletin* reported "just as the plane reached an altitude of 5,000 feet the hen cackled and laid an egg." The article continued, "a second afterwards [Chef] Victor [Hirtzler] had the newly laid egg cooking on an electric stove attached to the ignition system of the airplane. Swooping out of the clouds and cleaving the fog, the chef handed the fried egg to San Francisco's Mayor "Sunny Jim" Rolph." The mayor laughed, telling the crowd assembled at the air field, "I'll show you fellows what a good two-handed eater I am." He devoured "the delectable aerial dish" in seconds. "It was," reported the *Petaluma Daily Courier* "the first fried egg *a la* airplane."

One newspaper reported that the hen got nervous and flew out of the cockpit over San Quentin where it safely landed.

All of that was the official story dished up to the reading public. The historian DeWitt S. Copp gives us a completely different version. According to Copp, Hirtzler indeed took with him an electric frying pan to prepare the egg. Hirtzler, who was known for his thick French accent, goatee, curled handlebar mustache, showy costumes and always-present red *fez*, freaked out when he saw the open cockpit of the primitive de Havilland DH-4. Wrote Copp, "It took all of Hap Arnold's power of persuasion" to induce the chef to climb aboard. The hen, as dismayed as Hirtzler, did indeed "flap its way out of the cockpit" on the trip back to San Francisco and "when last seen was spiraling down into the Bay." The plane was traveling at a speed of 130 miles per hour. The prize hen never landed safely at San Quentin as reported—farmyard chickens have their wings clipped to prevent them from flying. The poor bird plummeted 5,000 feet to its watery grave. During its brief stay aboard the plane, the hen never did lay an egg and even if it had, to Hirtzler and Spaatz's dismay, there actually was no receptacle in the DH-4 into which the electric frying pan could be plugged. The normally exuberant chef, upon landing, was reported to have been "both crushed and shaken." Quickly regaining his composure though, he had a substitute egg surreptitiously cooked in his St. Francis Hotel kitchen. Even Mayor Rolph was a last minute substitute. The original recipient was supposed to be Admiral Hugh Rodman, the Pacific Fleet Commander. The fleet which was in route to San Francisco for Fleet Week was delayed by adverse weather conditions.

Despite the hilarious skein of blunders, the story was a first-rate public relations success for Arnold and Spaatz who both went on to long and distinguished military careers. Arnold would become the Commanding General of the Army Air Force during World War II while General Carl "Tooey" Spaatz would become the first Chief of Staff of the United States Air Force. History would be kind to Victor Hirtzler too, remembering him as the inventor of the Crab Louie.

Birds Do It, Bees Do It

In 1904 an article appeared about Ceylon (now Sri Lanka) natives who made wine from palm tree sap which drained into containers and fermented. Native parrots had "discovered this sap tastes good…and are frequently found drunk near the trees."

In 1912 Mrs. Andrew Welch, a San Francisco socialite, held a dinner for some of her uppity friends. The table was set with figures of lions, tigers, giraffes and elephants peering from a thicket. Live frogs, lizards, crabs, ducks, parrots and canaries "abounded" around the dinner table. The guests amused themselves by feeding champagne-soaked bread to the parrots, making them drunk. One parrot cheered "vociferously saying 'have a good time, have a good time but be home by 3!' …the other which was of the exaggerated profane type, consigned everyone to perdition in its swearing and shrieking."

During the nineteenth and twentieth centuries a number of articles expounded on the drunken bird phenomenon. A *New York Herald* article notes that "chickens and ducks after once tasted brandy, become absolute slaves [to it]…refuse to eat, grow thin, and exhibit symptoms of dejection when unable to obtain their favorite tipple." Birds routinely get drunk when eating overripe, spoiling berries and fruits which ferment as they spoil. The *Times* article claims the parrot "takes first place [among birds] as a habitual topper." They are most like humans, because they can talk, and "get louder and more boisterous the drunker they get." In 1913 Philadelphian John Maier's pet parrot was trained to say, "John, you're drunk again." John really was drunk one night when he "reached out, grabbed Polly and wrung her neck." John's wife had him arrested and a judge "sent him to jail for three months."

In 1918 twenty-five residents of Mattoon, Illinois brought suit against the city "for the alleged acts of a swarm of drunken bees made so through the carelessness of the police department." It was the eve of Prohibition and the local police raided "a number of illegal establishments… [and] confiscated a large quantity of liquor." They emptied the liquor into a sewage pipe at the rear of the building—the same place were William Welsh's bees watered themselves daily. "On the day the whiskey was emptied into the sewer, the bees made their customary trip to their waterhole." On their return to their hives at Welsh's yard, "an uprising such as never before occurred among the honey makers took place." A number of prominent citizens and a patrolman "were stung so severely" that some required hospitalization. Welsh claimed his bees "got crazy drunk."

A rather amusing story about a wily bear in Pikes County, Pennsylvania made the rounds in 1900. Uncle Jabez was "a bunged up man...his neck was scratched, his arm was in a sling, and all over his face and hands" were bee sting. A bear had killed three of his prize pigs and stole "some honey" from his bee hives. His dogs initially lost the trail but the following day he and his dogs started the hunt anew. They found his scent, but the wily bear "made tracks for a hole where a mother wildcat with her kittens lived." The wildcat, thinking her kittens in danger, attacked the dogs. Uncle Jabez, trying to save his dogs, got severely scratched and bitten on his arm. Confounded, he "kept thinking about the weaknesses of bears" when it occurred to him that "bears are as fond of honey as men are with Liquor." He soaked a "big lump of honey" in applejack in his barn—figuring to get the bear drunk "and avenge his numerous injuries." The following morning he heard a commotion and loaded his gun. Entering his barn he found his "hives overturned and all my good honey gone and...floor littered with bees." Looking at the applejack honey he saw bees "sticking" to it. His bees had been attracted to the applejack honey, got drunk and fell to the floor. "The scrupulous old bear...overturned the hives and gorged himself." The distraught farmer tried to "rouse the bees" by throwing water on them. The bees "got more and more awake...the livelier they got the madder they got...the whole swarm settled down to the job of making me unhappy" stinging him more than fifty times. When everything had calmed down, Uncle Jabez said he saw "that old bear...on his haunches...hugging himself with his front paws and chuckling to himself at the fix I was in" in a nearby clearing.

The Tipsy Butterfly

"The idea of a butterfly getting drunk...will not be welcomed by the poets with whom [the butterfly] has always been a favorite" alleged an 1898 article in the *Lafayette Gazette*. The article described the observations and experiments by Professor J. W. Tutt in his paper published by the South London Entomological Society. Tutt "shut up 12 males and as many females" in a greenhouse to observe the butterflies. He noted they spent upwards of an hour drinking muddy water. Tutt then isolated a male and female butterfly with flowers of "diverse species." He observed females quenched their thirst modestly "by sipping a few drops of dew in the calyx of a rose." They were he claimed "remarkable for perfect sobriety." The males on the other hand "indulged in characteristic intemperance [going] straight to the flowers whose distillation produced the most alcohol till they fell senseless where they stood."

Tutt observed that butterflies enjoyed "the vilest, foulest puddles to quench their thirst...and [even fed on] a cat five or six days dead." Collectors, it was revealed "entrap them by means of stale beer mixed with molasses" which they smear on trees. The "respectable" butterflies "get hopelessly drunk...and [collectors] crammed [them] in big handfuls into their collectors pouch" wrote Tutt. Further confirming his findings, Tutt put a glass of water and several glasses of brandy in the case in which he held the two butterflies. "Without hesitation [the male] chose the brandy" while the females alighted on the water glasses.

Tutt's observation wasn't something that was really new. Experienced butterfly hunters were well aware "beautiful butterflies subsist upon spoiled fruit...fresh fruit they won't look at...it must be falling to pieces with rottenness," claimed an article in *The Newport News Daily Press*.

The same year of Tutt's report, Dr. A. J. Weir observed butterflies alighting "on certain flowering plants...drink heartily from the calyxes of the blossoms, fall prostrate to the ground and after a while rise into the air and fly around like mad, just like drunken men would do if they could fly." Weir did not differentiate between male or female butterflies. In a kind of 19th century Timothy Leary experiment, Weir collected a half a teaspoon of the pollen from the plants. He swallowed the pollen "and after fifteen minutes [he related]…his pulse beat faster" along with a slight elevation of his body temperature. Later he gathered several of the blossoms, "distilled them in water" and injected himself with a hypodermic needle in his left arm. He found that "almost immediately his pulse accelerated and after a half hour he felt decidedly dizzy."

In 2013 Inga Piegsa-Quischotte visited the indoor Butterfly Garden of St. Thomas, U. S. Virgin Islands to "see the stages [egg-caterpillar-chrysalis-butterfly] and admire more than 1,000 species from all over the world." She learned that females mate only once, lay about 300 eggs and die. Males, on the other hand, can mate "many, many times," she reports. "After having done their duty, the males need to recover and do so by getting drunk, at the butterfly bar." She observed that the garden managers laid out "many sets of dishes filled with water, bright flowers and rotting pieces of banana which the male butterflies gobble up…and then start all over again."

Mathias Mugisha observed butterflies in their natural habitat at Lake Victoria and Mabira forest in Uganda which hosts 75% of all African varieties. He noted "some butterflies are natural drunkards." He watched certain species "take too much, get drunk and fail to fly and become vulnerable to predators." Many varieties are poisonous, while others produce repulsive chemicals that keep predators at bay." Still Mugisha reveals that the butterflies "with their dazzling dance…swaggering grace and jerky flight…have many natural enemies" even though poisonous. They are preyed upon by birds, reptiles and spiders while their eggs are eaten by beetles and birds—some birds crave their larvae.

Many studies suggest that adult butterflies live only a week or two. A nationwide project known as Butterflies and Moths of North America (BOMA) suggests a much longer lifespan for some species.

Total lifespan includes larval, pupal and adult stages. The project concludes that some species may live as long as eight to nine months depending on "annual flights" or migrations such as with the monarch species. The project concludes that of the species in the wild "only a minute fraction of larvae survive to adulthood." In direct contradiction to its human counterpart, the longer a male butterfly lives the more often he can and does get drunk, and the drunkenness appears to have no bearing on the insect's lifespan.

Lobster, Crab, Wine and Beer

John Reed filed a $10,000 dollar lawsuit against Alfred Jensen for stealing his wife Leone's affection. According to the 1913 complaint, "Alfred Jensen...insinuatingly introduced first the lobster and then crab and the bottle of beer [and wine]...and...adroitly introduced himself into Mrs. [Leone] Reed's life and incidentally into his own." The Reeds had been married for five years at the time of the lawsuit which alleged the "acts complained of" had occurred in December of 1911 and January and February of 1912.

During courtroom testimony, Reed's "misfortune to be employed at night" was highlighted. His night watchman job facilitated his wife and Alfred's amorous get-togethers. Miss Jessie Young, the Reeds' nanny, testified that Jensen "lavished presents upon Mrs. Reed and ...escorted her to the theatre and parties" after which "it was his custom to return to the Reed home for a midnight lunch." The presents included lobsters, crabs, beer, wine, and "a lavish Kimono." Leone Reed, in turn, "baked pies and cakes...and took them to Jensen's home."

Miss Young asserted that Jensen's courtship was "ardent and persistent" and that he "devoted time to the pursuit...of his love almost every day." Inevitably, Young saw Mrs. Reed "reciprocate by crossing the street to the Jensen house." Jensen was a widower with children. The Reeds had three children of their own. Young was sometimes asked to babysit his children at the Reeds' house so that Jensen and Mrs. Reed could be alone at his residence. In one instance she saw "Mrs. Reed, clad in a nightgown and kimono with a cloak for cover, steal out of the house after she had pretended to go to bed." Young also testified that she heard Mrs. Reed refer to Alfred as a "'dear man,' 'a rich guy,' and a 'good fellow.'"

Court testimony also uncovered that the Mormon Church became involved when Jensen, a Mormon, instigated a meeting between himself and Mr. and Mrs. Reed, the local Mormon bishop and other parishioners to address rumors within the Mormon community. At the meeting Reed accused Jensen of kissing his wife which Jensen denied. Mrs. Reed exclaimed "Oh yes you did, Alf! Don't you remember?" Reed also accused Jensen of putting his arm around Mrs. Reed to which Jensen said "I'll have the right to that someday."

Next door neighbors testified that almost "every night during last January, while Reed was at work, they heard loud laughter…emanating from the Reed home." Reed took the stand and said he became familiar with Jensen in 1911 when he "purchased a pig from him…[and]…when the pig grew up Jensen killed the pig as an accommodation." It was the pig killing incident which "gave rise to the friendship [by which] Jensen [stole] the affections of Mrs. Reed."

In February of 1913, the jury awarded George Reed $887 [$21,226 in current values]. It was the first case in the history of the State of Utah "where a jury actually placed a cash value on the affections of a woman." The jury had pondered for "many hours" and reported to the judge "that a verdict was improbable." The judge instructed them to "ponder a little while longer over the matter, which bore fruit at noon when the verdict was returned." Jensen's lawyers announced they would appeal the verdict.

The following month, Jensen's lawyers asked that the verdict be vacated and a new trial be set because the jurors had awarded the sum by "chance." Juror affidavits confirmed that five jurors sought to give Reed varying amount of damages while three favored acquittal. The jurors agreed to add the various amounts by the "guilty leaning" jurors and divided that number by the eight jurors which amounted to the $887—"a chance verdict." The judge set aside the verdict and ordered a new trial.

In May of 1913, Reed's alienation suit was dismissed when the parties reached an out of court settlement. The previous week Reed had been granted a divorce against his wife on the grounds of desertion. Leone Reed was granted custody of the couple's three children "with the understanding that John could "visit them at his pleasure." Research failed to disclose whatever happened to the scandalous romance between Alfred and Leone after the divorce, or whether he then felt the necessity to ply her again with lobsters, crab, beer and wine.

Drunk Fish

"Did you ever see a drunken fish?," a Sonoma County "wine grower" asked a group of San Francisco city slickers in 1896. One of them mockingly asked the country bumpkin farmer: "I suppose you are going to tell us about a drunken catfish staggering down through the orchard and catching a bird?"

Ignoring the insult, the farmer explained that his winery was alongside a creek and in the summer the water stands in pools full of trout, suckers and pike. "The other day a big vat of sour claret burst and... ran down into one of the pools," the farmer continued. He noticed a half hour later the pool "was crowded with fish floating belly up." Thinking they were dead, he pulled "a big pike out" and noticed it "wiggled and flopped around just like an old drunk trying to get up without anything to hold onto." He threw it back and noticed, "as the wine cleared up, one-by one the fish disappeared [into the depths of the pool] as they sobered up."

Was it just a fish story?

Further research clarified the Sonoma County incident was not an isolated one at all.

A 1904 *Washington Evening Star* article described a brewery in Trenton, NJ which regularly dumped beer refuse when cleaning its vats into an adjacent stream. "When the foaming malt pours forth...the Pickerel, eels, perch and catfish mingle in the festivities, and the meaning of the old saying, "He drinks like a fish," became evident. The fish, the *Star* reported "leap out of the water, and throw themselves high and dry at the water's edge." Comparing the scene to a crowded saloon, the article declared that when "[the] less bibulous fish starts to leave, with the idea that there will be trouble in the family if he stays longer, his companions...coax him back for "just one more."" As the fish got more plastered they drifted "slowly down the

35

river" oblivious to locals who waded in and "picked up the "plain drunks" in baskets."   Shortly "they are sizzling over a kitchen fire, victims of their own conviviality," the article continued.   The story concluded with a kind of "happy hour" depiction alleging "the fish come down stream in schools [in anticipation] of the weekly vat cleaning...patiently" waiting for the dumping to begin.   Was it a Pavlovian response or just plain jonesing?

A 1906 newspaper article reported that farmers along Benson Creek near Frankfort, Kentucky "have been catching with their hands thousands of fish rendered *hors de combat*" when a tank with 13,000 gallons of whiskey burst "into the stream...and the fish were made drunk."   The report continued, "fish in droves came to the surface of the water, sported around and cut the most fantastic capers...they seemed to be three sheets to the wind."

In 1913 two thousand barrels of beer were "turned into the Mississinewa River near Marion, Indiana" by order of United States revenue officers.   A crowd on a nearby bridge "laughed and shrieked" watching thousands of fish "disporting themselves in an extreme unfishlike way, leaping all manner of newfangled summersaults and flopping against each other in frenzied bunches."   *The Rockland Argus* reported "multitudes [of locals] are feasting on drunken fish hauled in by the bushel basketful" from the fish fest.

An inebriated visitor to Springville, Alabama was arrested and fined $5 in 1917.   A small cement-lined fish pond contained thousands of carp and was a local showcase. The fish were "quite tame and gather in ravenous, squirming masses whenever anyone feeds them," the *Hopkinson Kentuckian* reported.   The visitor decided to share his bottle of hooch and poured a quart into the pond. He told the newspaper "the sight of the fish while under the influence of liquor was worth the [fine]."

Even modern scientists have gotten into the act.   In 2014, researchers at the New York University Polytechnic School of

Engineering published the results of their experiment in *Alcohol: Clinical and Experimental Research.* The researchers exposed a single zebra fish to four different concentrations of ethanol in water. When left alone, the alcohol seemed to have no effect on the fish but when placed into a tank with other zebra fish, the cock-eyed fish "doubled its swimming speed." The team concluded "the presence of peers had a substantial impact on social behavior." Basically the besotted fish, like its human counterparts became a "show off" with its alcohol induced false sense of bravado.

Wine Confessions

In 1854 a kind of 'Amazing Grace' forgiveness story surfaced in the world's press about a London wine dealer who was on his death bed. The story, written by a "prohibitionist," relayed the unnamed wretch of a dealer's "distress of mind and agony." His torment was related to his decade-long practice of purchasing "all the sour wines he could...and by making use of sugar of lead and other deleterious substance, restored the wine to a palatable taste." The dealer dreaded his upcoming meeting with his Maker because "he had been the means of destroying hundreds of lives, as he had from time to time noted the injurious effects of his mixtures on those who drank them." He told friends he had witnessed hundreds of his victims "wasting and declining for years [who then] went to their graves...poisoned by the adulterated wines he had sold them."

The article editorialized that he would die rich "but alas, what legacy did he leave for his children! Wealth begotten by deceit, and that not of a harmless, but fatal nature."

Temperance leaders jumped on the story, demanding "wine fabricators" who dealt in "intoxicating poisons" quit dealing in such adulterated demon alcohol: "You all know [you] are poisoning and demoralizing all who drink them." Their plea had little effect on the numerous unscrupulous wine merchants and dealers who practiced innumerable dishonest deeds in marketing wines from adulterating liquors to mislabeling. Fixing the system would be left to government regulation which would gradually occur, beginning in the early twentieth century, with enactment of the Pure Food and Drug law (1906).

In March of 1885 Joseph Miller confessed that he "had a good time smoking [stolen] cigars and drinking [stolen] wine while they lasted." By way of explanation, a Patterson, Michigan warehouse had been "forcibly entered" three times by Miller. On his last burglary he left tracks in the snow which "led to the identification of the perpetrator"—Miller's residence. The Sheriff found a "piece of pork weighing seven or eight pounds," which Miller claimed to have purchased at a local store. Upon further investigation, the Sheriff found that the piece of pork purchased by Miller at the store was "of much less weight than the one found." Deputies returned to Miller's house and conducted another search which yielded two more pieces of pork "hid under a wash stand," a package of coffee and tea in a bag of carpet rags. The "clear evidence of guilt caused Miller to wilt" and he confessed to all three burglaries. Besides accounting for the stolen wine and cigars, Miller showed deputies where he had buried "the balance of the pork, caddy of tobacco and keg of syrup" near his water well.

Miller was arrested and jailed "with good prospects of serving [time in] the state prison." A surprised Miller told authorities that after turning over the stolen goods "he thought he would be allowed to go." He claimed he only took them because he was "hard up." He blamed the local marshal who happened to walk by the warehouse the first time he burglarized it and failed to notice him. Miller lamented that if only the marshal had seen him he would "have been caught in the act of breaking into the warehouse" the first time.

In the summer of 1922 Thomas Cushing "had been drinking wine" at his Morris, Illinois home. His nineteen year old wife chastised him for drinking which was, according to her, "something new for you" and forbade him to do it again. Cushing then "took a curtain stick of oak. It was two feet long and about two inches thick," he explained. "I wasn't mad. I was crazy and didn't know what I was doing. I hit her over the head two or three times." She fell against the door. Holding her head she told him "I forgive you Tom because you drank that [wine]. You are out of your mind." She then fell to the floor and "blood flowed and the sight of the blood frightened him." There was a can of gasoline and he "upset it…the gasoline went all over the floor" where his wife was laying. He struck a match and "threw it on the gasoline. The flames went all over." He went outside and called his neighbor. "I didn't know she was hurt bad." His wife died in the local hospital. Cushing was convicted of second degree murder.

Earthquake Wine

After the shaking had ended, a fire erupted that literally sent half of San Francisco up in smoke. 28,000 buildings were destroyed, 3,000 lives lost, 500 looters shot and two-third of the city's 410,000 population left homeless before the fire was extinguished four days later. Jack London, who was an eyewitness to the disaster wrote, "San Francisco is gone…nothing remains of it but memories…" Behind the disaster, though, there seems to have been a bit of a silver cloud for wine connoisseurs.

According to an August 25, 1906 article in the *Spokane Press,* when the fire reached "the vaults of the California Wine Association, the storehouse of the wine product of the entire state [of California], it ate away the cooperage of the great 80,000 gallon casks of sherry…stored in the upper part of the building." The burnt and weakened casks gave way and the sherry "fell through and submerged [a] half million bottles of wine [and champagne] lying in the recesses of the cellar." The heat from the fire boiled the sherry. The boiling continued "For two days and nights." Once the fire subsided and the "immense volume of wine had cooled, it was pumped out into the street"—a devastating economic loss.

It was then discovered that of the 500,000 bottles "which had been immersed for so long in the boiling sherry" about 50,000 had survived intact. Upon further investigation a "marvelous bouquet of the contents was discovered." It was estimated at the time "the process by which the wine was perfected" cost over $1,000 per bottle. The 50,000 bottles, it was believed, were worth $1,000 each [at today's value a staggering $141 million]. According to National Public Radio's Renee Montague, there would be more wine destroyed during the disaster when residents of the Telegraph Hill neighborhood "banded together…with barrels of wine that the Italians were fermenting in their basements [and] poured [it] on the fires that swept…up the hill…wine was even used to soak burlap sacks to cool down the roofs of houses." The wine saved the neighborhood.

The earthquake had an additional benefit—at least to Southern California wine interests. There had been a wine war between Northern and Southern California wine interests for several years. The result was that Southern California wine makers had "not made any money for several seasons" but now saw a chance to benefit from the earthquake's aftermath. Press reports revealed that two-thirds of California's entire wine production had been destroyed "in the conflagration." The "ruination of cellars and cooperage," it was predicted, would "have the inevitable result of enhancing the value of wines held outside San Francisco." The beneficiaries of San Francisco's misery would be the Southern California wine interests who had "large stocks on hand..." Southern California sweet wines had

still standing

been selling for 25¢ "a gallon naked—that is, not counting cooperage." The newspaper account reported "because of the destruction of millions of gallons of wine [in San Francisco]...the price is expected now to double."

One additional outcome of the earthquakes aftermath was a number of court cases waged by the California Wine Association against insurance companies which sought to avoid paying claims because the disaster was caused by an earthquake—an exclusion in virtually every insurance policy. The Association asserted the fire damage to its warehouse and inventory was caused by firefighters or vandals and not by the earthquake. Ultimately the California Supreme Court ruled in the Association's favor, forcing the payment of $268,446 in coverage [$7.5 million in current values]. The ruling set a major precedent in insurance exclusion law.

Numerous clergy in San Francisco insisted that the earthquake and subsequent fire was the wrath of God—divine retribution for San Francisco's wicked alcoholic ways. Ironically, one building that survived the fire was the Hotaling Whiskey Warehouse. It was saved because firefighters feared it's 1,700 plus barrels of spirits would further add to the firestorm that Jack London described as "heated air rising [that] made an enormous suck." The incident inspired local poet Charles Kellogg Field to write the following verse:

If, as they say, God spanked the town
For being over Frisky
Why did He burn the Churches Down?
And save Hotaling's Whiskey?

The Wine That Isn't Wine

Wine drinking in the Holy Scriptures was the subject of heavy debate from the mid-1800s through the 1920s. An intense religious-based argument raged whether sacramental wine should be alcoholic or nonalcoholic. The essence of the dispute was whether Christ drank wine or grape juice. If the Savior drank or made alcoholic wine, how could it be evil? The debate was a focus of the temperance movement, an organized effort by religious groups to abolish alcohol manufacturing and consumption.

An 1893 editorial of the *Asheville Daily Citizen* challenged one of Asheville's ministers, Reverend J. L. White, who contended that Christ made grape juice, not wine, at the Feast of Canaan and, likewise, drank grape juice at the Last Supper. The *Citizen's* editor, John Hoyt, disagreed writing: "Christ drank wine; that he made good, honest, wine at the wedding in Canaan, and not grape juice [is a logical fact]." Both sides hurled scripture at one another to bolster their respective arguments, e.g. Wine "biteth like a serpent and stingith like an adder" Prov 23:31-32; "I [God] give you new wine" Num 18:8-12. Things got so personal that in 1890 President Benjamin Harrison was censored by his church for imbibing and serving wine at the White House.

Charles (L) and Thomas Welch (R)

It was into this environment that Thomas B. Welch was born in 1825. By age 19 he had become a Wesleyan Methodist minister and temperance advocate. At the age of 26 he lost his voice and ability to preach. In rapid succession he enrolled in medical school, became a doctor and later changed his profession to dentistry, married and fathered seven children with his wife Lucy. In 1867 Dr. Welch took up residence in Vineland, New Jersey.

That same year Dr. Welch developed a process of pasteurizing grape juice which stopped the fermentation process by mimicking the process developed by Louis Pasteur four years earlier. It was revolutionary because grape juice naturally fermented when held too long. According to Eileen Bennett, a staff writer for *The Press of Atlantic City*, Welch's experiments were prompted by a "Sunday visitor to the Welch home who had a weakness for alcohol." Apparently the visitor "partook of the communion wine at church services but didn't stop with just the religious imbibing." The inebriated friend became rowdy and Welch "became upset." The result was Welch's grape juice which Welch promoted as "non-alcoholic wine" (he called it: *Dr. Welch's Unfermented Wine*) for communion services to local churches.

As his business expanded, Thomas Welch continued his fight against alcoholic consumption by organizing an anti-alcohol league in Vineland which forced the closure of liquor distribution facilities (stores and saloons). A prominent businessman in Philadelphia, he was also "sworn in as a special policeman" and caused the arrest of over a hundred and sixty "lawless liquor dealers" in that city.

Welch's Fruit Juice Company grew quickly. In 1890 his son Charles, who had been practicing dentistry, quit his practice to "devote his exclusive attention to [the company]." The juice, beside its use as a communal wine, was promoted by "Physicians in their practice, [sold] in [soda] fountains and for social gatherings," according to Charles. A 1912 national advertising campaign promoted the juice's medicinal attributes: "[its] delicate acid...the most refreshing to the sick" and "in convalescence Welch's Grape Juice creates an immediate vigor..."

As the temperance movement gathered steam, *Welch's Grape Juice* "really took off...Since it was the only nonalcoholic fruit drink on the market, it was a natural substitute for alcoholic drinks," according to Cumberland County (NJ) historian Delbert Brandt. The company's fortunes were further bolstered in 1913 when America's Secretary of State, William Jennings Bryan, held a diplomatic dinner for the British Ambassador to the U.S. and served *Welch's Grape Juice* instead of the traditional wine. The nation's press and cartoonist lampooned Bryan, calling his diplomatic endeavors "Grape Juice Democracy." "In the process, they made Welch's a household name," notes Bennett

Today Welch Foods, Inc. manufactures and sells a variety of products, but its primary product remains *Welch's Grape Juice* and its line of grape jams and jellies. In 2013 the company had sales in excess of $460 million.

Dr. Thomas Welch died in 1903, age 78. His son Dr. Charles Welch died in 1926, age 74. One can't help but wonder what the good Doctors Welch would think today if they found out that their "unfermented communal wine" is a popular mixer in several alcoholic drinks—such as the "Grapes of Wrath" cocktail—vodka, cranberry juice and Welch's Grape Juice.

Corn Wine and Virginia Ham

The only thing most of us remember about John Tyler is that his name was part of the political jingo—"Tippecanoe and Tyler too." His obscure presidency began when sixty-eight year old President William Henry Harrison (the hero of the Battle of Tippecanoe) died in 1841. Tyler, a Virginia plantation owner, was the first vice president to succeed to the presidency. The Battle of Tippecanoe was waged in 1811 between Native American warriors and the U. S. forces in the Indiana Territory.

John Tyler fathered the most children of any president—fifteen in all. He was the first President to be married while in office after his first wife, Letitia, died in the White House. Tyler and Letitia had eight children. At age 54, Tyler married his second wife, Julia, two years later in New York City with whom he had seven children. President Tyler died in 1862. Two of his grandchildren are still alive— making him the earliest former president with living grandchildren (Lyon is 92 and Harrison is 88).

John Tyler, Jr.

His third child was General John Tyler, Jr. In 1887 the president's nearly impoverished son was living on a pension of $8 per month [$261 in current values] which had been granted him by the State of Virginia for his service to the Confederacy. That year Frank Carpenter, a writer for *Lippincott's Magazine,* interviewed the then-68 year old "gray haired" officer who "gave [him] some interesting facts regarding the way the early Virginia presidents bought their wines" and the "evolution of the Virginia Ham."

According to Tyler, Jr. his father bought his brandy through a Norfolk wine dealer for $4 a gallon which by 1887 "was a quality [that] could hardly [be gotten] for $20 a bottle." President Tyler's rum was "imported the same way from Santa Cruz [Mexico]." The method of procuring the plantation's wine is the most intriguing tale of all. The Madeira wine "was the staple wine of the time" and was bought from the Portuguese Island of Madeira. Every year his father along with other prominent Virginians would set aside ten or twelve acres for Madeira corn. It was "a short eared corn, pearly grained variety noted for its hardiness...the only kind of corn...which would stand the long shipment across the ocean." Each acre would produce between fifty and a hundred bushels at harvest and then shipped to Madeira with a number of planters, such as [Supreme Court] Chief Justice [John] Marshall and others." The corn would be exchanged for wine. "The rate being one bushel of corn for one gallon of wine." The wine was delivered in barrels and "bottled at home."

He then related how his father "made [his] own ham, and the Virginia ham of those days was the finest in the world," he claimed. "Great care" was taken in breeding pigs. During the summer and fall, the young pigs "were allowed to run wild in the woods." Each morning and evening a little corn would be provided the pigs "to teach them the call of their master." During the winter they would be fed corn "but still kept out in the woods in the daytime [but] carefully housed and bedded at night." At eighteen months they would be let into the cornfields "which had been loosely harvested and [between] the rows had been planted black eyed peas," the general continued. They "grew fat" on the corn and peas. Towards the end of fall, "they were taken up and fed on selected corn...until Christmas...when they were killed and cured."

The curing involved salting them in brine and "and then hanging them in a smoke house...and smoking them for several months with fires made from hickory chips." Once removed they were taken down and rubbed all over with sugar. "The fat was now like white candy in appearance and the hams were ready for use."

The kind of detailed hands-on care and procedures involved in raising hogs and preparing hams in Tyler's day is pretty much a lost art. This is due to cultural changes and circumstances brought about by the Civil War, advances in animal husbandry and modern food technology. According to food editor and publisher Ed Behr there are still "some great Southern country hams." The Madeira wine made from grapes of the era and so popular in America's colonial and early post-revolutionary periods have dwindled in popularity. In 1851 the island's vines were attacked by mildew and later the phylloxera epidemic which earlier had ravished the European wine industry. Most of the vines were uprooted and fields converted to sugar cane production. However some survived and are still being grown producing some "great Madeira wines today," claims Behr. Continuing Behr says "Madeira is a great living wine of incredible longevity." He tasted an 18th Century Madeira "that still gave pleasure."

The same year Carpenter interviewed John Tyler, Jr., the latter suffered a stroke. He died four years later in 1891.

Jefferson, Hamilton, Madison
The Wine Deal

In 1790 Thomas Jefferson returned to America after five years abroad. He had been the United States Minister to France. He envisioned retiring to Monticello and a peaceful, pastoral life. Instead George Washington pressured him to become Secretary of State. He took up residence in New York City where the nation's first capital had been established.

Thomas Jefferson

The Constitution provided that the United States would have a national capitol. James Madison sought a location along the Potomac River. Northern interests favored New York—where the capitol had been situated. According to Thomas Craughwell in his book *Thomas Jefferson's Crème Brûlée,* the South "feared their influence would diminish if the [new] government's capitol] was established in a northern city." Unfortunately for the South, the North had the advantage because the number of congressional delegates was mathematically superior.

Alexander Hamilton

Of equal importance were the Revolutionary War debts which each of the thirteen original states owed individually. The debts, according to Craughwell, "were incurred… to outfit and provision troops provided to the Continental Army." These debts "were crippling the states' economies." Alexander Hamilton was Secretary of the Treasury. He was considered to be a financial genius. Hamilton believed America's salvation would be the federal government assuming the debts and then imposing taxes on the states to pay them off. By 1790 most of the Southern states had repaid their debts which meant such a federal assumption of the remaining Northern debts would force Southern states to help pay off their Northern brethren's debt.

James Madison

Accidentally running into Hamilton, Jefferson wrote, "[He looked] somber, haggard and dejected beyond description...even his dress uncouth and neglected." The concept of the assumption idea had created, according to Jefferson, "the most alarming heat, the bitterest animosities [in Congress]." Hamilton asked Jefferson to help him persuade Southern legislators to agree to the assumption. Believing that "men of sound heads" could achieve a "mutual understanding" if they discussed their differences, Jefferson invited his good friend James Madison to dine with him and Hamilton at his house the following evening.

Craughwell describes the likely menu of the dinner gleaned from research conducted by author Charles Cerami and Monticello research staff: green salad with wine jelly; capon stuffed with truffles, artichoke bottoms, chestnut puree and Virginia ham served with Calvado sauce; *boeuf á la mode*--a pot roast slowly cooked in a Dutch oven with onions, carrots, bacon, parsley and thyme with a veal knuckle bone; small plates of macaroons and meringues; and, for desert warm pastry puffs stuffed with vanilla ice cream. A different wine was served with each course, respectively: Hermitage as an aperitif; a white Bordeaux with salad; Montepulciano with the capon; Chambertin with the beef; and, Champagne with the sweets.

Craughwell writes that the cuisine and wine "put all three men in an amiable, reasonable, lets-get-things-done frame of mind."

At dinner's end, Madison agreed not to oppose Hamilton's bill but, according to Craughwell, "he would not vote in favor of it." Without Madison's opposition, the assumption bill was assured passage. The ever politically astute Jefferson recognized that Hamilton would need to offer Madison a *quid pro quo*. He suggested moving the federal capital to a site on the Potomac River. Hamilton agreed and the trio further agreed to move the capital temporarily to Philadelphia from New York while the District of Columbia was being laid out and built.

It would be the only time the trio were able to agree with one another. Within a short time, Jefferson and Madison were politically aligned against Hamilton whom they considered a royalist. Jefferson felt Hamilton and his Federalist Party were "panting after...crowns, coronets and mitres." In reaction Jefferson and Madison formed a political party—called the Democrat-Republican Party which evolved over the centuries into the Democratic Party. In 1796, Jefferson was elected Vice President and in 1800 was elected President—a position he held for eight years. Jefferson's Vice President, Aaron Burr would kill Hamilton in a duel. James Madison would be elected president upon Jefferson's retirement and serve for eight years (1809-1817).

Washington, D. C., as we know it today, finally located the nation's government there in 1800. The White House was built between 1792 and 1801. John Adams was the first president to occupy the structure from November 1800 till March of 1801. Thomas Jefferson became the second occupant. Madison became the third occupant (1809-1817). Jefferson became famous for his lavish intimate dinners at the White House while Madison's wife Dolly is still remembered for her opulent White House banquets and dinners.

Venom From the Vine

In 1896 an article made the rounds which was a combination of an O'Henry twist-ending story and religious parable. A story about criminal conspiracy, redemption, forgiveness—then banishment. Whether true or a 'snake oil' tale, we'll never really know. The article started with a discussion of Benjamin Gooch, an 18th Century physician who authored an early medical text entitled *Medical and Chirurgical [Surgical] Observations* in 1771. In it, he discussed a common practice of West Indies medicine. One therapeutic method was "the use of animal poisons" for their curative powers. In the text he recites the case of one of his patients who had been suffering for a "long duration of severe pains, spasms, etc." Unable to help the patient, he was forced to tell "[the poor] wretch [that he] could do nothing for him." In a last gasp effort he sent him a bottle of rattlesnake wine," telling him to take "a glass frequently."

Three nights later the cured patient came by to see Gooch claiming "you cannot be so much amazed as I am, nor half so much pleased; I come to thank you and, if not criminal, to worship you."

Gooch claimed he learned "the virtues" of rattlesnake wine from a wealthy "old gentleman of the West Indies." The old man was suffering from leprosy. Prior to the development of sulfone drugs in the 1940s, leprosy was incurable. A diagnosis was a certain death sentence. The body literally decayed over time with various pieces simply falling off until the individual expired.

The old gentleman, wrote Gooch, was in his final days and executed his will leaving "a large legacy to a female servant." The devoted servant had lived with him for years.

Apparently, he told the servant of his appreciation and that he was leaving her a sizeable inheritance. What happened next is reflective of one of those irritating contemporary television advertisements: "It's My Money and I Want It Now!" According to Gooch, she and her paramour decided to hasten matters along. They cautiously decided that putting the heads of rattlesnakes in the old man's wine "would be an infallible poison" and "raise the least suspicion to make away with him."

The old man drank the wine and seemed to get better. "The criminals, imagining the poison was not strong enough, added more snake venom." Instead of dying "he was restored to perfect health."

Foiled in their attempt, "conscience finally put this servant upon her knees before her master, confessing to her crime." The old gentleman forgave her, gave her a sum of money and then ordered her "to depart and never to see him more."

A search of the literature found no reference to rattlesnake wine in the West Indies. However, snake wine has long been in use in traditional Chinese medicine. The drink was first recorded to be consumed about a thousand years before Christ. According to one article, snake wine is "an important curative and [is] believed to reinvigorate a person." There are three varieties of snake wine. A large venomous snake is placed in a glass jar of rice wine with medicinal herbs and left to steep for several months and then drunk in small cups. The other varieties involve slicing a snake along its belly and draining the blood directly into the wine which is then consumed immediately in the form of a shot. Snake bile wine is prepared by draining the contents of the snake's gallbladder and likewise consumed immediately in the form of a shot. Contemporary scientists have demonstrated that the snake venom is actually denatured by the ethanol in the wine and "its proteins unfolded and therefore inactive." One other problem—a few users have reported the snakes survive their wine bath and have been known to bite. In 2013, a Chinese woman opened her 'home-made' bottle of wine to add more alcohol when the viper bit her, requiring her hospitalization. A similar incident occurred in 2009 and in 2001 a snake bite caused one user's death. Scientists speculate the snakes may initially hibernate when placed in the wine.

Today, snake wine can be found in Vietnam, Southeast Asia and Southern Chine. Under traditional Chinese medicine, snakes are advertised as a basic cure-all for ills ranging from farsightedness to hair loss, as well as to increase sexual performance. Since many of the snake types (such as cobras) used in the preparation of the wine are endangered species, the wine cannot be imported to many countries.

'Hi' on Cronk @ 102

102 year old Hiram Cronk "keeps up his strength on tobacco, wine and milk...he has used tobacco from boyhood...He consumes a gallon of wine each day." Cronk was one of four centenarians interviewed by the *New-York Tribune* in 1903.

At the time Hiram "Hi" Cronk was the last survivor of the War of 1812. When born in 1800 in Frankfort, New York, The U.S. Constitution was just eleven years old and John Adams was America's second president. There were only sixteen states. When Cronk was three Thomas Jefferson engineered the purchase of the Louisiana Territory. During his lifetime he saw "coal oil supersede the candle, only to be passed in turn by gas and electricity," an article in the *Minneapolis Journal* read. "He saw his country pass through its various baptisms of blood [the War of 1812, The Texas Revolution, the Mexican-American War, the Civil War and the Spanish-American War]," the article concluded.

Hiram Cronk

As a boy of thirteen he fought in the War of 1812—America's first foreign conflict. He enlisted with his father and two brothers. His actual service lasted about 100 days at Sacket's Harbor, New York. According to one newspaper account, the teenage boy was of such "extreme frailty... [it] made him the butt of many jokes... [his fellow soldiers] claimed if exhausted or wounded...his father could pack him away in his coat pocket." However "in one skirmish he behaved in such a soldierly manner" that his captain commended him.

Initially he was discharged after five weeks and was staying overnight at Watertown before going home. He heard "the sound of cannonading at Sacket's Harbor where a British warship was bombarding the fortifications." Within a few weeks he was "back in the ranks...serving as a private, assisting in the construction of barracks." Sacket's Harbor was an important Lake Ontario naval base. In November of 1814, he was honorably discharged from military service.

Cronk made his livelihood as a shoemaker, spending his working career around Watertown making and fixing shoes. In 1825 he married Mary Thornton. The couple had ten children—of which seven survived to adulthood. When Mary died in 1885 the couple had been married sixty years. According to the *Daily Capital Journal*, Walker also had a 120-acre farm upon which he lived until he died in 1905. His seventy year old daughter, Sarah, and son-in-law moved in and took care of him his last eighteen years. Sarah was able to get her father an $8 a month pension which was raised to $12 in 1886. In 1902 a special act of Congress raised his pension to $25 and the New York Legislature in 1903 voted him a pension of $72 a month. All told, the pension "money made it possible for him to have proper care," concluded the article.

Through 1903 various articles attest to his sprightly demeanor, good hearing and sight. He was "up and about and sat on the veranda a good deal...he chewed tobacco constantly and [drank wine]." Besides his wine, tobacco and milk, Cronk also indulged himself in Duffy's Pure Malt Whiskey of which he admitted he "took a dessert spoonful...three times a day with [his] meals, and when [he] went to bed." His testimonial was included in a Duffy's advertisement promoting the medical and health benefits of the whiskey which allowed the centenarian to be "out every day and take extended tramps." A dessert spoon is equivalent in size to a tablespoon.

Hiram Cronk died in May of 1905 at the age of 105. Debra Groom of the *Syracuse Post-Standard* commemorating the 100th anniversary of the War of 1812 wrote "three ministers performed his funeral in his house... [then his body was]...moved by train to New York City where it laid in state at city hall." An estimated 925,000 paid their respects. The New York City government several years before his death voted funds for a funeral procession to honor his life which included horse cavalry, a brigade of the Rough Riders, uniformed Civil War veterans, a marching band and mounted NYC police. An early film reel of the event was recorded which can still be viewed today on YouTube.

Whether or not Cronk's affinity to milk, wine, whiskey and tobacco had anything to do with his longevity is debatable. It is apparent though that he enjoyed his "little nips" and "plugs."

A version of this story was published as "The Last Survivor of the War of 1812" in the July 2016 edition of ARMY *MAGAZINE* a publication of 'The Association of the United States Army' (page 49)

Carrots and Wine

In 1897 the Barnum & Bailey Circus had the "finest menagerie in the country," extolled the *St. Paul Globe*. The Circus had arrived in town and the menagerie was scheduled to give a "free street parade" the following morning. It's worth noting that at the time radio, movies and television hadn't been invented. Circuses were major entertainment and a big deal when they visited America's cities and towns.

The *Globe* claimed the most exciting animal was the "educated Gorilla Johanna, whose 'human-like' actions" were extolled by the paper.

Johanna had "so much sense as to increase believers in the Darwinian Theory," the *Globe* continued. Next to her cage was the giraffe who "stretched numerous feet of spotted neck through the top of its cage."

Johanna gave a little exhibition of her talents to the assembled newspapermen. Her trainer had "accomplished wonders with her." He set a table and chair inside Johanna's cage. On it he placed a bottle of wine, a plate full of carrot pieces, a knife, a fork and napkin. Johanna "took the bottle and uncorked it." Pouring the wine in a glass she took "copious draughts between bits of carrot which she conveyed to her mouth on a fork." She was every bit the lady following "every rule of polite dining room etiquette." When finished she re-corked the wine, crossed her knife and fork across the plate, "wiped her mouth with a napkin and picked up one toothpick from a glassful and nonchalantly picked [her] teeth."

After the meal, she was given a mirror which she held up to "her anything but pretty face" and brushed back her hair. She powdered her face and put on her hat and "smiled sarcastically at the chattering monkeys in the cage across the way."

Another article pointed out that she smoked too.

Barnum & Bailey advertisements touted Johanna as the "only gorilla in captivity." She had been procured in Lisbon in 1894 to serve as "the bride" to a male gorilla named Chiko who had joined the circus in 1893. Once together, it was the first time "that a male and female gorilla had ever been so exhibited," claimed an article in the *Washington Times*.

Before Johanna, the lonely Chiko often became enraged. In one instance he broke out of his cage and attacked his handler. Three of the circus' elephants were finally able to corral him back into his cage which workmen had hurriedly repaired and furnished with "a mattress, blankets, a chair and small table." *The Scranton Tribune* described his diet as consisting of "tropical fruits, milk, rice, fresh eggs and port wine." Even though his hands made a "veteran baseball player's look like an infant's" he was capable of breaking open an egg shell at one end and sucking out the contents. Then he held the empty shell out "to be filled with wine to wash it down." Chiko was 5' 7" tall with a reach of 6' when he extended his arms. Like Johanna he was considered civilized because "he sleeps on a decent mattress, uses knife, fork, spoon and plate at his meals, and sits up at the table."

Chiko died of "green apple poisoning" in 1895 leaving Johanna the sole surviving gorilla in captivity. Research failed to discover any information about "green apple poisoning attributed to be the cause of Chiko's death. His body was stuffed and put on display at New York's American Museum of Natural History. "Johanna possessed," claimed another era newspaper, "a convoluted brain and the organ of speech...considered...to have the facility for talking...lacking only the inherited power to speak." Even so the article claimed she "ejaculated strange sounds phonetically approximating closely to words."

Johanna died in October of 1900.

There was one major problem with Chiko and Johanna. Neither of them were gorilla's at all—they were chimpanzees. According to Ted Gott and Kathryn Weir in their book *Gorilla*, "...deception was nothing new to P. T. Barnum..." In 1867 when he displayed another chimpanzee which he claimed was a gorilla he brought in an acknowledged expert who certified to the public that it was a gorilla.

The first real gorilla to be brought to the U.S. was in 1897. The primate was brought to the Bronx Zoo but died three days later.

Freak Dinners

They were the days of uniquely opulent banquets by the very rich. Gatsby-like stories abounded in the nation's society columns about dinners that left the average working stiff shaking his head. One 1903 dinner in New York featured a tuxedo-clad monkey trained to eat with a fork and knife sitting at the head table. A Chicago "zoo" dinner featured ten guests with an animal seated with each guest—including a parrot, dog, cat, goat, rooster, dove, chameleon and a pig. The cat and dog got into a scrap. The nation's press dubbed it a "banquet of beauties and beasts."

The *New York Sun* reported that the industrialist C. K. G. Billings planned on throwing a dinner for thirty-three friends. Billings had just been elected president of The Equestrian Club. The club elected a new president every two months. Each time the winner was obligated to throw a dinner for the members. It was the custom at the time for each new president "to provide a more novel affair than that given by his predecessor."

Billings originally wanted to hold the dinner at his new 25,000 square foot trotting stables which he had built at a cost of $200,000 [$6.1 million in current values]. Newspaper reporters who caught wind that the dinner was be on horseback spoiled the surprise. The

club members met instead at Sherry's Restaurant which catered to New York's social elite. After the first course of soup, Billings sadly told the guests that he "had been forced to call off the affair." He asked them to follow him to the ballroom where they would finish their dinner and enjoy privacy.

The nation's press discovered to their dismay that Billings had outwitted them after all. One unknowing reporter misled his colleagues, writing that the dinner guests would meet at Manhattan's Hotel Netherland and would then "be conveyed by automobile to…the big driveway at his palatial stables." There they would be treated to dinner on "thirty six wooden hobby horses gaily caparisoned awaiting them." Instead he had secretly relocated his opulent banquet to the Sherry's fourth-story ballroom. He provided a photograph to reporters which clearly showed that the men dined "on horseback' in the grand ballroom. The horses had been secretly loaded onto the restaurant's passenger elevator two at a time and "tethered in the ballroom…Each horse was equipped with a white quilted satin saddle and bridle, martingale and shoulder hangings in gold and white." Gold lettering for each guests name was embroidered on the saddle. The horses were arranged in a horseshoe shape around a mound of green turf "surmounted by a mass of flowers." The mound sloped off into a lawn which "spread to the horse's feet." Each horse had a three stair step-up to facilitate servers and riders.

The ballroom was replete with fountains, potted flowers and real grass. Added scenery made the room seem like "a bit of open country." Partially hidden behind the mound was a full orchestra.

Fastened to each saddle horn was a table. To ensure the horses wouldn't "curvet [leap] or prance or shy" and possibly spill or toss the meal "a liveried groom stood at each horse's head" holding the reins. While the guests ate so did the horses who munched "oats from individual satin covered mangers." The banquet consisted of twelve courses after which the tables were removed and the "guests lounged over their cigars in the padded saddles." One article reported champagne was served through rubber hoses attached to iced champagne in saddlebags. The guests were reported to still be in their saddles at midnight.

Billings revealed he had spent $50,000 on the soiree [$1.5 million in current values].

Cornelius Kingsley Garrison Billings was born with the proverbial silver spoon in his mouth. He had grown up in Chicago. His father was one of the principal founders and owners of Peoples Gas Light and Coke Company which provided gas lighting to Chicago before electricity. After graduation from college he went to work for his father's company. When his father died, Billings inherited the bulk of his father's wealth and retired at the age of 40. He devoted the remainder of his life to stabling thoroughbred horses. In 1901 he moved his family and horses to New York City. He is considered one of the fathers of matinee racing (trotting).

Billings moved to Santa Barbara, California in 1917 where the weather there enabled him to "more fully indulge his love of fast horses." He died there in 1937 at the age of 76.

A Seafarers Fare

"Two broad-shouldered, swarthy-faced men, with brown beards edged with yellow" were spotted at a junk store in Honolulu in April of 1886. One of the men picked up "a substantial iron spoon," looked it over and gave the dealer 5¢. A young man who "recognized the two" as sailors, asked why.

The sailor answered: "That ere spoon" is to eat my scouse." He continued, "Generally, I uses my knife, but my mate here says a spoon is more perlite and enables a feller to git to the windward of the rest of the mess when they hogs it."

At the time sailors were served on a "mess clothe" laid down on the deck. "A dozen sunburned, brawny arms…stretched… [for] the [food]." Before refrigeration, sailor's food was comprised of salt-cured pork and beef, dried fruits and hardtack. Hardtack was a biscuit made from flour, water and salt—hard like a dog biscuit. It was baked four times, then stored six months before sailing. Barreled salt-cured meats, were cured using saltpeter.

1880s sailor

"Scouse?" inquired the young man, "What's scouse?"

Scouse was the most common food fed sailors of the era. Made from hardtack, it was broken up and soaked in water to soften it before use in a variety of dishes. Left over "Odds and ends of meat" would be mixed (1 lb. meat to 10 lbs. hardtack)—"then baked and sent to the men in the [mess] in the dish it was cooked in." Then men scooped it out "into little tin pans and eat it with their knives." When the hardtack was combined with potatoes, the dish was called "lobscouse;" with beans it became "bean scouse." When onions were added it made a "good dish," said one of the sailors.

Another popular dish was "Dandyfunk"—a mixture of flour, softened hardtack and molasses baked in a pan. One sailor reported, "It is not an appetizing dish, but it is a nourishing feed." Sailors received coffee for breakfast and dinner and tea for supper [lunch]. Additionally, they were provided an ample supply of vinegar, "when the meal is bad it helps the men to eat it."

The sailors got dessert once a week. "Duff" was made from flour boiled in a bag with lard and salt. "On rare occasions a handful or two of raisins" were added. The "duff" was served to the men with molasses. "Pumpkin funny" was a "sea luxury," according to one of the men, "made from dried pumpkin stewed up into sauce and sweetened with molasses." He continued, "ships vary…in the matter of grub…but [not] in the cheapness of the stuff…and in its lack of good quality."

Sometimes ships' cooks could be inventive. One cook "made mince pie" around Thanksgiving. He soaked salt beef and minced it. Instead of cider he used grog [watered down alcoholic spirits], added raisins and dried apples.

A special treat was given the men whenever they caught a whale. A barrel of flour was mixed with molasses and shaped into doughnuts which were "dropped into kettles filled with boiling blubber."

"In the fish oil?," inquired the young man. The sailor told him it wasn't offensive at all, "fresh blubber is as sweet to the smell and taste as any leaf lard you ever saw." "Sea donuts" he claimed, "are better than shore doughnuts every day in the year."

Sea pie was made from hashed-up beef, pork and vegetables boiled and thickened with flour. When done it was baked in a pie crust and served to the men who "scaffs it up quick."

According to the article, Congress enacted legislation in 1872 regulating a sailors "bill of fare." Sunday, Tuesday, Thursday and Saturday: 1 lb. bread, 1 ½ lb. of beef, ½ oz. of tea, ½ oz. coffee, 2 oz. sugar. Monday, Wednesday and Friday: 1 lb. bread, 1 ½ lb. of pork, 1 lb. of flour, ½ pt. of peas, ½ oz. of tea, ½ oz. coffee, 2 oz. sugar. Molasses could be substituted "for sugar, and it is almost always preferred. It's cheaper." Sailors were also entitled to rice and barley "but," added the sailor, "as quantity is not mentioned, it is frequently infinitesimal."

While navies served their men different forms of "grog"—an alcoholic drink made of rum, brandy or whiskey heavily diluted with water, merchant sailors typically did not receive the concoction. Ship owners were given a substantial discount in their insurance premiums on voyages performed "without the consumption of spirits."

Elephant Sausage

Between 1904 and 1910 a story made the rounds about an elephant named Jack. One version suggests that Belgium's Ghent Zoological Gardens was shut down and Jack was its last inhabitant. Another was that Jack "became unruly and it was necessary to kill him."

According to the *Shenandoah Herald,* "an enterprising German pork butcher contracted for the carcass" of Jack. He "proceeded to transform the huge carcass into Frankfort sausages." The 3,800 pounds of sausage sold well "owing to their novel origin." The elephant's fifty pound heart was sold in slices.

A 1909 *New York Tribune* article acknowledged the elephant sausage had "been sold at high prices in the land where sausage has great popularity." Another reporter claimed there was a story making the rounds that Parisian butchers used the "carcass of a lion for making 'Lyons sausages.'

Jack would not be the last time that Germans enjoyed elephant meat. A 1917 *Harrisburg Telegraph* article by Marie Bonini Brown relates that she ate elephant meat in Leipzig. Apparently the Germans were "pinched" during WWI and authorities slaughtered the local zoo's elephants to cover meat shortages. Bonini ordered the elephant meat in a local restaurant—the portion was "very small" which came with "two tiny potatoes." The cost was 75¢ but she found it "very good tasting...a little like beefsteak...with a little wildness. It reminded me of venison." It wasn't the first time elephant meat was served up during war according to a follow up article by the newspaper five months later. Turnabout was fair play—during the siege of Paris in the Franco-Prussian War in 1871, "animals in the [Paris] zoological gardens were slaughtered for food." The result was that Parisians found elephant meat was relatively cheap selling for $4 a pound compared to ducks which sold for $30 apiece. The cheapest per pound cuts were horse meat ($1), followed by dog meat (60¢) and rats which sold for 35¢ apiece.

Today the value of elephant meat in Central Africa exceeds by far the value of the elephant tusks. Elephant meat is a delicacy in Africa and "can earn a poacher $6000 for the meat" but only $180 for the tusks. A 2007 *Associate Press* article quotes wildlife photographer Karl Amman who is "convinced the poaching of forest elephants in the Central African region is for the meat and ivory has become a byproduct." It's not the first time such an allegation has been made. In 1909, Captain Fritz Duquesne, a South African professional big game hunter turned writer went on a hunt with Congo natives. He opined "the hunt...was not conducted for ivory... it was for food." Duquesne was sickened watching the natives start a circle of fire "five miles in diameter" which converged on a herd of about one hundred elephants. The fire forced the elephants "towards the center of the slowly narrowing circle." The smoke became "suffocating." Finally the natives attacked—running back and forth shoving spears into the crazed elephants. "One after another they fell...bodies quivering as they bled to death." Natives "also met death" as defending elephants "tusked and crushed" them. Duquesne estimated "30 natives" and "100 elephants" were killed in the massacre. "Then came the feast," he continued as thousands of natives began hacking the carcasses. He wrote "Every bit of the dead elephants was cut off the bones and taken to the villages to be smoked and kept for future use." Just as Amman observed in 2007, the ivory was secondary to the meat, it was later collected and "divided...amongst the village chiefs and hunters."

There has been only one attempt to raise elephants as domesticated animals for slaughter in the United States. A rancher named Anson Newbuary in 1891 described his plan to develop such an industry in California. He planned on developing elephant herds some of which would be slaughtered for their meat claiming "All African explorers speak highly of elephant meat...steaks as big as mattresses...and elephant chops six feet long," he verbally dreamed. Besides, there "would be value in elephant hides and ivory ...the powerful and intelligent [pachyderms]...can be harnessed as a beast of burden" just like in India, he exclaimed. He also believed elephants could be sold to orange growers—"[an elephant] could readily reach all over the trees with his trunk and carefully pick the fruits and place it in a bag in his back." Nothing came of Newbuary's pipe dream.

Brut for the Brutes

"But the most radical of all innovations by [Yale football coach Frank] Butterworth was a liberal supply of champagne with every dinner," announced an 1897 article in the *Hawaiian Star* newspaper. The story broke when a local "Hawaiian lad" received a letter from a Yale student friend with an enclosed clipping announcing the unusual champagne training implemented by the coach. The innovative Butterworth radically departed from the rigorous athletic diet of oatmeal, rare steak, potatoes and temperance. Instead he dished up soup, fish, meat and sweets of all kinds with "a liberal supply of champagne with every dinner"—allowing his players to eat "anything they cared for that was within the bound of reason," the article read. The article went on to report that whenever a player showed any signs of "his hard work turning on him the coach increased his supply of champagne…and he rapidly got back into condition." Yale's other coaches were appalled by the radical regime, but Yale's football  team had a 9-0-2 record that year which seemed to vindicate Butterworth.

Three days later *The Hawaiian Gazette* blasted the *Star's* story as "irresponsible journalism" claiming its disbelief that their publishing competitor would dare to use "flaming headlines" to extoll that alcohol in any form was in anyway a "virtue" for athletes. The *Gazette's* chief objection was that their cross-town rival had dared to even run the story which could possibly influence young Hawaiian high school football players into believing the liberal use of champagne should be "a part, and a generous part" of a football player's diet. If it was true that champagne actually helped athletes, the *Gazette* reasoned facetiously, then "young mothers can best make stalwarts of their male babes by bringing them up on the bottle (of champagne)," adding their rival "should advocate the opening of a training table, with free liquor for athletes in some central spot [in Hawaii]."

Two weeks later Albert Judd, Jr., a Yale alumni (class of 1897) and local lawyer, tried to calm the controversy in a Letter to the Editor published in both papers. Judd claimed the story was a "yarn" and that "such a story hurts football and especially the institution with which the story is connected." Judd tried to explain away the champagne diet by writing coach Butterworth did not serve champagne at the Yale training dinner table but that he would take "two or three players who were... too tired to relish their dinner, down to Heublein's [tavern] across the [campus] green and give them enough champagne and crackers to stimulate their appetites for the regular [team] dinner that followed with the whole squad."

Judd went on to claim that Butterworth's methods were vindicated because Yale's same eleven man team "played the veteran teams of both Harvard and Princeton" both of which were forced to use five or six substitutes because of exhaustion. Yale beat Princeton and tied Harvard. American football was actually developed by Yale Coach Walter Camp circa 1880. He is considered "the Father of American Football." At the time of the champagne controversy, football was in its infancy and the best eleven players generally played "both ways," i.e. no separate offenses or defenses.

Butterworth was an All-American football player for Yale before becoming its coach. He coached at U. C. Berkeley (1895-1896) amassing a 9-3-3 record. He returned to his alma mater as its head football coach where he coached for two years (1897-1898). His 1897 "champagne guzzling" team went undefeated with two ties (Army and Harvard). He left coaching after the 1898 season with an overall record at Yale of 18-2-2. He changed his career and went into banking and real estate. Butterworth served two years as a Connecticut State Senator and was a Second Lieutenant during World War I. He died in 1950 at the age of 70.

Saving Caruso's Chickens

In September of 1919, Enrico Caruso, along with his new bride, arrived in New York harbor aboard the passenger liner *Giuseppe Verdi*. Suffering from a cold, reporters noted he was "blowing his nose three times a minute" as the ship was moored to its dock in Jersey City. The forty-six year old operatic tenor had married twenty-six year old Dorothy Benjamin the previous year.

Caruso was returning on the passenger liner which had begun in Genoa, Italy with stops in Naples and the Azores. The ocean voyage had taken twenty-one days. He and his young bride had just spent time at his sixteenth century "Villa di Bellosguardo" described as a "palatial country house near Florence." He purchased the villa in 1906.

Enrico Caruso

At the end of World War I, Italy, like many European nations witnessed civil unrest and government collapse. The country was in such debt that it couldn't even pay its national legislators—leading to wide scale bribery and corruption. For a while local Soviets—communist enclaves—took over government functions. This was the case in Florence and the area surrounding Caruso's villa. The unrest led to the rise of Dictator Benito Mussolini and his Fascist Party.

When Caruso and his wife arrived at the villa "a hundred and fifty of the neighbors came to the gates and cheered—a touching welcome home," he told reporters. He went down and talked to them and they told him "with tears in their eyes that they had been without

73

wine and cheese all through the war." The compassionate tenor "opened the gates" and invited them in and had "wine and cheese brought out to them and they feasted," he reported.

An hour or so after the initial crowd had gone home another crowd of three hundred arrived with official looking papers imprinted with "wax seals and ribbons." The documents asserted the crowd's leaders represented the 'Public Commissary' "with authority to confiscate all 'surplus' food and wine."

Caruso objected to the confiscation and offered to sing for them. "I sang as well as I could... [and]...they applauded," he told the assembled newspapermen. Then they broke down the gates to the villa and "swarmed through my house [carrying away] two tons of wine...a hogshead [63 gallons] of the best olive oil...four dozen of my finest hams...and I know not how much cheese," he continued.

Dorothy Caruso was able to avert "one tragedy." Caruso proudly related how the crowd was "about to take away all my chickens and wring their necks and cook them and eat them." The chickens were his wife's pets. "Many of them she had named...she could not have their necks wrung." Dorothy pleaded with the proletariat and, according to Caruso, "they relented. The chickens were saved."

In his day Enrico Caruso was a superstar equivalent in our times to Elvis Presley, Michael Jackson or Mick Jagger. He was the first singer in history to sell a million records by capitalizing on the then new phonograph record technology. He affiliated himself with the New York Metropolitan Opera (Met) in 1903 and remained there until his death. Besides his regular engagements with the Met he sang opera throughout the United States, Canada, South America and Europe. In 1910 he participated in the first public radio broadcast in the United States.

The Naples, Italy born tenor was the third of seven children. He started his musical career as a street singer in Naples and also performed at cafes and private parties. In 1895 he made his professional operatic debut in Naples. He was 22. In 1902 he made his first sound recordings—ten discs—all of which became best sellers. As noted he joined the New York Metropolitan Opera in 1903, quickly becoming its superstar. His recordings made him immensely wealthy and gained him worldwide fame. In 1920 he was paid $10,000 a night to sing in Havana, Cuba [$120,000 in current values].

Enrico Caruso died in August 1921 at the age of forty-eight-following seven surgeries resulting from purulent pleurisy and empyema. When he died, his chickens at "Villa Bellosguardo,"  were reported to still be alive.

Wine Bath and Beyond

A story about bathing in wine was first published in 1859 in numerous U. S. periodicals. Variations were republished over the next three decades. At first blush, it seems a good yarn replete with Mark Twain dialects and ante bellum humor.

The original story relates that an American tourist in Paris saw a sign advertising a 'wine bath.' Curious, he took the bath which cost seventy-five cents. He wondered how a wine bath could be so cheap. He knew the bath's attendant who had been a slave in Virginia but in France was a freeman. The attendant explained as follows:

"That wine has been in the bath room for one week, and you, is the thirty-eighth person that bathed in it." "Well I suppose they throw it away when they are done with it?" replied the tourist. "Oh no, they send it down stairs for the poor people, who bathe for twenty-five cents," replied the bath attendant.

"Then of course, you throw it away," exclaimed the traveler, "who thought this was going even beyond Yankee profit." "No, indeed," was the "indignant reply, accompanied by a profound bow; "No indeed, we are not so 'stravagant as dat comes to; we just bottle it up den and sends it to 'Merica, for champagne!"

An 1890 article by Shirley Dare in the *Pittsburg Dispatch* reveals that certain "California beauties know the tonic effect of wine baths." The girls bathed first in warm water and when their pores were opened "they enter a wooden tub containing a cask of red wine [for fifteen minutes] which does duty over and over again." Miss Dare writes: "The wine bath is very refining and refreshing to the skin."

A 1902 article In the *St Louis Republic* advocated "for the wealthy a wine bath is recommended." The article claims a twenty minute bath in "100 liters [26.5 gallons—the average bathtub holds 24 gallons] of Malvoisie wine can be used a hundred times without losing its invigorating properties." The article continues, "[after which] the Malvoisie may be distilled, and the result will be a delicious brandy." The previous year, Malmsey [a variety of Madeira] was the preferred variety—"It takes a hundred quarts of the wine for a bath… [which] is poured back in the barrel and used over again for the next bath."

By 1910, external wine applications were the vogue. A popular French technique was to wash the hair occasionally with wine—"white wine for blondes and red for brunettes." A 1911 article, though, suggest wine baths were still around but because "so few women could indulge in such extravagance," the article suggested women "sponge [their] faces in wine," red or white was fine but the author touted "sour claret [as] especially beneficial" for the complexion.

Wine baths of a sort are still in vogue today. A recent *Huffington Post* article suggested wine baths were beneficial but a modern wine bath consists of adding a mere 16 ounces of red wine to one's bath water. *Les Sources De Caudalie* which claims to be "the first wine spa in the world," extolls wine baths as part of their new vinothereapy "which involves being wrapped, massaged and smothered in extracts from some of France's finest wines." The Bordeaux, France spa offers a "hot red wine bath fitted with strategically placed jets designed to boost circulation." The bath is actually water "enriched with red wine extracts." They also offer a "Barrel bath" which they describe as "bubbly and enriched with gently exfoliating grape marc [i.e. pulp residue after grapes are pressed]." A reporter who examined the spa writes, "Although many dermatologists agree that red grapes can play a role in preventing serious diseases such as cancer when eaten, they remain skeptical of claims that the body can absorb anti-ageing chemicals and affect its appearance."

Susie Leung of *Absolutely Fabulous* discovered a red wine spa in China which does have a communal red wine bath and she wondered "can just sitting in wine even have any health benefits?" She wondered, "How often are they going to change the bath water?" She never thought to ask the real question—will the wine be reclarified and bottled—because today the thought is simply out of the question. But is it?

The Frenchman and the Sponges

1889 engraving of a turner

"The Frenchman's face was hacked and notched," was the beginning line of a newspaper article that appeared in much of the world's press in the summer of 1906. The old man's scars were so prominent that they sparked questions from passer byes—one of whom asked him if he was "a duelist?" The man's response was that he "was a champagne maker" in Rheims and that the "honourable nicks" were "champagne scars."

The scars, he claimed, "decorated the visages [faces] of all the workers in the underground champagne mills of Rheims." It was in these caves that champagne bottles burst "as the turners move along the racks—each turns 35,000 bottles daily—they are continually saluted with explosions," the old man continued. When the explosions occurred "Bang! And the glass splinters fly, and a little fountain of champagne perfumes the air," he added. Several million bottles were turned every year in the miles and miles of caves cut into solid limestone rock where the temperature averaged 45 degrees. The Frenchman claimed that about "one bottle out of every ten bursts" during the refining and ripening process.

At the time the bottles were turned by workers, fifty times in all, during the ripening process. As the champagne ripened, the sediment "mounted up and concentrated itself about the cork." The corkers then removed the cork, and the sediment which had collected around the neck of the bottle would blow out and the workers would "skillfully replace the cork again." The procedure called *mise sure pointe* involved placing the bottles neck "downward at a depth of three inches in a refrigerating mixture which causes an icicle to form in the neck"—the icicle then blew out when the corkers removed the cork

"The workers down there smell nothing but champagne all day long, champagne escaping from burst bottles, and as the turners move along the racks, they are continually saluted with explosions," the Frenchman explained.

"The corkers' and turners' work is dangerous. These men are nearly all scarred like me," he concluded.

A year later the world learned that the Rheims champagne mills had developed a new process to protect the workers and salvage a good part of the burst champagne. A 1907 article in the *Lafayette Advertiser* noted "champagne makers of Rheims buy a lot of our sponges, said a wholesale dealer." In an effort to save the champagne which "breaks the strongest bottles," according to the article, "they pack the bottles in clean sponge[s], and every day or two they go over the plant, and if any of the bottles have broken, they squeeze into casks the wine that the sponges have retained." The casked wine was "reclarified, refined and bottled again [which made] a very good second quality drink," the sponge wholesaler told the reporter. He estimated "in a year's course, 1,000,000 bottles of champagne" was being wrung out of the sponges.

While a few champagne makers still manually turn the bottles, most have abandoned it because of the high labor costs and product loss. Mechanized riddling machines (gyroplatte) are used in their place. Modern disgorgement machines have replaced the "corkers." The sediment is frozen in the neck of the bottle and the plug of "lees" is removed mechanically, a small dosage of *liqueur d'expédition* is added and the bottle corked.

Whatever Happened to
The Pie Girl?

Susie Johnson's mother and father were beside themselves with grief. Mr. Johnson had murder on his mind. Unbeknownst to them, their fifteen year old daughter had become one of the "prettiest artist models" in New York City. She had posed "first for the face and neck only, but at last for the altogether," the 1895 edition of the *New York World* reported. She was wined and dined by the artists and "was dazzled by the glitter of the new life," the *World* continued. By October she went missing and her parents suddenly discovered that their daughter had been concealing "the questionable part of her life" from them.

They were shocked to learn that earlier that year a group of thirty-three of New York's most prominent businessmen and artists ("men of note") had held a sinfully opulent banquet in which their daughter was the featured dessert—"the queen of the night." The banquet included thirteen courses and each course, of course, included champagne—144 bottles of the very best champagne in all. "An average," the *World* noted, "of nearly four and half bottles for every guest." The dinner it was reported cost $3,500 [in today's values $120,500 or $3,790 a plate]. It was the tail end of what Mark Twain called 'The Gilded Age' (1870-1900)—a time when the ultra-rich, labor exploiting 'robber barons' (Rockefeller, Vanderbilt, Carnegie, Gould, et al) ruled financial empires and publicly flouted their obscene wealth.

The *piece de resistance* occurred when coffee and cigars were passed out. Four waiters "came in bearing an enormous pie" which they placed in the center of the horseshoe shaped table. The band began playing *Sing a Song of Sixpence* and the raucous guests all began singing the popular nursery rhyme. As the "headwaiter cut the crust, the pie fell apart and [out popped] Susie Johnson, dressed in filmy black gauze." In addition "a great bevy of [24] canaries that he been imprisoned in the pie with her flew about the room."

Her father "a well-to-do mechanic" was furious and was reported to have threatened to "murder the man who enticed her away." Her mother was desperately searching the city's "artist studios for her."

The banquet guests were members of the who's who of American art including the sculptor Augustus St. Gaudens, artist Charles Dana Gibson (the Gibson Girls), painter Robert Reid and John Ames Mitchell (founder of *Life Magazine*). One of the guests was the renowned architect Stanford White. He designed numerous buildings in New York and had a near monopoly on designing homes for New York's ultra-rich.

Eleven years after the banquet, White was shot to death at the premier performance of a play aptly named *Mam'zell Champagne* by millionaire Harry Thaw. Thaw was jealous that White had seduced his wife (before they were married) when she was sixteen and White was forty-seven. Thaw's 1906 murder trial was dubbed 'The Trial of the Century' by William Randolph Hearst whose tabloid newspapers sensationalized the story. During the trial it was learned that White had a penchant for teenage girls—one of whom was Susie Johnson who had become his mistress after the pie incident. The affair lasted three years. Like numerous others, according to the press, when he tired of her he simply kicked her out. It was reported during the trial that she later

Menu
Champagne...Clams
Champagne...Potage Marmite [Broth]
Champagne...Timbales a la Rothschild [Truffles w foies gras]
Champagne...Hors d Oeuvres Assortis
Champagne...Planked Shad [Fish entrée]
Champagne...Aloyau aux Champignons [Steak, wild mushrooms]
Champagne...Farci, Pommes Chateauf [Persian stuffed potato]
Champagne...Ris de Veau Cheron [Sweetbreads of Veal]
Champagne...Jambon aux Epinards [Ham with Spinach]
Champagne...Sorbet
Champagne...Pluviers sur Canapés [Bird breast on bread]
Champagne...Asperges a la Russe [Mold cake gelatin/cream]
Champagne...Glace [Ice Cream]
Champagne...Turban de Fraises [Cake with Strawberries]
Champagne...Gateaux et Bonbons [Bonbon Cake]
Champagne...Fromage [Cheese]
Champagne...Cafe

married but when her husband found out she was the infamous "Pie Girl," he abandoned her—leaving her impoverished. According to Thaw's trial testimony, the abandoned Susie got sick and died of consumption. She was buried in potter's field. Thaw was ultimately found innocent by reason of insanity.

Two years later (1908) Susie Johnson's resurrection made national headlines. She was still alive. Susie told a reporter that White had paid her off when he no longer desired her services. She added that she never got married, and "I've never been sick a day in my life." At the time of the interview, Susie was thirteen years older (28) and a professional dancer. She also disclosed she had reconciled with her parents whom she hadn't seen "for a long, long time" after the notorious pie incident.

Teddy Roosevelt's 'Occasional Nip's'

Teddy Roosevelt was undoubtedly our most physically energetic president. Born into a very wealthy New York family, the asthmatic TR barely survived adolescence. As a teenager he worked out diligently with barbells and boxed to build up his body. He studied biology at Harvard, graduating magnum cum laude. Even with asthma, a weak heart and a bout with cholera he joined the boxing team becoming an intercollegiate boxing champion.

Teddy did big things. He authored 35 books. He was a speed reader with a photographic memory who read a book almost every day of his adult life before breakfast and, time permitting two or three more after dinner. According to his own estimates he read tens of thousands of books during his lifetime. He was multilingual, having a command of French,

Theodore Roosevelt

Italian and German as well as classical Latin and Greek. He was an ardent conservationist and naturalist who helped create the Forest Service setting aside 230 million acres of public lands for parklands, monuments, game reserves and bird sanctuaries. So many other things: daredevil military man with his charge up San Juan Hill and "Trust Buster." He began the construction of the Panama Canal and led two scientific expeditions—one to equatorial Africa and one to Brazil. He was the first president to fly in an airplane and the first to invite an African American to dinner at the White House (Booker T. Washington).

Like everything else, TR ate big. He described himself as "an abnormal eater." According to Edmund Morris in his book *Colonel Roosevelt,* "It was not unusual for him to consume 12 eggs for breakfast along with potatoes, toast and large quantities of breakfast meat." On one occasion, his daughter Ethel, "was amazed at the amount of lunch he could put away." She noted that "he had 2 plates of tomatoes, 2 plates of applesauce, 1 plate of potatoes grouped around...spare ribs of pork." She counted "18 which he ate and then he refused to let me count further!!"

Teddy put his wine preferences on the record—literally. In 1913 Roosevelt brought a $10,000 libel lawsuit against George Newett of Ishpeming, Michigan. Newett was editor of the *Iron Ore* newspaper in which he had printed an article alleging TR "got drunk, and that not infrequently, and all his intimates know it." According to one era journal Roosevelt took the witness stand "and launched into an account of practically every drink he had taken in his entire life."

The article recounts that his testimony recounted a "trail of occasional "nips" from the Dakota badland's cow camps, to Cuba, Africa and through his numerous political campaigns. TR "bared his famous teeth, and barked a crisp denial [to the jury] that he is not a drunkard or ever has been under the influence of drink." He admitted he wasn't a teetotaler but "I am abstemious to the extreme," he said. He claimed he never drank a cocktail or highball in his life. He never drank whiskey or brandy unless prescribed by a physician. He noted he didn't drink beer or smoke because he "dislike[d] smoking, and dislike[d] the taste of beer."

He preferred white wines, Madeira and champagne and an occasional glass of sherry. With dinner he often had "a glass or two of Madeira. In summer, instead of Madeira I will often drink a tall glass of white wine and Poland water [i.e., bottled spring water from Poland, Maine]," he testified. At public dinners "I sometimes drink a glass of champagne," he continued—adding on rare occasions he had enjoyed a "mint julep." On campaign tours he "sometimes drinks a goblet of milk containing a spoonful of brandy" before bed to soothe his throat. The total-recall Roosevelt finished his testimony claiming he could give a detailed account of every drink he had had the previous fifteen years. "Since I have been of age I have never under any circumstances been in even the smallest degree under the influence of alcohol," he concluded.

As the trial drew down, Newett retracted his charges saying "In the face of the unqualified testimony of so many distinguished men...I am forced to conclude I was mistaken." TR in turn withdrew his claim for damages asking the jury to pay him only "nominal damages." The jury awarded him six cents—worth $1.43 today—not nearly enough for even a cheap glass of wine.

Two Bottles of French Wine and a Harmonica

John Raschitsch was described as a model tenant. The bartender, "short and plump," had rented a room in Andrew Gippner's Kansas City, Missouri home for five years.

On September 4, 1905 John came home after work with two bottles of French wine and a harmonica. He shut his bedroom door and commenced drinking the wine and playing his harmonica. According to Gippner, John "played the mouth harp [harmonica] so long and hard" that he and "his family couldn't sleep." According to Gippner's court testimony, he knocked on his door and "begged him to be quiet," whereupon John "seized his Springfield rifle and threatened to fill me with bullets."

Gippner called the police and John was arrested. The following morning he appeared before Justice Casimir J. Welch and pled guilty. He attempted to explain the previous night's debacle saying "That French wine—" but Justice Welch cut him off, banged his gavel and said "Ten dollars." He then instructed the court clerk to call the next case. John interrupted, telling the judge he didn't have the necessary money and was immediately locked up in a holding cell adjacent to the courtroom until he  could be transported to the city jail to serve his ten days in jail. The Judge continued hearing other cases.

"Suddenly music was heard, emanating from the John's cell." The music must have been entrancing. The judge was reported to have "smiled and nodded his head, keeping time to the strains." And the other courtroom occupants enjoyed the lively tune, too. The tune John was playing was a popular Irish song of the era: *Ireland Must be Heaven, for my Mother Came From There*. The song had been a big hit for Charles W. Harrison, an era recording artist better known today for his *Peg O' My Heart* and *I'm Always Chasing Rainbows*. He had, it was reported, a "distinct and riveting tenor [voice]." He made his last recording in 1954 at the age of 75.

The smiling Justice Welch was of Irish heritage (the Irish surname 'Welsh' means 'wise' in Gaelic) and couldn't help but be moved by the song about the Olde Sod. He asked the court attendant to "bring out that person who is playing." John reappeared, still playing his harmonica and the nostalgic Irish song. "Justice Welch listened until John, almost breathless, ceased his efforts.

The enlivened Justice Welch exclaimed, "You're not Irish, but you sure got all the ways." He vacated his previous verdict and told the court clerk "cut that fine to $5."

John paid the fine and was freed. Further research failed to find if John ever drank French wine again.

Ireland Must Be Heaven

I've often heard my daddy speak,
Of Ireland's lakes and dells.
The place must be like heaven,
If it's half like what he tells.
There's roses fair and shamrocks there,
And laughing waters flow.
I've never seen that Isle of Green,
But there's one thing sure I know.

Ireland must be Heaven,
For an angel came from there.
I never knew a living soul,
One-half as sweet or fair.
For her eyes are like the starlight,
And the white clouds match her hair.
Sure Ireland must be Heaven,
For my mother came from there.

I've pictured in my fondest dreams,
Old Ireland's vales and rills.
I see a stairway to the sky,
Formed by her verdant hills.
Each wave that's in the ocean blue,
Just loves to hug the shore.
So if Ireland isn't heaven,
Then sure, it must be right next door.

Ireland must be Heaven,
For an angel came from there.
I never knew a living soul,
One-half as sweet or fair.
For her eyes are like the starlight,
And the white clouds match her hair.
Sure Ireland must be Heaven,
For my mother came from there.

Wine Controversy in Christening Ships

It seems silly now, but beginning in the 1890s the custom of christening ships with bottles of champagne or wine became controversial. As the temperance movement gained steam and prohibition became inevitable—anything associated with alcoholic spirits became politically incorrect. A 1904 newspaper article condemned the custom of christening ships with wine "[as] a survival of barbarism." Apparently "in the olden days...in sacrifices to the gods of nations...it was the practice to select some person [cut his throat] and spill his blood over the prow of a new vessel." Over time "wine was substituted" for the bloody practice.

In 1896, Iowa Governor Drake's daughter Mary was selected to christen the nation's newest battleship—the *USS Iowa*. The people of the town of Moulton, Iowa "at a meeting adopted resolutions...asking the governor to have his daughter use water instead of wine in christening" the ship. The governor and his daughter ignored the resolution and christened the ship with a bottle of wine. A number of newspapers, though, endorsed the idea of using water thinking it "wicked to waste so much good wine."

Two years later, at the launching of the new battleship *Illinois,* an article in the *Kansas City Journal* highlighted the controversy, commenting as to whether "wine or water should be used" in christening the new ship. The article noted it wouldn't "make any difference in the fate of the vessel whether water or wine or beer or catsup is spilled over its bows...there is the traditional element which clings to precedent...[and] the total abstinence element [which] will be shocked by dignifying [the ceremony with] wine."

Water Christening of USS

The article facetiously suggested "opening a can of beans over the bow of the *Illinois*" would cement the friendship between Illinois and Boston.

Water from Minnehaha Falls was used in christening the battleship *Minnesota* in 1905. Governor Johnson had received numerous letters "from temperance advocates urging the water instead of wine" be used. Miss Rose Marie Shaller, a university student selected to christen the ship, urged the governor to use the water "unless there was too strenuous objection from the shipbuilders."

The dreadnaught *USS Arizona* was christened in 1915. When a bottle of "undefiled Hassayampa [River] water" intended for the christening failed to break, controversy erupted. "Suspicion exists that developments took place in accordance with a deep-laid plot—someone "padded" the receptacle to insure against its breakage." "It is an established fact," continued the article, "that sailor-folk are exceedingly jealous of a tradition which calls for the use of wine, and wine only, in christening a ship." The editors of the *Bisbee Daily Review* expressed their opinion that the conspiratorial allegations were expressed by zealots "who overplayed the game and hurt the cause" of temperance by their fanaticism. It was considered "a bad omen in the superstitious seafaring trade." The ship would be destroyed and sunk twenty-six years later by Imperial Japanese forces at Pearl Harbor.

By 1918 ideas of what constituted the proper medium for a ships christening had really turned bizarre. In Portland, Oregon "bottles of milk [were] substituted for bottles of wine," newspapers around the country reported. A new custom had developed whereby "coins contributed by the [Portland shipbuilding] workers for French and Belgium orphans [were] put in the milk bottle." How the new procedure benefited war orphans was never explained. The christening of the submarine *Nautilus V-6* was accomplished with a bottle of apple cider in 1930 although she was decommissioned with a bottle of champagne in 1945.

In 1920 General "Black Jack" Pershing, commander of U. S. Troops during World War I, put his two cents in when witnessing the champagne christening of the army transport *Chaumont* at the Philadelphia Shipyard. His uniform was splattered with the champagne and he jokingly commented that the bottle ought to have

89

been opened and half of it consumed before the actual christening. "Half a bottle is plenty for the christening," he commented.

One temperance supporter claimed he didn't object to using wine to christen ships. He noted "immediately after the first bottle of wine the ship takes to water, and sticks to it ever after."

The use of champagne—"the King of wines"—became commonplace after prohibition ended, although the use of whiskey and brandy has also been recorded.

T.J.'s Gift-French Fries
and Mac and Cheese

He gave us so much. The Declaration of Independence which enunciated our human and political rights; the Louisiana Purchase which doubled the size of the United States; and, the University of Virginia which helped set the standard for higher education. These are but a few of Thomas Jefferson's contributions to America. On a less grand scale he is credited with introducing French cuisine and French wines to America, including French fries and macaroni and cheese— "dishes which have become American classics," according to Thomas Craughwell in his book *Thomas Jefferson's Crème Brûlée.*

Jefferson was appointed Minister to France by the fledgling United States. Living in Paris from 1785 until 1790, he brought with him his slave James Hemings. Desiring to develop an appreciation for French cuisine and gourmet foods, he apprenticed James to the chef of the Prince of Condé at the prince's Paris palace and country estate. Jefferson paid twelve francs a day for James's schooling which included his room and board. He also made a deal with Hemings that when they returned to America and after Hemings trained another slave at Monticello his French cooking techniques, Hemings would be freed.

According to Craughwell, the Prince of Condé "lived almost as lavishly as King Louis XVI and Marie Antoinette." A supper party of eight guests commanded twenty-five servants. Hemings' training "in the culinary arts under the prince's chef meant that he was learning the most sophisticated techniques of French cuisine from an absolute master," concludes Craughwell.

During his apprenticeship, he learned to operate kitchen equipment non-existent in the United States such as a macaroni maker and copper cookware of all sizes and shapes (e.g. sauté pans and molds), corkscrews, egg poachers, etc. He learned to make multitudes of gourmet dishes, including French fries and macaroni and cheese— two dishes that colonial and post-revolutionary America hadn't yet savored.

Potatoes had been introduced into French cuisine about the time Jefferson arrived in France and had become very popular with the upper classes. Marie Antoinette often wore potato flowers as a corsage. French fries became increasingly popular after Jefferson returned to the U.S. We know that Jefferson delighted in serving French fried potatoes at his Parisian dinners and later at Monticello. One Jefferson document which has survived notes that he had "potatoes served in the French manner" at an 1802 White House dinner. According to Craughwell, Jefferson knew

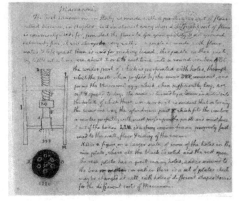

French fries as *pommes de terre frites à cru, en petites tranches."* (Potatoes deep-fried while raw in small cuttings).

Additionally, Hemings introduced Jefferson to macaroni and cheese which he learned to make in the prince's kitchen. Historians disagree as to whether or not Jefferson and Hemings were the first to introduce the dish to America, but we do know that it became a favorite of Jefferson's and, like French fries, was frequently served at the White House and at Monticello. At the very least, Craughwell claims they "established its popularity in America." Meriwether Lewis, who often dined at the White House, was served mac and cheese in 1802 and later wrote "[it] tasted very strong and not agreeable."

When Jefferson returned to the United States in 1790 his crates of goods shipped home included a pasta-making machine from Italy. Jefferson had toured Italy during his ministership to France. An undated document at Library of Congress depicts a "macaroni" press design with a narrative description of its use and workings which he drew in 1787 while in Paris. According to the Library of Congress, the machine "was not very durable" and his kitchen staff resorted to "cutting rolled dough into strips, which were then rolled by hand into noodles."

Upon his return to the U.S., Hemings continued to perform as Jefferson's chef. By then Jefferson had become Secretary of State. In 1796 after teaching his brother Peter, French cooking, Hemings was freed by Jefferson. He moved to Philadelphia where he obtained work as a cook. When Jefferson was elected President in 1801, he invited Hemings to serve as White House chef, which he declined. At the time he was in Baltimore working as a chef. Shortly afterward, thirty-six year old James Hemings committed suicide—"He had been drinking heavily for several days" and became delirious, relates Craughwell.

Thomas Jefferson's Macaroni Recipe

This recipe is among the Jefferson documents at the Library of Congress and was written in Jefferson's own hand.

6 eggs. Yolks & whites.
2 wine glasses of milk
2 lb. of flour
a little salt
work them together without water, and very well.
Roll it then with a roller to a paper thickness
cut it into small pieces which roll again with the hand
into long slips, & then cut them to a proper length.
Put them into warm water a quarter of an hour.
Drain them.
Dress them as macaroni,
but if they are intended for soups they are to be put in
the soup & not into warm water.

A Barrel of Fine-Bodied Rum

In 1805 Admiral Horatio Nelson was killed at the Battle of Trafalgar during the Napoleonic Wars. The naval battle was one of the greatest naval victories of all time. Nelson had routed a combined French and Spanish fleet with his smaller fleet—sinking or capturing 20 enemy ships without suffering a single ship loss of his own.

Nelson, who ironically suffered from chronic seasickness, requested that he not be buried at sea. He had dictated that he wished to be buried at St. Paul's Cathedral in London. His body was placed in a barrel of rum to preserve it and then lashed to the mainmast of his flagship *Victory*. During the long voyage home, it was discovered the barrel was almost empty. The sailors on board had drilled a hole in the bottom of the cask and were drinking the rum. For propaganda purposes, authorities claimed they drank the rum "for good luck…[and hoped] to inherit some of Nelson's traits." The hole was plugged and the barrel was topped off with brandy and placed under guard. Thereafter, Nelson's Blood became an acronym for rum.

The same year French General Model was killed at the Battle of Austerlitz. Napoleon decided to erect a "memorial building…on the Esplanade des Invalids in Paris" in his honor. His troops put his body in a barrel of rum and shipped it to Paris. After Napoleon's defeat, the project was forgotten. The barrel was left in a room at the Paris School of Medicine where in 1814 "The barrel broke through decay…[and spectators] were surprised to find the rum had made the general's mustaches grow… to such an extraordinary extent they fell below his waist." Somehow the general's body got into the possession of a scientist who "made a curiosity of it" and set the body up "in his library between a rhinoceros and a stuffed crocodile." His family had to sue the scientist to claim the body for its proper burial.

There any number of newspaper articles in the 1800s about use of alcoholic beverages to preserve bodies. In 1854, a body was discovered in a cask of alcohol unloaded in Madison, Indiana. The body was addressed to 'A. Kelly' and had a knife wound in the neck and "the effects of a blow upon the head." Police determined it had been sent for dissection at a local medical school.

Admiral Horatio Nelson

In January of 1884 police seized three whiskey casks containing bodies which had been shipped from Baltimore to Chicago. The police arrested John Carisen, a veterinarian surgeon who paid the express charges. The bodies were to be sold to "[a medical school] dissecting room."

Another rummy story, as famous as Admiral Nelson's, occurred in 1886 when thirty-five year old George Atherton died of a kidney failure. He was the son of the wealthy real-estate tycoon Faxton Atherton for whom Atherton, California is named. George was the husband of novelist Gertrude Atherton—the Danielle Steele of her day. George and Gertrude's marriage was on the rocks, so he decided to take a trip to Chile with his cousin, the captain of the Chilean man-of-war *Pilcomayo*—to get away from his wife. According to Gertrude's biographer Emily Leider "Instead of burying him at sea...[he] was embalmed in a barrel of rum." Legend has it that the barrel was unceremoniously delivered to Gertrude's San Francisco home and the butler, unaware of its contents, opened it and was horrified. Gertrude, who had a good sense of humor according to Leider "would repeat with glee the tale of his containerization" the rest of her life.

In 1897 Charles Bramel asked that he be buried in a stone coffin with "whiskey poured over [his] body." Bramel's mourners "were disappointed. His body was buried in a beautiful rosewood casket." It turned out that Charles had gotten so fat that the stone coffin "was found to be too small to contain his body." The press speculated that the whiskey to be used to pour over his body "will probably go inside the living bodies of some of his relatives."

As prohibition began to take hold, the Tennessee Coffin and Casket Company and one of its employees was convicted of shipping "bottled whiskey in coffins to consumers "in dry communities" whenever they ran short of their "mournin's mornin."

Rum seems to be the "spirit" of choice for body preservation. In 1921 a cemetery vault in Tuscaloosa had fallen into decay. The vault contained the bodies of a prominent couple—the husband died in 1847 and his wife in 1867. The bodies were encased in lead coffins "filled with rum and hermetically sealed...[even though] the elements had obliterated the brick walls ...the caskets were found to be in perfect condition."

Poisoned Communion Wine

From time to time we read about "angels of mercy," nurses or doctors who shorten the lives of the incurable by assisting in their deaths. The most famous was Dr. Jack Kevorkian who openly promoted and campaigned for physician-assisted suicide in the 1990s. Ultimately he was convicted of second-degree murder and imprisoned. The practice of assisting the death of the terminally ill has undoubtedly gone on for millennia. Evidence of the use of sacramental wine can be traced back to at least 1865 when a Swedish Clergyman named Linbach was condemned to death for murdering (euthanizing) "several of his parishioners by putting arsenic in the communion wine." In his confession, Linbach claimed "he became witness of much misery and hopelessness…[of] the incurably sick and dreadfully pained fellow creatures." A sort of nineteenth century, Dr. Kevorkian, Linbach felt justified in "releasing [incurable parishioners] from their heartbreaking misery." He told the court, "I believe that the merciful God will not condemn me if I shortened the sufferings of a miserable fellow creature."

It was not the first time, nor would it be the last, that poison in communion wine made the world's press. In late 1889 Father James Kelly, pastor of St. Patrick's Roman Catholic Church in Oneida, New York, was the victim of two murder attempts. Kelly was described as "a young man, full of energy, life and spirit…the most popular priest…that Oneida" had ever known. During an October communion service he drank two tablespoons of wine (laced with arsenic) from his chalice, he then rinsed the chalice with water which he also ingested. He said "I knew at once I was poisoned, the burning seemed to extend" throughout his body and "up and down" his esophagus. Regardless, he "persevered" and completed the Mass. A nearby druggist and physician ran to his aid. The priest remained bedridden for two weeks in recovery. About three weeks later, someone tried to poison several horses, feeding them apples laced with cyanide. The horses belonged to a good friend of Father Kelly's. On New Year's Day, at 4 AM someone rang Kelly's priest house doorbell. Thinking it a sick call, he opened the door and a man "raised an iron bar" and hit him in the arm and head. "Stunned and shocked" he was able to yell

"Help!" Several house guests came to his aid. Kelly told reporters he didn't have a clue who had attempted to poison or attack him. He concluded they were the acts of some "crank...whose brain has been turned by sectarian jealousy or some fancied injury."

Fourteen years later a similar attempt was made on the life of Father Giuseppe Lops, an Italian priest, at his Youngstown, Ohio Catholic Church. Father Lops drank wine laced "with strychnine...before administering communion to his flock." A few days before a "shot was fired through a window" at the priest house. Lops survived both.

In 1904 a report from Greece reported that "insurgents placed a large quantity of strychnine in the [communion wine] of the Greek [Orthodox] church in Macedonia." Fortunately the "priest tasted the fluid and detected a peculiar bitter taste" and disaster was averted.

Just about every altar boy claims to have sinned by tasting communion wine—it's a kind of rite of passage. Sometimes their mischief goes too far. In 1910 two altar boys in Germany were sentenced to several years' imprisonment in a reformatory school. One boy stole some highly corrosive hydrochloric acid and the other put it into the priest's chalice at Mass. The "first person who tasted the wine" gagged. A doctor in the congregation administered a "strong emetic." The parishioner survived.

Sometimes wine poisoning was purely accidental. In January of 1922 a "new elder" of the Seventh Reformed Church of Grand Rapids, "by mistake picked up a jug of stain varnish" which was served as communion wine to ten elders. "The men," it was reported, "staggered...reeled in front of the pulpit...and dropped to the floor." Two of the elders died while the eight others recovered.

As late as 1979 incidents of communion wine poisoning were still being reported. Father Giuseppe Murs noticed a "bitter taste" when he sipped wine during Mass at his Sardinia Catholic church. He immediately "felt ill and was taken to the hospital where his stomach was pumped out and he was dosed with an antidote." Police said there was no apparent motive and noted "the church was always open."

Two Glasses of Wine, a Cigar—
End of the Line

Emanuel Ninger stopped by a New York City saloon in 1896 and ordered a glass of wine and a cigar. A pleasant man, he spoke with a German accent with which he conversed with the bartender. He ordered a second glass of wine, puffed on his cigar, seeming to enjoy the barroom comradery. Suddenly he glanced at his watch, gulped the last bit of wine explaining that he feared missing his train. He hurriedly exited. Suddenly he reappeared at the door and asked the bartender if he could cash a $50 bill—explaining he had to pay his farm hands the following day. The bartender complied and handed him the change which Ninger hurriedly grabbed and left.

The bartender thought it odd that the German hadn't counted the change given and picked up the $50 bill [$1,750 in current values] to examine it. When he rubbed his wet thumb across the serial number it smeared. The bartender told his assistant to take over, grabbed his coat and ran out in search of Ninger. Along the way he grabbed a policeman. They found Ninger at the ferry terminal counting the change he had been given. Ninger was taken into custody.

The Secret Service took over the case. Ninger gave his name as Joseph Gilbert of Wilkes-Barre, Pennsylvania and denied any knowledge of the counterfeit bill—claiming he got it in a stock transaction earlier that day. A few hours earlier, he had purchased a bottle of whiskey with a bogus $20 bill at a local grocery store. The woman grocer identified him as one and the same. Additionally authorities found three more counterfeit bills in his pockets. Realizing the game was up, he identified himself and confessed to the crime. He and his wife had emigrated from Germany to New Jersey twenty years before. He had been employed as a house painter in Hoboken. Later they bought a farm in Flagtown, New Jersey

The U.S. Secret Service did not know who Ninger was but had been pursuing him for fifteen years. The case had "baffled them...because the notes were of a free hand drawing with pen and ink, and yet [their] likeness was so close to the genuine as to practically defy detection," according to a 1900 *St. Paul Globe* article. Authorities took him to his New Jersey farm where he lived with his wife Adele and three children. He led them to a "little room on the second floor of [their] modest cottage" where he crafted his bills, continued the *Globe*.

He explained that he bought bond paper similar to currency paper. He cut it to the exact size of the bills and then doused it in coffee to give it an aged appearance. While still wet he laid the coffee stained paper exactly over the bill he would copy and then placed the two on a piece of glass at an angle against the window frame—"the light, of course, rendering the tracery of the genuine engraving distinct." Using "an extremely hard and sharp-pointed pencil" he traced the bill's intricate minutiae. When the paper was "thoroughly dried" he used pen and ink over the pencil tracing and "applied colors with a camel hair brush." Slowly and meticulously he produced an exact duplicate of the $20, $50 and $100 bills including replicating the red and blue fibers within the real currency paper. At the end of each month he would travel to New York City with his months' work and unload it. Author Murray Bloom in a 1984 article speculates Ninger "turned out some $300 worth a month [$10,335 in current values]."

Emanuel Ninger

At his trial he was asked why he omitted the imprint of the 'Bureau of Engraving and Printing'. "[He] laughingly said: "They did not make them." His attorneys argued that he hadn't defrauded anyone because his greenbacks were really "works of art and as such [were] worth more than [their] face value." In fact since his arrest collectors were buying his so-called artwork and paying "five times their face value."

Ninger was convicted and sentenced to six years in prison and fined $1. He was released after serving fifty months in prison. He reportedly did counterfeit some British 5 Pound notes but he quit because it upset his wife. He died impoverished in 1924 at the age of 77—living with one of his sons.

Rush for Food

In 1806, 192 Russian settlers living in Sitka, Alaska (then a Russian territory) were experiencing a scurvy epidemic. By mid-February eight had died and sixty "were unfit for duty," according to the naturalist George Von Langsdorff in his book *Narrative of the Rezanov Voyage to Nueva California in 1806.* They were living on a diet completely deficient of Vitamin C—dried fish, whale and seal blubber, whale oil and sarana root (a bulbous lily root pounded into flour). A decision was made by Count Nikolai Rezanov, Czar Alexander I's ambassador plenipotentiary, to sail to San Francisco "to secure a supply of fresh provisions."

George Von Langsdorff

The Russians had purchased the *Juno*, an American merchant ship, which had needed repairs and sought refuge in Sitka's harbor earlier in the year. They hastily put together a crew of thirty-three of which fifteen were suffering from the scurvy. According to Langsdorff, the scurvy ridden seamen "were so diseased and enfeebled," instead of being able sailors "they themselves needed assistance." Midway through the trip one sailor died and "fifteen more…lay sick in such a pitiable manner…it seemed as if six or eight more [would] inevitably perish," wrote Langsdorff. Rezanov prepared a kind of punch for the crew with brandy, vitriolic acid and sugar syrup. During the trip they were able to kill a vast number of sea birds to augment their diet.

The *Juno* arrived in San Francisco on April 8 after thirty two days at sea. Langsdorff was able to communicate with one of the mission padres in Latin and explain their situation. Spanish soldiers immediately provisioned the ship with "4 large fat oxen, two sheep, onions, garlic, lettuce, cabbage and other vegetables." It was wrote Langsdorff, "more supplies than our debilitated [sailors] could consume in several days."

Spanish California had so much food that it dumfounded the Russians. Just a few months prior to their arrival the Spanish, fearing pasturage erosion, had killed 20,000 steers. They had multiplied from the five "original oxen" brought by the Spanish to the Bay Area thirty years earlier

During their thirty-day stay in San Francisco the Russian officers were "received in the most hospitable manner" and treated with great cordiality. They were daily visitors and frequent dinner guests at the Presidio and Franciscan mission. The ship's seaman, though, were forced to remain onboard the *Juno.* Rezanov feared they would abandon their ship and remain in San Francisco. Two sailors did desert and five attempted to leave. They were lashed and imprisoned on Alcatraz until the ship departed on its return trip to Sitka.

Langsdorff describes several of the meals they enjoyed. On their first trip to *Misión San Francisco de Asís* (aka Mission Dolores) they feasted "on a very appetizing soup seasoned with herbs and vegetables of different kinds, roast fowl, leg of mutton, different kinds of vegetables dressed in different ways, salad, pastry, preserved fruits, and many fine sorts of food dishes prepared with milk…the wine offered was of poor quality…after dinner we were served with tea of poor quality, and chocolate of super excellence." He continued: "All these were things to which our palates had been so long strangers, that we were not a little pleased with them."

Langsdorff visited the *Misión San José* and was overwhelmed at the amount of "grain in the storehouses…[which] greatly exceeded [his] expectations." Wheat, barley, corn, beans and peas were in abundance and stored in cavernous storehouses—in direct contrast to the Russian settlement in Alaska.

The crew of the ship, after "being fed on wholesome meat and pulse [beans] were soon entirely cured of the scurvy," relates Langsdorff. He marveled at how quickly even those "who had scurvy to the most frightful degree" assumed "a healthy appearance." Within two weeks "nobody could have supposed them to be the same beings" that had left Sitka "such miserable, pale, lean, emaciated figures."

The *Juno* left San Francisco on May 10, 1806 laden with foodstuff acquired from the Spanish—thousands of bushels of "wheat, flour, corn, peas, beans...casks of salted meat...salt, soap [and] tallow." On the 8th of June they arrived back in Sitka where they were met by their comrades who "looked like living skeletons, they were so wasted, forming a striking contrast to the plump, well-fed sailors" returning from San Francisco—"all well and healthy," concluded Langsdorff. California's cornucopia had saved the settlement.

California's Misión Indians' Diet

California's twenty-one missions were founded by Franciscan padres sent by the Spanish king to convert the indigenous people to Catholicism. The Christian conversion included educating and "civilizing" to bring them into compliance with European standards and morals. A number of European explorers visited Spanish California. The English voyager George Vancouver, the French explorer Jean-Francois de la Perouse and Russian naturalist George von Langsdorff have left us journals filled with descriptions and their opinions of the mission culture.

La Perouse spent eight days in Monterey in 1786 where he toured the mission. He was very critical with what he saw, opining the natives "were like prisoners in a penitentiary…their lives, their bodies,

 even their thoughts no longer their own." But he left us little detail of their diet.

Vancouver gave us a colorful description of San Francisco during his visit in November of 1792. He noted the mission Indians "are well fed… [the padres] securing [for] them plenty of food" as a means of keeping them at the mission.

Langsdorff in his book about his 1806 experience at the San Francisco's *Misión San Francisco de Asís* gives us a detailed description of the diet of the twelve hundred neophytes residing there. The principal food, he relates was "a thick soup [stew] composed of meat, vegetables, and pulse [beans]." Ironically he noted the scarcity of fish at the missions because they lacked "the proper means of catching them" in San Francisco Bay which was overflowing with edible aquatic wildlife.

The mission Indians were served the stew three times a day in "large ladlesful." They were called to their meals by the ringing of the mission bells. He observed the feeding of the stew "and it appeared incomprehensible to me how anyone could consume so much nourishing food three times a day." The missionaries told him they killed between forty and fifty steers a week to feed the Indian community. "Besides this meal, bread, Indian corn, peas, beans and other kinds of pulse [legumes] are distributed in abundance, without any regular or stated allowance," Langsdorff wrote. Besides religious studies and prayer, the Indians were trained in a variety of trades: animal husbandry, blacksmith, locksmithing, cabinetmaking, weaving, soap making, butchers, etc. and housed in comfortable quarters. Men and women were kept in separate quarters. Married couples were properly housed.

Grinding corn and wheat into meal or flour was done entirely by the women using mortars and pestles. "Although the flour made is very white, the bread is very heavy and hard." He noted that La Perouse gifted the mission a hand mill during his 1786 visit to better grind the flour. The mill would facilitate the making of a lighter bread but "it was never used." One of the padres explained it was for economic reasons that the hand mill was not operated as "they have [more] Indians of both sexes under their care than they can keep constantly employed [and]...the mills would only be productive of idleness."

Langsdorff observed that the Indians living outside the mission were "living in a moderate and equable climate...where there is no lack of food and no care about habitations or clothing, where by hunting they can obtain sustenance...roots, seeds, fruits, and the products of the sea." Underlying the abundance of natural foods, on one occasion he went on a rabbit hunt with thirty Indians. He described the natives using "a peculiar kind of snare...within three hours, without firing a shot, we had taken seventy-five, and most of them alive."

He found the San Francisco Indians "small, ugly, and of bad proportions...and heavy and dull in their minds." He was confused by their size and proportion in the midst of such abundant nourishment.

"These pigmies" living in "such a mild climate and, with an abundance of food, is to me a puzzlement."

The invasion and conquest of California's native peoples and Spain's religious and educational policies of "civilizing" them was largely a failure despite the abundant and nourishing diet provided. When the Spanish first began colonizing California in 1769 there were an estimated 300,000 native Californians. European diseases decimated the mission and native populations. By 1842 the population was halved and by 1850 with American conquest there were less than 15,000 California Indians alive—disease, homicide and a falling birthrate resulting primarily from rampant European introduced venereal disease.

A Wine Tart for the Virgin Mary

In 1898 a story about an unnamed married couple residing in Kempton, Bavaria made the rounds in the nation's press. The couple, who were well-to-do farmers, had recently lost their daughter. The wife, the press reported, had baked a wine tart for the Virgin Mary to thank her for the many interventions with their daughter Crescence in her afterlife. Kempton is located in Southern Bavaria in a region known as the Allgäu. The area is well known in Germany for its beautiful landscapes and farm produce, especially dairy products--including 'herdsmen' cheese.

According to the *Los Angeles Herald*, a couple who lived nearby, the Wohlfarts, convinced the farmer that that their daughter, Agnes, "received frequent visits from the Virgin Mary, who told her that Crescence was not in heaven but in purgatory." Frau Wohlfart convinced the bereaved and obvious deeply religious parents that Agnes could arrange for Crescence's "release from purgatory." They promptly paid the Wohlfart's 300 German marks, which we are told was the amount the Virgin Mary charged to facilitate the cross-over. "A little later" Agnes was alleged to have received the news that Crescence had not only entered heaven "but had married an angel." Agnes related that the new bride would like to have her dowry together with 1000 marks sent to her in heaven. The farmers without hesitation promptly ponied up the money.

A month or so later, Agnes claimed she was told by the Virgin Mother that Crescence was pregnant. The joyous farmers who would soon be proud grandparents doled out more money to help their daughter and her angel husband with their heavenly paternal expenses. After the birth Frau Wohlfart suggested they voluntarily pay another 200 marks to celebrate the special occasion. They were told "All the angels in heaven blew their trumpets when the money arrived." There was no mention as to whether or not the new baby angel needed to be baptized. Documents unearthed by the local authorities included a receipt for 150 marks which read "from the Mother of Christ" along with a number of personal letters from the Blessed Virgin to them about their daughter, angel-in-law and their precious new grandangel's life in heaven. On one occasion the farmer's wife was asked to provide the Virgin Mother with a sack of potatoes which was promptly given to Frau Wohlfart to be passed on to heaven.

It wasn't only money that passed between the farmer couple and the Blessed Virgin. The *Mohave County Miner,* an Arizona newspaper that also covered the story related that the relationship was far from being a unilateral one. Gifts had been exchanged between the Holy Mother and the farmers. The Blessed Virgin had actually given the farmers "a sofa and a loaf of milk bread and other things which [Agnes] declared she had received from heaven." It was a gesture of appreciation that the farmer's wife "personally baked a wine tart for the Virgin Mary."

The *Miner* called the report "an incredible instance of nineteenth century gullibility." The farmer was "bled in this manner until he was ruined," the *Miner* continued. When authorities discovered what had happened, they arrested the Wohlfarts accusing them of fraud. The court determined that "Frau Wohlfart was the guiding spirit in the fraud." She was convicted and sentenced to two years in prison.

A wine tart? The press report doesn't indicate which kind it was—white or red wine. There are numerous varieties, e.g. sweet potato tart with red wine; red wine poached tart, peach with white wine tart and the like. Such tarts involve numerous steps—making a pie crust dough, cooling and rolling the dough and inserting ingredients consisting mainly of wine, sugar, flour and cinnamon and then a two-step baking process. There can be little doubt the farmer's wife put a lot of tender loving care into hers with deep appreciation for the Blessed Virgin's intervention which greatly assuaged her and her husband's grief. Discovering the fraud that had been committed must have broken their hearts.

A Bottle of Champagne in Nome, Alaska

French Count G. Des Garets had just returned from Cape Nome, Alaska Territory when he was interviewed by Chicago reporters about his Alaskan experience. He gave us a first-hand report of kinds and types of food and beverage in the earliest days of a gold mining camp.

Des Garets was one of the first hundred gold miners to visit Nome shortly before its gold find made international news and it's population swelled to 20,000. The adventurous aristocrat reached the cape in June of 1899 and saw "a picture of desolation...the beach swept by terrible storms." He had to wait out the storms in a ship forced to lay offshore several days before attempting to go ashore in a small boat. There was no harbor, piers nor wharves. His boat "overturned [with] billows rolling over it and me" washing him ashore, he told the reporters.

Nome Miners

He found Nome "a terrible place...the food was nauseating, the cold was horrible and only the rudest accommodations existed." "But," he continued "gold was everywhere...it was mixed with the sands of the seashore for at least 30 miles along the beach." Within three months of his arrival another 4,000 people followed. Des Garets described the miners (men and women) who "can go down to the beach when the tide ebbs and pan out from $10 to $20 [$325 to $700 in current values] from the sands...before the tide flows again." With a rocker box recovery was "from $15 to $150 a day [$500 to $5,000 in current values]." He claimed there were 500 rocker boxes along the beach and anticipated 5,000 by the next summer.

Nome he claimed "is the best poor man's camp in the world...whenever a man is hungry or thirsty and has no money...[he simply gets] a pan...and he can wash out gold enough to pay $2 for a meal and 50 cents for a drink."

"Good food" in Nome in the summer of 1899 was "rare, and bad food is very dear." He paid $10 for a bottle of Mumm champagne [$325 in current values]. He was embarrassed and told the newsmen he didn't want his French friends to know he paid so much although "it was," he said "good to taste once more the wine of France." Today a good bottle of Mumm retails for $35.

Garets opened a leather pouch and showed the reporters "several chunks of yellow metal" which he picked up from his own claims. He bragged about buying $20,000 in lumber in Seattle and selling it for $125,000 in Nome—despite his lack of business experience and knowledge. He swore "The world has never seen anything like Nome."

The French count was right. Nome was one of the most unique gold discoveries in the world and the site of one of the greatest gold frauds in history. In 1900, Federal Judge Alfred N. Noyes was appointed by President McKinley to oversee the law in Nome under the new Alaska Act passed by Congress. A political operative by the name of Alexander Mackenzie came to Nome with the Judge.

Two days after his arrival, the Judge ruled that several mining claims legally owned by three Scandinavians were illegally held because they were not U.S. citizens (actually two were and the other was in the process of becoming a citizen). The mines were producing in excess of $15,000 per day [$500,000 in current values]. Vacating the Scandinavian's title, Noyes then appointed his crony and personal friend Alexander Mackenzie as receiver to operate the mine until legal title could be established.

Noyes and Alexander ignored a court order from the U.S. Federal Appeals Court in San Francisco and continued to operate and pillage the mine of its vast wealth. Finally U.S. Marshalls were sent from San Francisco and they arrested Noyes and Mackenzie and took them back to San Francisco were they were placed on trial. Mackenzie was convicted and sent to prison. Noyes was found in contempt of the Appeals Court orders and removed from office. Mackenzie was pardoned a year later by President McKinley on health grounds—he lived another twenty years.

The episode prompted Rex Beach to write his best-selling novel *The Spoilers*. The story with the same name has been portrayed five times on the big screen—1914, 1923, 1930, 1942 and 1955. Over the years the various versions of the movie have starred such well-known actors as John Wayne, Anne Baxter, Marlena Dietrich, Noah Berry, Gary Cooper and Randolph Scott.

"Diamondfield" Jack Davis'
Wine Spree

In 1905 "Diamondfield" Jack Davis left Rhyolite, Nevada after having "made his 'pile.'" He proceeded "to spend it in the most approved fashion," newspapers across the country reported. Before he left Rhyolite "he flooded the town with wine." As Davis wound his way north from Rhyolite to Reno in a stagecoach with his wife, "he stopped at every mining camp during his journey and bought up all the available wine in town for the miners before continuing on," the newspapers reported. In Goldfield he presented his partner with title to the stagecoach line which he bought in Rhyolite before he left for

Jack Davis

$15,000 [$450,000 in current values]. Arriving in Reno, he purchased a $7,000 automobile [$210,000 in current values] and headed for San Francisco. At the time roads were rugged cattle and animal trails interspersed with rutted dirt roads. In San Francisco the Hawaiian press announced that Davis intended to hire a steamship, "in order to establish a new, trans-Pacific record" If he couldn't hire a ship "he would

offer a large bonus to the captain if he would shove his vessel fast enough to break the [existing speed] record to the Orient [Hawaii]." Davis had earned his nickname in the mid-1890s while prospecting for diamonds in Idaho. He never found them, but according to *Murderpedia's* Juan Ignacio Blanco, "he talked so much" about the elusive diamond field he "earned the nickname."

Just three years prior, Davis had been on death row in Idaho—convicted of murdering two teenage sheepherders. In a kind of Billy the Kid story, Jack had been hired by cattle ranchers at $50 a month [$1,760 in current values] to keep sheepherders off of their land. The year before the murders, Jack had shot and wounded a sheepherder in the pursuit of his job and had left Idaho until the heat settled down.

Prior to moving to Idaho he had served time in Arizona Territorial Prison for a shooting incident and he had bragged about shooting sheepherders. Those facts, plus additional circumstantial forensic evidence regarding his gun and bullets used in the murders, led to his conviction in 1897.

He was sentenced to hang on June 4, 1897. The day before his execution, two other cattlemen confessed to the shootings which led to a reprieve. Despite their confessions, the two were tried and acquitted—leading authorities to demand Davis' execution. After exhausting all appeals, his execution was rescheduled for July 3, 1901. The Idaho Board of Pardons extended the execution date to July 17th. Three hours before his execution the State Board of Pardons commuted his sentence to life imprisonment. On December 17, 1902, Governor Frank Hunt pardoned him.

After his release Davis moved to Nevada "with but a few dollars between himself and the cold world," the press reported. He arrived in Rhyolite, a new mining camp. A couple of dirty shoe prospectors had just discovered gold in a green—almost turquoise-colored rock (rhyolite). The rock was "spotted with big chunks of [gold] and looked a lot like the backside of a frog." The miners named their new find The Bullfrog Mining District. Davis is considered the father of the camp because he was able to arrange for grubstakes from several wealthy miners—including Nevada Governor Tasker Oddie. He received a piece of the action from the prospectors and investors. Additionally, he filed several claims of his own which he worked and finally sold his interests and thus "made his pile."

Davis associated himself with several prominent bankers and miners and was involved in other dramatic mining finds in Nevada, California, and Mexico after his Rhyolite success. In 1910 he led a mineral exploration expedition to Brazil comprised of 200 native scouts and fifty mining experts.

In March 1913, Diamondfield Jack was reported to have been executed in Mexico by Federal authorities for publicly expressing his sympathies for rebels attempting to overturn the government of

President Victoriano Huerta. He was in Sonora negotiating mining claims and did escape a reported death attempt by government troops. When he showed up in Salt Lake City, the *Salt Lake Tribune* which had run the original story acknowledged "Davis was too lucky to be killed."

Davis made a fortune as an explorer, miner, stock promoter and investor. Davis' luck finally ran out—of all places in Las Vegas when he was killed by a taxicab while walking across a street in 1949. He was 85.

The Raines Law Sandwich

In a New York City "tenderloin saloon one of the patrons picked up a sandwich and ate it. The waiters and bartenders scowled at him," read the opening line of a 1908 *New York Tribune* article. The patron's act was bothersome because the bartenders had to go find another "time-worn sandwich," the article continued. When the patron asked for another beer he was told to "be on your way...for diminishing the supply of sandwiches is considered an unpardonable offense."

Senator John Raines

In 1896 the New York legislature passed the so-called Raines Law which was designed to curb alcohol consumption. One of the provisions closed all local bars and saloons on Sunday. Alcohol could only be served at hotels when in the course of a meal. The law defined a hotel as a facility having at least ten rooms for lodging. A meal must consist of at least a sandwich. Numerous saloons added rooms in attics or outbuildings and applied for a hotel license as a means of staying open on Sundays.

These Raines law hotels served a sandwich with every drink. Patrons understood they were not to eat the sandwiches—they were merely a legal prop to comply with the loophole in the law. Jacob Riis, a nineteenth century social reformer and muckraking journalist, wrote about "saloon keepers who mocked the law by setting out 'brick sandwiches,' two pieces of bread with a brick in between." On one occasion he witnessed "an altercation in a saloon when a customer" tried to eat the sandwich "and the police restored the sandwich to the bartender and made no arrests."

State officials were overwhelmed with complaints by temperance reformers. Tax authorities found one hotel created out of a barn that had been built in 1850. The bedrooms were in the loft where guests had to climb over two huge beams three feet thick formerly used as perches by chickens. The walls had one inch gaps causing lodgers to freeze in the winter. In another instance an enterprising saloon owner added a facade with windows painted on it to give the appearance of hotel rooms.

Newspaper reporters periodically wrote funny articles about the law and the courts regularly intervened, declaring Raines sandwiches a violations of the intent of the law, but to little avail. One 1897 article related how an "absent-minded" patron sat down and "buried his face at once in the newspaper." He was delivered a ham sandwich and a "large paste board check." The absent-minded man complained to the waiter that the sandwich was "as dry as a bone." It turned out the patron had eaten the paste board check. Another article referred to the sandwiches as "indestructible...flourishing in its mocking but strictly legal simulation of a meal." Numerous hotel saloons reused their sandwich props "keeping [them] in the icebox from week to week until they [were] worn out."

The law also created an unexpected boon for the saloons. The rooms quickly became cribs for prostitutes or convenient places for one-nighters. Fifty-year old canalboat Captain John White docked his boat at the foot of Adams Street in Brooklyn. He spied a "Raines law hotel on Cherry Street where he sampled the wet goods and ate part of a Raines law sandwich," the *New York Sun* reported. "Then he met Annie Mackey, an English woman of 35 hard winters" who, continued the *Sun,* had a room upstairs. White believed he had been robbed of $29 by Annie and yelled for help. The police arrived but found no money on Annie. They did find $28.60 in White's pocket. Annie was locked up for prostitution and White who "wanted to be released, saying his canalboat was unprotected...was also locked up, charged with intoxication."

In 1906 London adopted its own version of the Raines law—giving true meaning to "a quick one." A patron could buy one pint of ale but only with a "chaser sandwich." He could only remain in the bar a sufficient time for their consumption. Consumption of the sandwich was compulsory. A patron could not loiter on the premises after his pint and sandwich.

Over the years New York Courts periodically ruled that the Raines law sandwich violated the intent of the law and periodically police departments would raid establishments as a show of good faith. In reality over the twenty years of its existence it had a negligible effect on reducing liquor consumption. The Raines law was extinguished when the eighteenth amendment to the U.S. Constitution was implemented.

Wine and Outhouses

Wine and outhouses became big news in Virginia in 1916. That year Virginia adopted a state prohibition law (the Mapp Act) in anticipation of the enactment of the Eighteenth Amendment to the U.S. Constitution. The Mapp Act banned the manufacture, sale or storage of intoxicating liquor in the state of Virginia. Specifically, the law forbade the storage of alcoholic spirits in any home. M. H. Hatcher of Danville, Secretary of the Danville Creamery, was arrested and tried for storing "several [60] gallons of ardent spirits [in his outhouse]."

The *Richmond Times-Dispatch* reported on the adjudication of the case against Hatcher. In addition to the home itself, the Virginia law forbade keeping "or storing any amount of whiskey or wine in an outhouse, stable, barn or storage room that does not constitute a part of the residence and this is true no matter for what purpose the said whiskey or wine is kept or stored."

Hatcher argued that even though he owned the premises, he was a bachelor and because he was unmarried and without children had no home. The court rejected his argument and he was convicted of violating the law and sentenced to thirty days in jail and fined $50. He appealed the court ruling and put up a bond of $1000.

In May of 1917, he failed to show for his court date and Hatcher's bond was forfeited. It was also disclosed that "according to reliable accounts, Hatcher is now in Canada." He returned to Danville later that year and petitioned the governor for a pardon. Seven hundred Danville citizens including ministers, doctors and even the judge that presided over the case against him "joined in a petition to the Governor for a pardon." His doctor said he was in poor health "and if he was confined to jail the results would undoubtedly prove serious." Virginia Governor Crook granted a conditional pardon which relieved Hatcher of the jail time but required that he pay the $50 fine.

The Hatcher case wasn't the first which involved storing wine in an outhouse. In December of 1911 an article appeared in the

118

Bismarck Daily Tribune criticizing the number of pardons being granted in North Dakota. The article referred to an editorial in the *Larkin Journal* which had castigated the state pardons board which had just commuted the sentences of 37 inmates in the state prison. Two of those pardoned, James Kelly and Joseph Law, were "two of the most despicable murderers in the history of the state," related the *Tribune*. In 1894 the duo had robbed a "storehouse of a cask of port wine, thought by them to be whiskey." When the intenerate drifters discovered their mistake they returned "to secure the whiskey" and were interrupted by a security guard whom they shot and killed with a Remington rifle. According to the article the rifle was found and traced back to the killers and "the remains of the port wine cask they attempted to burn was found in an outhouse while the wine itself was found in Law's quarters." The two were pardoned because they were "exemplary prisoners, in other words a snitch and lick-spittle of prison guards," concluded the *Tribune*. A prison magazine published by the inmates further confirmed Law's snitching led to his pardon lamenting he used "his slick tongue and petting ways to officers."

An on-topic story which at first blush appears to be a tall tale, but in reality it turns out to be a freakish coincidences goes as follows:

An 1899 article in the Lordsburg, New Mexico *Western Liberal* reported that Jerry Wines, Superintendent of the Superior Mining Company had resigned his position "as he had other and more important business interests." In his place J. E. Outhouse had been selected to replace Wines as superintendent. Outhouse was described as an "experienced mining man...who for many years had been the superintendent of the Shafter silver mine in Shafter, Texas." There really is a Shafter, Texas, now a ghost town with a population of 11 persons.

Pope Leo XIII's Endorsement of Cocaine Wine

In 1900 an advertisement appeared in newspapers worldwide in which Pope Leo XIII endorsed *Vin Mariani Wine Tonic*. Cardinal Mariano Rampolla, Pope Leo's Secretary of State, announced the endorsement and further that "His Holiness has even deigned to offer Monsieur Mariani a Gold Medal bearing his venerable image" which could be used on *Vin Mariani* advertisements

Vin Mariani was a wine tonic developed in 1863 by a Corsican chemist. It was a French Bordeaux altered with coca leaves. *Vin Mariani* contained the equivalent of 7.2 milligrams of cocaine per liquid ounce. According to Darryl Mason, Leo carried "a personal hip flask to fortify himself." Mason implies the wine was responsible for the pope's demeanor, writing he was "known for his happy personality."

Besides the *Vin Mariani*, Pope Leo used snuff. "He takes large pinches of it…[dropping] a good part of it over his soutane [shoulder covering] and on the carpet," relates a 1901 article in the *Virginia Enterprise*.

During his twenty-five year papacy, Leo led an extremely disciplined life. He rose every morning at seven, dressed and performed his morning devotions after which he celebrated a forty-five minute Mass in a small oratory next to his bedroom. He then attended a second Mass celebrated by one of the Vatican prelates along with other inhabitants of the Holy See, after which he had breakfast.

According to an 1898 *Washington Evening Star* article the meal consisted of a cup of soup and "a few chocolate pastilles [medicinal lozenge]." Another newspaper claimed he also had two soft boiled eggs and noted he had no teeth and a "feeble stomach" which made him "a light eater." Over the next two hours he attended to church business. At noon his lunch consisted of an omelet, bread roll, cheese and a single glass of wine. The wine was "an excellent Bordeaux" produced by a nearby convent which "he cut with water." A 1901 newspaper article noted "when the dishes are" removed "it is seen that what he had eaten would hardly be enough for a child of 6."

Lunch was followed by "his constitutional [exercise] in one of the numerous Vatican halls" which was followed by a visit to the Vatican garden. He was a frequent visitor to the *Cascata dell' Aquila* where he enjoyed strolling through a Catholic vineyard which produced 1,500 gallons of wine annually. He amused himself by catching "small birds with nets, a sport" which he mastered as a "young lad" but which he was still fond of at 90. Every day he spent several solitary hours in the dungeon at Rome's eighth century Tower of the *Citta Leonina*. According to one newspaper, "what he does there nobody knows." It was speculated he took a nap, worked on his literary works or simply meditated. At sunset he returned to the papal apartment, said a rosary, and worked on church business till midnight when he retired. Era newspaper articles assert he was mentally alert: "nothing escapes him and his remarks, although always calm, are short and to the point. There is no relaxation in him."

Pope Leo XIII

Leo was one of the most learned of all Catholic popes, speaking fluent Latin, German, English, French, Spanish and Italian. He issued eleven papal encyclicals (position papers) during his papacy of which *Rerum Novarum* [revolutionary change] is the most famous.

It spelled out the Catholic Church's position in support of labor unions, rejected communism and unrestricted capitalism and affirmed the right to private property ownership. The encyclical specifically addressed "the misery and wretchedness pressing so unjustly on the majority of the working class."

On a daily basis the multilingual pope read dozens of the world's newspapers "without glasses." He preferred nighttime reading "in the gentle glow of a candelabrum with three candles," even though electric lights were available.

As to his cocaine wine addiction, Pope Leo was in good company. *Vin Mariani* was a medical tonic touted as an energizer comparable with today's energy drinks. It was used by an international group of literary luminaries including: Emile Zola, Jules Verne, Alexander Dumas, Robert Louis Stevenson and Arthur Conan Doyle. Users among aristocratic and political leaders included: Britain's Queen Victoria, Greece's King George I, Spain's King Alphonso XIII, the Shah of Persia and America's President McKinley. The Grand Rabbi of France exclaimed "Praise be to Mariani's wine" and Pope Leo's successor Saint Pope Pius X was also an exuberant user. Thomas Edison claimed it helped him stay awake longer.

Pope Leo XIII died in 1903 at the age of 93, distinguishing him as the oldest pope.

Salvaging Wine from the Sea

Over the centuries innumerable ships laden with wine have sank. Over the past hundred years or so, with the advent of modern diving equipment, archeologists and explorers have found ships dating back to the Phoenicians and Greeks as early as 350 BC—many with containers of wine.

In 2010, Alasdair Wilkins, in an article for *Archeology of Booze*, wrote about crates of champagne and beer found in a sunken ship "at the bottom of the Baltic Sea." Divers found 186 bottles of champagne in the ship which dated to the second quarter of the 19th century "making its cargo...the oldest alcoholic drinks in existence." When they brought the champagne to the surface changing pressures caused some of the corks to pop off and "a diver decided to take a sip...he was shocked to discover the wine still tasted fine." The beer was "just as phenomenally well-preserved as the wine." In May of 2013, six bottles of rare wines salvaged from a ship that sank off the coast of Holland in 1735 went on auction at $2600 each. The auction director tasted the wine from another bottle which had cracked and commented "it had a buttery smell and [was] a very oxidized wine—it did taste like wine—secondary acids and some bitter notes," he commented.

Hundreds of articles graced the pages of the world's newspaper during the nineteenth and twentieth centuries about wine salvaged from sunken ships—some funny, and some not so funny and some in between.

In 1897 Captain Alfred Le Cato was overseeing a salvage of the ship *Frances* off Little Egg Harbor, New Jersey. The *Frances* was in ninety feet of water and its cargo consisted of wine and whale oil in casks, fish oil, canned fruits and salmon and marble soda fountains. Daily, Le Cao descended into the hold to inspect the diver's work. "On this occasion... [he was] let down to the [*Frances'* submerged deck]," read an article in the *Rock Island Argus*. Two men on deck manned air pumps which fed oxygen "so necessary to life" the article continued. About a half hour into his dive "something struck him that all was not right on deck." He noticed his air supply was coming in a "jerky manner" and then stopped altogether. His brain "throbbed" and the fish which passed "grew larger and larger" as oxygen deprivation intensified. He realized he was "suffocating." When he came to on the deck of his tugboat, he was told a sailor had opened one of the casks of salvaged wine, drank it and became "a crazy seaman running about the deck." The drunken sailor attacked the chief mate with a knife, who in turn took him down with "a handy barrel stave dropping him to the deck...instantly there was pandemonium...the whole crew rose up in revolt...the men on the [air] pumps forgot the captain below and joined in [the melee]," related the *Argus*. Finally when order was restored "they regained their senses and began pumping air" while another diver went overboard to bring the captain up. Captain Le Cato discharged the entire crew with the exception of the chief mate.

Eight years later "tugboats plying the Hudson River held joyous "Bacchanalian revels" picking up "some hundred kegs of claret floating [in the river]," read a front page article in the *New York Tribune*. The wine came from a lighter which "suddenly turned turtle and sank," continued the article. "It seemed like every tugboat in the harbor was coming to the rescue of the lighter [i.e. a small boat]...but it was not the lighter which attracted, but the claret...[which] they salvaged as fast as they could...tasted, then drank deeply," related the *Tribune*. The article revealed that the following day "was a day of dull headaches, of pains of lethargy upon the river."

In 1912 heartbroken sailors aboard the steamer *Francisco* in route to Boston from England related how they saw a thousand cases of champagne drift by their ship. The *Francisco* "was fighting her way...through a heavy gale...[the big Atlantic waves] were breaking over the deck." All was not a loss, one sailor managed to "pick off a [single] bottle which had broken loose from one of the cases."

In 1917, fifty barrels of wine washed ashore at Bodie Island, North Carolina from the steamer *A. A. Raven* which grounded and broke up. The barrels were seized by "beach dwellers and a force of Coast guardsmen." The dispute was resolved when the IRS seized forty of the barrels and auctioned them off. What happened to the other ten barrels remains a mystery.

The White House Basement Wine Racks

In June 1892 and April 1905 two different articles appeared in the *Omaha Daily Bee* which described the White House and how presidents lived and what they drank. One subtitle covered the White House basement. "There are no end of wine closets" which had "seen good liquor in the past," we are told. It was there in the basement wine closets that the presidents kept their favorite spirits.

Andrew Johnson stored his favorite Robertson County, Tennessee bourbon and sherry in the closets. John Tyler stored his "Jamaica rum and Madeira wine" which "he imported himself, trading ship loads of corn from his Virginia plantation."

Thomas Jefferson, we are told, filled the basement wine closets full of "bottles up to $11,000 [$425,000 in current values] worth of champagne and other liquors which he served up while he was in the White House ...Jefferson spent more on liquors than any other president on record." At the time presidents had to buy all food and liquor, pay for domestic help, heat etc. out of their own salaries. Jefferson was paid $25,000 annually.

Besides Jefferson, President Chester Arthur "was noted for his fine wines" and also enjoyed John Chamberlin's apple toddy [apple cider, dark rum, cinnamon sticks heated and served warm]. "Old Hickory"—President Andrew Jackson was fond of "punch...and drank rum, brandy, whiskey and applejack." Ulysses Grant, known for his drinking and public inebriation, "was fond of whisky punch and champagne." President Van Buren, we are told "indulged in liquors and Madeira wine" while Presidents James Polk, Rutherford Hayes and William Henry Harrison "used liquors less than others; yet all three knew good grog when they tasted it." Harrison's son, Benjamin, like Chester Arthur, was "appreciative of John Chamberlin's famous apple toddy."

President James Garfield "was fond of fine wines and once in a while indulged in brandy and ice." Honest Abe Lincoln was known to take a "snifter of bourbon occasionally... [sometimes] a glass or so of sherry or port." President Buchanan "took to Monongahela [rye] whiskey and was fond of fine wines." Franklin Pierce "was happy over" mint Juleps and "rum, brandy or whiskey" while Presidents Taylor and Millard Fillmore "were fond of a glass of good Madeira or brandy."

A few oddities about the basement were noted. Andrew Johnson's daughter owned a dairy and churned her own butter in the White House basement and "gave her guests a drink of buttermilk." Mary Todd Lincoln "peddled out extra milk of the White House" from the basement and President Buchanan's servants "ate him almost out of house and home" giving "some of the best porterhouse steaks to feed the stable dogs." Ike Hoover who spent forty-two years as the White House usher

White House Kitchen in 1891

describes the basement he first saw in 1891 when he started there: "Blackened with dirt and grime, the floor covered with slimy bricks." He wrote about "the old open fireplaces once used for broiling the chickens and baking hoecakes [cornbread]...the old cranes and spits still in place...there still remained the old wine vault, the meat house and smokehouse." Mary Brigid Barrett in an article published by *Our White House* observes that open hearth cooking (in the fireplace) was done until Millard Fillmore's presidency (1850-1853). "Bread was baked first in the [firewood and coal charged] bake ovens...and as the temperature dropped...in went the pies, and later the cookies and custard...knowing how to control the cooking temperatures was an art."

The basement until recent years was a stark place where servants lived. William Stoddard, a Lincoln aide, described it as having "the air of an old and unsuccessful hotel...perennially overrun with rats, mildew, and foul smells." When Teddy Roosevelt moved in he found a dingy kitchen with "a meat room, servants' chambers...servants' bedchambers, a housekeeper apartment and storage rooms piled with discarded furnishings." He installed a modern kitchen which has been altered and renovated by succeeding presidents.

The modern White House Kitchen is capable of serving dinner to as many as 140 guests and hors d'oeuvres to 1,000. It is manned by five full-time chefs. It actually has three kitchens—main kitchen (ground floor), diet kitchen (3rd floor) and family kitchen (2nd floor). Chefs and servants haven't lived on premises for several decades. The White House still maintains a wine cellar, the key to which is under control of the White House usher. Since Lyndon Johnson's presidency only American wines can be served at the White House and the basement is now known as the ground floor.

More Presidential Wine Stories

In 1894 Frank Carpenter, a well-known author-journalist, decided to seek out former servants of the nation's chief executives. His intent was to interview "the servants of the presidents...[men] who have lived with them...and who have known them as only a servant can know a master." He found them "the most interesting men about Washington."

These men's White House careers were long over by 1894 as Carpenter tracked them down one by one. Carpenter found them as clerks in government departments, "others [who] run little business establishments...[another] has a restaurant...perhaps the most interesting of all, drives bridal couples and tourists about Washington in his [horse drawn] cab." The latter was President Franklin Pierce's groom who stayed on—taking care of the White House stables through the presidencies of James Buchanan, Abraham Lincoln and Andrew Johnson. He told Carpenter that Pierce's favorite horse was "blind as a stone wall...[President Pierce] liked to ride fast...and gallop through the streets [of Washington alone] at night."

President James Buchannan had good horses, but never rode them. Buchanan was extravagant, Carpenter was told. He "brought food in [to the White House] by the wagonload, and the servants carried [stole] it away in basketfuls." He had ten dogs and the stable servants "often received a whole leg of lamb to feed the dogs" Additionally Carpenter reported Buchanan's "wine cellar was open and the servants took whatever they pleased."

The unnamed servant denied that President Andrew Johnson was a drunk. "No," he said, "I never saw President Johnson under the influence...and I drove his horses and met him every day I never smelt it upon his breath." One evening after driving Johnson to a dinner, he had to wait outside to take the president back to the White House. The servant was "nearly frozen" and Johnson invited him up to his room and offered him "a glass of wine to warm me up" which he declined. Instead he asked for a glass of whiskey to which Johnson "smiled and brought me out some of the best whiskey I have ever tasted." Arthur, another of the retired servants, told Carpenter that "Mistah Johnson had the best pale sherry that ever came into the White House…[whenever] the president had me serve lunch…the wine [served] was this pale sherry. It was might good." Once someone gifted Johnson a case of Scuppernong wine from North Carolina. After sipping the wine, he gave the case to Arthur who was from North Carolina, telling him "that wine will suit you better than it does me…"

Carpenter found one of Abraham Lincoln's coachmen working at the War Department. Mrs. Lincoln had discharged him for being absent when she called for her carriage. Lincoln's ten-year old son Tad was fond of the man and intervened with his father who "wrote him a card asking the Secretary of War to give him a position, and he got it." Carpenter relates that one of the most "affecting stories" was told him by a Mr. Pendie who had been employed in the White House for a generation and was still there at seventy when he tracked him down. He remembered how "little Tad [Lincoln] ran in and told him they had killed [his] papa."

Another former White House steward, Billy Crump during the administrations of Rutherford Hayes and James Garfield recalled that Garfield came into the White House suffering from dyspepsia [chronic indigestion] and could "only eat the plainest food…one of his favorite dishes was baked potatoes…he would press the mealy mass out of the skins with his hands and pour cream over them…[believing them] more digestible than potatoes and butter." He always had potatoes for breakfast along with steak which he also always ate for dinner. At the time of the interview, Crump owned a Washington, D.C. boarding house.

President Hayes we are told "always had candy on his table and Mrs. Hayes doted on angel's fruit cake [i.e., angel food cake filled with fruit]." Breakfast was normally fruit and oatmeal or grits followed by mutton chops or steak. "We always had cakes and President Hayes particularly liked corn bread." Lunch normally consisted of salads, cold meats and bread and butter. Dinner always began with oysters with a typical *entrée* consisting of fillet of roast, game and vegetables followed by dessert. The Hayes's were big coffee drinkers. Neither Garfield nor Hayes ever had wine at their tables.

President Chester Arthur, on the other-hand, always had wine at his table. His days started with "light breakfasts and his dinners [were] always late and we always had to wash the dishes in the early morning...he was a hard man to work for."

Wine Bottles as Hollywood Props
Bergman and Grant

Ingrid Bergman, Cary Grant, Claude Raines and Alfred Hitchcock—four of Hollywood's golden era greats.

Hitchcock directed Bergman, Grant and Raines in his movie *Notorious* which was released in 1946 exactly one year after the end of World War II. Hitler's insidious Nazi regime had been defeated just a year earlier. The world gasped on a daily basis as the Nuremberg Trials revealed Hitler's evils—Auschwitz, Treblinka, torture, humiliation, baskets of teeth with gold fillings and stolen artworks.

The cold war was just festering and the communist world and the west still had a shaky detente. Rumors circumnavigated the globe that Adolf Hitler, his chief aide Martin Bormann and hundreds of hated SS officers had escaped to South America in German U-Boats. The rumors insinuated that large caches of Nazi gold had been smuggled out of Germany along with its wicked genius scientists—the money to finance a Fourth Reich headed by a new cabal of evil masterminds.

Notorious fed on these rumors and fears. Its plot involved secret German nuclear activities in Rio de Janeiro.

Ingrid Bergman and Cary Grant--The Kiss

The story starts with Bergman's father having just been found guilty of treason for his espionage activities during the war. As a result of their undercover investigation, Alicia Huberman (played by Bergman) was known to the American intelligence community as a wealthy promiscuous floozy. T. R. Devlin (played by Cary Grant), an American intelligence agent, is ordered to woo her and enlist her to work as an undercover agent. Early into the movie Hitchcock has the couple kiss—considered one of the most erotic kisses in movie history—they fall in love. The kiss lasted two and a half minutes. At the end of the kiss, Devlin leaves to meet an associate promising to come back that evening. He asks her if she wants him to bring anything, "What about a nice bottle of wine? We'll celebrate." she responds. The kiss is still a favorite on YouTube.

Devlin's job is to recruit her to spy on a Nazi spy ring in Rio de Janeiro. She is specifically instructed to seduce Alex Sebastian (played by Claude Raines) who is the neo-Nazi group's leader and a former associate of her father. Recognizing her, Sebastian invites her to dinner at his opulent Rio home with some intimate "business associates," who are part of the secret Nazi group. She notices one of the guests became nervous when seeing a certain wine bottle. The guest tries to leave but is assassinated by Sebastian's "business associates." In the meantime, Devlin leads Alicia to believe he is married which distresses her. Heartbroken and bitter she marries Sebastian but continues to perform her undercover duties.

Together Devlin and Alicia investigate the wine cellar to look for the bottle of wine "that rattled the fellow at dinner." Devlin accidentally breaks the wine bottle which contains a sandy ore. He takes a sample of the contents which turns out to be uranium ore.

When Sebastian figures out that his wife is actually a U.S. agent investigating his activities he conspires with his mother to poison her. Together they put poison in her coffee, a little every morning, slowly and methodically in their conspiracy to kill her. Devlin figures out what is going on and rescues Alicia from the house leading Sebastian's associates to figure out that he has compromised their conspiracy. Devlin confesses to Alicia that he is not married and the two swear their love to one another. Sebastian realizing the gig is up, begs Devlin to take him with them to the hospital—"please take me! Please!" he pleads. Devlin tells him there's no room in the car: "But they're watching me," Sebastian begs again. "That's your headache," Devlin coldly responds.

As the movie ends one of Sebastian's associates ask him to return to the house saying "I wish to talk to you." As Devlin and Alicia speed off to the hospital, Sebastian is seen walking back into his house—presumably to his death.

Francois Truffaut interviewed Alfred Hitchcock for over twelve hours in 1962. In his 1967 book *Alfred Hitchcock—A Definitive Study* he writes that in *Notorious* "there is a constant feeling of intoxication about the film." He also noted the recurring prop theme: "bottles of wine figure significantly in several episodes."

Whale and Dog Meat

The U.S. entered World War I in April of 1917.

The nation was asked to send nearly two million soldiers to assist the Allied war effort against the Axis powers. One of the sacrifices the home front was expected to experience was a beef shortage—war planners anticipated at least ten percent of the nation's beef would be diverted to our European allies.

By February of 1918, marine biologists started touting whale meat as a way of overcoming beef shortages. Roy Chapman, curator of the American Museum of National History declared "Americans [should] make...use of the 15,000,000 pounds of whale meat" wasted annually. He contended the meat "is very much like venison...[with] an exceptionally fine flavor peculiarly its own." Chapman "tendered a luncheon...to thirty representatives of a somewhat hungry America," claimed an article in the *Washington Times*. Chapman's proposal was heartily endorsed by Herbert Hoover, chief of the Federal Food Administration. Several of the guests told reporters the luncheon "was equal to many and far better than others they had attended in New York." The *Times* article noted that the Japanese had eaten the sea goliath's meat for centuries and dairy shortages in Norway and Denmark led those governments to use whale fat for margarine and lard.

The *Times* related that statistically, one 350,000 Rorqual [Baleen] whale "would release 500 cattle that would yield 250 pounds [each] of beef for the American army in France."

The article also promoted dog meat as another source to minimize meat rationing: "Looking toward utilization of some of the millions of useless dogs...for food [is] likely." The article concluded "a choice cut from a dog should be just as palatable as from a hog...[nor] would the plain hound dog or common cur...depreciate the value of sausage any more than the use of left-overs of slaughterhouses." During the previous year the District of Columbia had "impounded 4,288 dogs [which if] fattened might have been used for food."

H. F. Taylor of the U. S. Bureau of Fisheries reported "muskrats were being eaten for food [in Michigan]." Michigonians referred to the creatures as "marsh rabbits." Taylor asserted "Millions are caught annually [for their fur], in traps and otherwise, but only 10% of the catch is eaten," He also proposed large ocean populations of shark and eel were available for human consumption, "people [must] disregard unpleasant names," he asserted

Even "the little English sparrow" was expected to do its part for the war effort. Introduced into America in 1869 to eat caterpillars in city trees in Philadelphia, sparrows were suggested as a good food source. Their flocks had multiplied into a "pest because [they] eat [farmers' grain]." Home economists invited dignitaries in Washington to dine on "an English sparrow pie." The pie, we are told "was pronounced delicious and each sparrow was found to be a toothsome morsel." The effort to check the growth of the sparrow population by exploiting it as a food source was endorsed by the U. S. Department of Agriculture.

A year later, the Bureau of Fisheries continued hyping using whale meat as a way to "beat the high cost of beef." Whale meat, the bureau contended, was "suited to steaks, soups, stews, roasts and curries." The Bureau published a series of recipes developed by government domestic scientists and others "donated to the government...[by] hotel chefs and home cooks." New York's Delmonico's Restaurant contribution: 'Whale Patties.' The government subsidized and oversaw fresh whale meat distribution to markets in refrigerated railroad cars. Additionally consumers could buy the meat canned "or corned like beef." "There are no bones in whale and no waste," contended a government spokesmen.

By 1920 the *Richmond Times-Dispatch* declared "when the armistice was signed the bottom of the market [had] dropped...the whale meat fashion has flivvered." The *Dispatch* went on to explain that the meat had "a certain oily flavor reminiscent of blubber and a whale ships [deck]…and [had] little appeal to the palate of fastidious." The same year, though, Captain John B. Loop of Long Beach raised the possibility of a whale milk dairy in Los Angeles. Loop claimed whale milk was "richer and more palatable than cow's milk." He received an order for a supply of the milk from an Omaha dairy and asserted if demand warranted it, he would "bring the cow whales to [Los Angeles] so they can be herded into a dairy." Nothing came of the idea but one can't help but wonder how they would have been milked—let alone fed?

In 1921, war ravaged Germany imported whale meat from Vancouver for use "in the manufacture of hamburger" for its starving population.

A Glass of Tokay and the Baby's Rattle

The two men met at a snake exhibit in a museum. Afterward they retired to a local restaurant where seventy-something Thomas Wilman conveyed this snake story to an unidentified "young man." Relaxing over a bottle of Tokay, "Wilman lifted his wine glass between his thumb and finger [and] watched the exquisite light playing in the red depths of the glass" as he proceeded to tell the story. It was 1884.

Thirty-one years before, Wilman had married his sweetheart Katie in Great Barrington, Massachusetts. "We were young and had the world before us, and [in 1853] we concluded to go west... [to make our fortune]." He explained, "In those days going west didn't mean going beyond the Mississippi."

They settled in Cattaraugus, New York where he established a saw mill in Skinner Hollow. The hills "were covered with a first class pine,'" he remarked. He built a saw-mill "right down in that hollow" on a stream to power the saw. Next door he built their house. Over the next couple of years business was good and they prospered. They had a son, Harry.

"Katie," Wilman said "used to think the saw-mill was just about the pleasantest place in the country. Hour after hour she'd stay out there with me." "Lost in happy reverie" he remembered how "she used to jump on the log and ride up pretty close to the saw to scare me...nobody was ever happier than we were."

"There were snakes then...rattlers [came] around the mill... In the country we expected to find snakes." As long as the snakes "kept their distance...we didn't mind them," related Wilman.

He had built a bedstead that "had neither a head nor footboard...one end was raised a little like a couch, and that was the head." Wilman, Katie and baby Harry slept under "bearskins and blankets" in the "chilly nights" of fall and winter.   Their heat was a fireplace "parallel with the bed." They had an English shepherd dog named Leo—"a black and white beauty" whom they had brought with them from Massachusetts. Kate loved the dog which she had raised from a pup.   Leo was trained to come whenever Wilman whistled. Wilman told the young man "We let him sleep in the room at the foot of the bed...in the morning he'd wake up Katie by licking her face."

One cold fall night Wilman threw an "extra pine knot on the fire...went to bed and fell asleep." He couldn't sleep, got up and threw another pine knot on the fire. As he walked back to the bed, "Leo gave me a loving look as I stooped down and patted his head."   He fell into an "uneasy sleep" when "all at once" Wilman "awakened with a start... [he] saw his Katie asleep and Harry" in his baby slumber between the two of them.

As Wilman's eyes focused he saw "a dark object glide down from off the baby...a rattlesnake fully five feet long, had slipped down from between my wife and myself, where it had been stretched out...to get warm."   Startled by Wilman's movement, the snake threw itself "into a coil...at the baby's feet and just opposite" Wilman's knee.   He wondered if he "would ever see tomorrow." Lying motionless on the bed Wilman saw the snake's head rise and "for the first time sounded its rattle."   The noise awakened Katie who "opened her eyes...every vestige of color left her face, but she did not move a muscle." Death "lay between them in a more horrible form than" they had ever dreamed of. Her eyes spoke in a way "a man does not see more than once in a lifetime...[saying] for the baby's sake ," Wilman relayed. Then he slowly "and with infinite care raised" his head until he could see Leo.   "The hideous head of the snake swayed to and fro," he continued.

He whistled. "Leo as quick as thought...sprang to his feet and bounded on to the bead." Katie grabbed the baby and rolled out of the bed while Wilman rolled out on his side and grabbed his rifle. "The dog and snake were rolling together on the bed" when Wilman shot the snake.   Leo "staggered off the bed...shivered, moaned and looked from" Wilman to Katie "with more love than [Wilman] ever saw before or since in any animal's eye and died."

At daybreak the next morning they buried the dog, sold the mill and the house and "before the sunset" were on "their way [back] to Massachusetts." Wilman built another mill in "the East" and "prospered and got rich." Katie and he had "other children and there were grandchildren now," he told the unidentified young man.

Torrents of Italian Idioms

Prohibition created numerous Italian gangsters—"Scarface" Capone, "Lucky" Luciano, "Fat Joe" Pinzolo, "Joe the Boss" Masseria and the like. Italian-Americans missed their wine—so did native Italians when visiting the U.S.

As prohibition took hold, a number of regulatory problems arose. A 1919 Philadelphia incident was reported which "brought tears to the American workmen's eyes making repairs on the" Italian steamship *Corca*. The *Corca* which was described as being "six nautical inches from Philadelphia," by the *Philadelphia Evening Public Ledger* was unloading a load of cork at Pier 34. When the Italian sailors, thirsty from the cork dust, "knocked off for chow each seaman broke out his bottle...happily chatting in their native liquid tongue...they stretched out bronze hands grasping [their empty wine bottles while] the steward put a funnel in the neck of each bottle and filled it from a bucket of wine," continued the article. "The scene" the Ledger concluded "was from a happier world, enacted in the clear, bright sunlight on the Delaware [River]" to the chagrin of the American shipwrights who were prohibited by law from imbibing.

The following year, federal authorities had become more rigid in applying the prohibition laws to foreign vessels. When the Italian liner *Regina d'Italia* and Spanish steamer *Prince de Satrustegui* docked in New York in January of 1920 all liquor aboard "was placed in quarantine [by customs officers]," according to the *New York Sun*. The liner's labor contracts required "that a certain quantity of wine should be served to officers and men daily." Ships officials claimed that the United States had no right to "interfere with the feeding of the crews, wine being regarded as much a part of the meals as coffee and tea are to American repasts," reported the *Sun*. The Spanish captain whose ship was laden with a large cargo of Spanish wine destined to Havana said the ship "should be regarded as practically at sea, in the circumstances, and that their right to drink [wine] at meals aboard ship...should be the same here as [when at sea]." The sailors claimed it was the first time in their lives "they had been forced to eat without wine." Both the Spanish and Italian captains asserted the matter would be taken up by the Italian and Spanish embassies in Washington.

In 1921 things had loosened up a bit. The Italian steamer *Vindobona* arrived in New York harbor. Their contract called for a bottle of wine a day which was provided aboard the ship at mealtime. However the ship's chandlers were unable to purchase wine for the return trip to Italy. Midway across the Atlantic the ship's crew was informed their wine ration had been exhausted. Two days and 600 miles out "they forced the skipper back to New York, claiming the ship was leaking." When the ship docked the sailors insisted their agents provide them with a fresh supply of wine but all that could be had was 150 cases of near beer which "they grudgingly accepted and once more went to sea," an article in the *Washington Evening Star* reported. As they sailed home, "torrents of Italian idioms and thundering comments about the near beer drenched the [airways] with such wireless messages as no one ever received before...[the crew wired:] We pledge ourselves never to return to America while its laws against good wine remains in force...[we will] never [again] meet these horrors," concluded the *Star's* report.

Secretary Mellon resolved dispute

By 1922 all of Europe was up in arms over perceived American threats that they would seize foreign ships with wine, ale or other alcoholic spirits onboard. One editorial reasoned Americans would be equally upset if foreign laws "forbid our ships to bring ice water or buckwheat cakes into [European] ports..." "Besides," the editorial reasoned if American passenger liners carried only water while foreign ships carried wine, "our ships won't carry any passengers."

The problem was finally resolved in November of 1922 when Andrew Mellon, Secretary of the Treasury, ruled that crews on foreign ships could drink their wine "even when tied fast to prohibition American docks."

Vodka and Holy Water

In 1958 Catherine McClure and Miranda Doyle were expelled from Catholic grammar school in Lewiston, New York. Their expulsion resulted from their spiking the holy water font with vodka, turning Father Flanagan into a raving lunatic while saying Mass. Catherine Gildiner (nee McClure) confessed it all in her 1999 best seller--*Too Close To The Falls*.

The incident occurred shortly after the Irish priest had run into the twelve year old girls at a local variety store. They were buying pre-teen makeup—"wax fingernails filled with cherry Kool-Aid." Flanagan innocently insulted them by putting one arm on each of their shoulders while saying in his cheerful Irish brogue: "A-ha, here we have beauty and brains walking abreast.'" "Public school boys," writes Gildiner, overheard the remark and snickered which only served to intensify the girl's embarrassment.

Catherine McClure

The girls swore revenge—McClure—the smart one—was piqued: "stores sold makeup, not IQ points." Doyle—the pretty one—was equally upset: "Father Flanagan had no right to say she was stupid." "Besides" chimed in Doyle "he's a drunk." McClure's mother called his affliction "a weakness for the sacramental spirits." The following Saturday Doyle went to confession and made sure she was the last in line. She drained the holy water from the font, replacing it with vodka after studying Father Flanagan's routine. He dipped his crucifix in the vodka, made the sign of the cross and kissed it—"the taste of vodka." He repeated the process several times before each Mass. By the noon Mass, he had a good heat on as he started his homily. The priest got "red-faced, banging the pulpit, rocking the goose-necked lamp, shouting in Irish lilt...'the bloody Limeys have reigned over the Irish for how long, *how long*?'" His outraged, chest-beating damning of the English continued until Mother Superior Agnes signaled the "bewildered" altar boys to ring the communion bells.

Not long afterwards, the girls were summoned to the rectory. Father Flanagan, holding his "liquid refreshment" chastised the two girls telling them "this is your last chance...can you ask God's forgiveness?" Both said yes. There was no forgiveness with Mother Superior Agnes, though, who emphatically announced: "I run a Catholic School, a temple for young souls, and just as Jesus expelled the merchants from His temple in justified anger...you are expelled."

The same year in San Francisco, Arthur Castle had his own run-in with vodka and holy water. Castle was the printing-production manager for the *San Francisco Progress* newspaper. His son Buddy relates that Arthur was born a Presbyterian. When he proposed to his wife-to-be Kay, she insisted he convert. He and his wife Kay had two children, both of whom were raised in compliance with Kay's wishes—attending Catholic grammar and high Schools. Arthur never really took to his new religion but Kay was as rigidly devout a Catholic as there could be—Mass and rosary every day—a volunteer for all church and school events. On one occasion her devotion took her to Europe where she visited several Marian apparition sites of the Catholic religion—Fatima, Lourdes, La-Salette, Knock and the like.

While in Lourdes she filled a bottle of spring water from the grotto in which the Virgin Mother had appeared to St. Bernadette. Since the 1858 apparition which created the spring fed lake, there has been over 7,000 unexplained cures of which 69 have been recognized and documented as "truly miraculous." When she arrived back in San Francisco, Kay put her "treasured" bottle into the refrigerator, periodically dipping and blessing herself.

One day Arthur hurt his leg at work. The doctor prescribed aspirin and a temporary cane and sent him home for the remainder of the day. He decided to fix himself a cocktail. Spying the unlabeled bottle of water in the refrigerator he drained it into a glass of vodka and placed the empty bottle on the sink. When Kay came home she blew her top. Arthur apologized, but she continued to snipe at him the rest of the day for his irreverent and blasphemous deed. The following morning as he left for work he threw his cane down in front of Kay claiming the Lourdes holy water had miraculously cured his ailing leg. Kay watched him limp out the front door. She chuckled the rest of the day. All was forgiven.

Kevin O'Donoghue was a Peace Corps volunteer to Latvia in 1994. He relates how one of the local Catholics in the village of Bemani filled an empty vodka bottle with holy water from a bucket inside the local church. Like Kay he was struck thinking "what an obscene mingling of the sacred and profane." Later that evening at dinner he discovered it was a local tradition to drink a glass of holy water with Easter dinner.

The Wine Brawl

In 1902, the French ship *Charles Gounod* docked at the Long Island City pier. The three-masted steel barque had sailed from Cherbourg and London with a load of ballast.

After docking, Captain Jules Oger threw an on-board banquet for his crew. According to a *New York Sun* article, "wine flowed freely" at the banquet. Afterwards the Captain and most of the sailors went ashore. The crew "tried to get more drinks in the Long Island City saloons but failed because the saloonkeepers did not understand French," continued the *Sun*.

The thirsty and very disappointed crew returned to the ship around 9 P.M. and asked the first mate, Caesar Lugie, for more wine to continue their partying. Lugie, it was reported, refused and a heated argument followed with "members of the crew declaring that they would take whatever they wanted." Lugie and two of his loyal sailors "tried to prevent the men from getting at the wine, and a free [for all]...followed."

Typical three masted Barque like the Charles Gounod

The article asserted "It was the liveliest sort of fight. Knives were drawn and crewmen chased each other upon the deck and down into the forecastle" and through the ship's passageways between decks. Lugie's two stalwarts were forced to "take refuge in the hold of the vessel."

Lugie resorted to using his pistol with which "he kept up a steady fire" in his efforts to keep the drunken sailors at bay. His use of the pistol only served to intensify the sailor's anger "and they hurled iron spikes at him" forcing him to hide in the forecastle (i.e. the sailor's living quarters). Then they hurled firewood at him and threatened "to set the [ship] afire to force him from his hiding place."

Lugie kept yelling for help. After about a half hour his cries were finally heard by a dock watchman who telephoned police headquarters. A half hour later a squad of thirty policemen arrived and "found the sailors shouting, fighting and trying to get at the first mate." The policeman finally were able to board the ship and found themselves "in hand-to-hand battle with the sailors." The ship's cook attacked one policeman with "a knife raised to stab him." Another cop "hit the cook on the head with a club and knocked him senseless." All told, the battle with the police lasted another half hour and ended with the arrest of seventeen sailors. Five of the men were charged. The remaining twelve were freed and returned to the ship. The *Sun* article reported that "all the members of the crew were cut and bleeding" and needed doctors' care.

Four of the crewmen charged by police were arraigned the following day and sentenced to five days in the city jail. The cook who had threatened the police with a knife was bound over for a grand jury indictment.

The *Sun* article concluded by describing the ship as looking "like it [had] passed through a cyclone." Broken bolts, logs of wood, "and other things the sailors had used in the fight" were strewn "all over the decks." The Captain, who had been ashore when the melee erupted, told reporters "he would leave everything in disorder until the French Consul could see for himself just what sort of time the men had in his absence."

The ship was named after the famous prolific French composer. Today Charles Gounod is best remembered for his opera *Faust*—one of the most frequently staged operas of all time. He composed innumerable religious opuses—his version of *Ave Maria,* based on Bach's first prelude, is the one most often in use today. A deeply religious man, Gounod, who had died nine years before the wine brawl incident, would have been horrified and appalled by the fight on a ship named after him.

Chicken and Wine

Chicken and wine go together like peanut butter and jelly or bacon and eggs. There's nothing more refreshing and satisfying than a good glass of wine with a roasted chicken.

But what about chickens drinking wine? Is it beneficial or harmful or just plain humorous?

In November of 1911, French agriculture Professor M. Joubert reported the results of an experiment which the press claimed "would cause the poultry keepers of [America] to chant anew the virtues" of wine. According to an article in the *Yale Expositor,* Joubert was investigating why egg production declines during the winter months. The professor pondered if the decline was attributed to the hens "growing lazy or the early hours they keep in the cold [prevented] proper attention to business." At the time, French egg production during winter months had declined "in recent years...with a growing [dependency]" on foreign eggs. The professor wanted to rectify "this condition of [economic] affairs," and newspapers claimed "he seems to have been successful."

Joubert "selected a dozen young hens and divided them into two indiscriminate lots of six each," Both groups were served the same diet with the exception that one group was given "a daily ration of a glass of wine per head." Joubert was amazed with the results. Egg production during the four month period October 1910 through January 1911 by the hens who did not receive a ration of wine was twenty-seven. In contrast, the wine-drinking hens produced one hundred and forty-eight eggs during the same four month period. Joubert's report claimed the wine "greatly improved [egg] quality."

The *Expositor* noted that Professor Joubert didn't report "what sort of wine" was used in the experiment: "If he used the best champagne, the cost would exceed the profit... [but if the cheaper] *vin ordinaire* was used...a new and important field of consumption [of wine] will open up." French wine sales had declined in recent years and Joubert's experiment could come as a great relief to "French wine growers," the article concluded.

A different result, to a degree, was experienced by Mrs. S. A. Thompson of Louisville, Kentucky whose Preston Street house "took on the appearance of a trained animal show" one Sunday afternoon in 1909. Earlier in the day Mrs. Thompson went to her cellar and "discovered that [her]...blackberry wine had soured." Not wanting to discard it, she took it to her chicken yard and "poured the wine into their trough," according to the *Crittenden Record-Press*. "A big buff rooster strutted up to the trough and, taking a sip, sent out the call that brought the entire brood [of 100 chickens] hurrying to the feast," continued the article. The chickens drank until the trough was empty. "Then the fun began. Mothers fought with sons and daughters. Hens cackled and roosters crowed while the battle was on," the *Record-Press* reported. The rooster which started the affair collapsed "with a farewell crow [when] he stumbled over on his side."

When Mrs. Thompson heard the commotion she looked outside and saw the "chickens wobbling about in their drunken frenzy...some [were] lying on their backs apparently dead...she called her husband [to help but] by the time the majority were down and out." The couple thought the chickens would be ok within a couple of hours—at least before nightfall but "nearly everyone had to be carried into the hen house." Fortunately all recovered by the morning with the exception of "one old hen, who so far [had] forgotten her motherly duties...leaving her brood of thirteen chicks to the mercy of the rats, cats and dogs," concluded the article. There was no mention of egg production increases or decreases.

Not exactly on point but of sentimental interest was a story in the *St. Paul Daily Globe* about a "big...cat playing with a... hen...[the cat] was purring at the hen." When queried the hen's owner Mrs. Linchley of East St. Louis related that "that cat is the mother of that chicken." Apparently the cat had chased a sitting hen [the real mother] off her nest in order to give birth to her kittens. The next thing Mrs. Linchley knew "there was a nest full of kittens and one chicken...from the time the 'chick' struggled through the shell to the present day it has been a member of the feline family," the *Globe* reported. Continuing the cat's "feathered ward...has frequently been seen perching beside its foster mother [and they were] frequently together in the barnyard [enjoying] each other's company."

Duel Purpose Wines

For hundreds of years duels were fought over minute points of honor such as dogs, geese, a pinch of snuff or "trumps in a game of cards." *The [1829] Dueling Handbook* describes a duel between British General Barry who was challenged by Captain Smith "for declining [dinner] wine on a steamboat... [even] though the General had pleaded...that wine [at sea] made him sick." In 1777, a couple of British soldiers engaged in a duel over eating an ear of corn, "one contending that the eating was from the cob" while the other asserted "that the grain should be cut from the cob before eating." The cob proponent was shot in the arm which "had to be amputated," reported the *Louisiana Democrat.* R. J. and A. W. Bodmer relate the origination of the custom of clinking glasses. It started "[in] the days of Roman gladiators [who drank] a glass of wine before the combat...[continuing] through "the days when dueling was considered the only method of settling an affront." The challenger "or his friends provided the wine," explains the Bodmers. A fear of treachery "had to be considered...[the challenged] insisted the wine be poured from one glass into the other before drinking...[thus] if poisoned both dueling combatants would die." Neither

German student with scar

dueling nor pouring wine from one glass into the other is any longer customary. Still "the friendly spirit is shown...[by] the mere touching of glasses," concluded the Bodmers.

A duel between Colonel J. M. Robinson and John Carrell about a Fordham [Bronx] Village widow exhibits one humorous incident in 1872. They chose "seven-barreled navy revolvers" for the combat. The event occurred behind the Fordham Hotel where "it so happened that a large willow tree stood at each end of the ground paced off, and just to the left of each principal." The two men shook hands and the referee counted off one, two three. "Before the three could be pronounced both [men]…dodged behind the trees and fired." The shots went wild—one "going in the air" and the other "went into the ground." The men decided to call it quits, "shook hands [and] invited their friends into the hotel" treating them to wine according to an article in the *Orangeburg News*.

The most sophisticated dueling in the world developed in the German Universities during the 1700s and continued through World War I. At Heidelberg University dueling with swords was a kind of early form of fencing. The all-men student body was regulated according to military customs. Classes were divided into Korps. Each "had several students" who were considered good duelists and intramural duels between the different Korps were "fought each day," according to a 1911 article in the *Orangeburg Times and Democrat*. The events were held in a campus "fighting house" which contained a zinc bowl, chair and surgeon's table. "After the duel the men are placed in" the chair "while their wounds are being dressed" and the zinc bowl was "to prevent the blood" from running onto the floor. The duelists were "well covered" with eye, neck, nose and leg guards. The legs and body were covered in chamois leather pants and the "right arms…[padded with a soft silk material]." Table and chairs were placed around the `sides of the room "where [Korps] members…[sat] with their wine" to watch the duels. The duelist's objectives were to give each other "cuts" in the face. A scar was regarded as an honor "and no effort was made to efface the mark after it" healed. "Blood often flowed at the first slash…[and duels were often] stopped to examine the wound and wipe away the blood" before resuming.

Dueling was not only a man's sport. In May of 1889 a "most unusual and sanguinary encounter took place…between two young ladies," reported the *Sedalia Weekly Bazoo*. Misses Rucker and Kyle fought a duel over "a young man." Each girl "obtained a knife and they attacked each other with the utmost fury, using the weapons with such scientific and murderous effect that they were soon covered with blood." Rucker gave up the fight and ran off "with Kyle in hot pursuit…[but who soon] fell to the ground exhausted." Kyle was taken home by friends who discovered a "dangerous cut from her spine to the forearm." The two girls were arrested but the judge discharged them on the grounds of self-defense. While called a duel it was really just a chic fight. The *Bazoo* did not report if any wine was drunk before or after the incident.

Wine Bricks

When prohibition became the law of the nation in 1920, a statutory provision provided that families could produce up to 200 gallons of wine for home use consumption. Grape growers capitalized on the loophole by packaging grape concentrates in brick-like packages for sale. The bricks would then be dissolved in water and fermented into wine. Wine brick makers cautioned buyers: *After dissolving the brick in a gallon of water, do not place the liquid in a jug away in the cupboard for twenty days, because then it would turn into wine.* According to an article by drink historian Reid Mitenbuler, "The makers of the Vino Sano Grape Brick even dutifully indicated what flavors one's careless handling of grape bricks would result in: burgundy, sherry, port, claret, riesling, etc." The wine brick makers also cautioned: *To prevent fermentation, add 1/10% Benzoate of Soda.* Another loophole product sold was a type of grape jelly called "Vine-go," which like the bricks could be fermented into wine by the simple addition of water.

When lawmakers crafted the law they anticipated use of the loophole by including a provision "that if the shipper knew that the final buyer was going to use the grapes for making wine then both buyer and seller could be charged with a conspiracy," according to an article by Kelsey Burnham. It was virtually impossible to file criminal complaints, though, because of the chain of commerce involved in selling wine bricks, i.e. growers to processors to wholesalers to retailers to consumers.

As an interesting sidelight, Mitenbuler's article sheds light on how Cesar Mondovi, a Minnesota grocer was sent by an Italian social club to California to acquire a suitable supply of the wine bricks for its members. "Mondovi," he writes "quickly abandoned the life of a Minnesota grocer and moved his family, including young son Robert, to the Golden State." The rest, of course, is history.

Eric Hwang, who publishes the *Bricks of Wine Blog*, writes that to meet demand for wine bricks, "growers increased their production by seven-fold." Home winemaking grew nine-fold. Prior to Prohibition, U.S. wineries sold 141 million bottles a year. According to *Wine Folly.com*, "many wineries shut their doors and poured out their barrels." Within a very short time, speakeasies opened across America—New York City alone boasted 30,000 individual facilities. Special "Booze Cruises" were inaugurated which took shiploads of passengers beyond U. S. territorial limits where imbibing was legal.

Several wineries, bucking the trend, remained in business by specializing in sacramental wine which was not criminalized under prohibition laws. Georges de Latour, founder of Beaulieu Winery, made a deal with the Catholic Archdiocese of San Francisco (which, at the time, included virtually every parish in Northern California) to provide sacramental wine. By 1924, though, *Wine Folly* explains government officials became "highly suspicious of sacramental wine…due to the rampant growth to nearly a million gallons in two short years." Several permits were cancelled because, according to *Napa Valley Register* writer Kelsey Burnham, of the perception "that priest and rabbis were acting as bootleggers for their congregations…their titles effectively shielding them from prosecution." Between 1922 and 1924 sacramental wine sales increased by 800,000 gallons annually. Ms. Burnham's research also confirmed that between 1920 and 1933 (when Prohibition ended) "[Napa Valley] grape production actually increased and the savvy business people who figured out how to work the system became exceedingly wealthy."

Another common less-than-legal practice, according to Burnham: "Wineries would also bottle new wine and switch it out with bottles in their cellars, which were locked and routinely inspected by the government to make sure bottles did not go missing."

Whiskey, rum, brandy and gin had their own loophole—they could be dispensed with a doctor's prescription. The AMA, capitalizing on the potential new revenue source, declared whiskey and other ardent spirits useful for twenty-seven medical maladies including diabetes, cancer, snake bites and even old age, according to Daniel Okrent in a 2010 *Los Angeles Times* article. Distilleries, such as Jack Daniel's, simply inserted "unexcelled for Medicinal Purposes" on its label and peddled their product through pharmacies. Okrent relates how a doctor's liquor prescription cost about $40 in today's value and the same amount to have "it filled by the local pharmacist." All told a "legitimate" bottle of distilled spirits cost $80. These high costs only served to drive up sales of cheaper illicit booze sold in speakeasies and through other illegal outlets. Still, it is estimated doctors grossed $40 million in medicinal hooch office visits during Prohibition [$543 million in current values].

Roasted Peacock and Carp Tongue Pie

In the late 1880s and early 1900s a number of culinary experts complained about the decline in banquets and joviality in civilized society—especially at Christmastime. Article after article waxed nostalgic about exquisite meals prepared over the "twelve days of Christmas" in yesteryear. The feasts stemmed from medieval times and the *pièce de résistance* was always a roasted peacock. References to the dish were cited during Roman Emperor Caligula's reign.

Typically the peacock was carefully skinned, making sure all plumage remained intact. The bird was then stuffed "with spices and sweet herbs" and roasted (Caligula liked his stuffed with hummingbirds). When it was removed from the ovens it "was carefully sewed up again in its gorgeous plumage," relates one newspaper account. The bird was then carried into the banquet room on a gold plate by the "fairest lady" and carved by the "most honored guest." Another article attests that the bird had to be frequently basted with butter or lard to keep it from being too dry. In order to moisten the meat, after the bird was re-sewn, a sauce made of equal parts of "port wine and strong beef gravy mixed with a cupful of currant jelly" was carefully poured into the body "from the neck allowing the same to permeate slowly into the bird."

Another version was the peacock pie "common to Shakespeare's day…the stately pye." The cut-up bird was mixed with seasoning, herbs and other meats and cooked as a pie. The head of the peacock was "elevated above the crust" on the front side of the pie and "the beautiful tail spread out to its full extent" on the back side of the pie related another article.

Any number of other medieval side dishes was served up along with the peacock. "Brawn" sausage was made by capturing wild boars which were penned to fatten them. According to an 1884 *Harper's Magazine* article by Charles Warner, while fattening, the boars were cruelly strapped and belted tight "in order to make the flesh dense and brawn." Other dishes included mince pie, mutton, beef, pork veal, goose, turkey, cheese and apples to name but a few. Specialty pies included carp tongues (an average tongue is 4 inches), smoked cow tongue and mutton. Another pie served was a *Tartee* which was comprised of sliced boiled pork mixed with eggs, raisins, sugar, ginger powder, "white grease and small birds covered with a crust made of "prunes, saffron and salt." A 1906 article published in the *Hartford Republican* nostalgically relates the banquet of 14th Century marriage of Violante Visconti to England's Duke Lionel Plantagenet in Milan. The dinner consisted of eighteen courses including "suckling pigs wrapped in a thin coating of gold [and] veal roasted and trout encrusted in gold."

A popular desert of medieval times, still served well into the nineteenth century, was *Viande Royale*. The dish consisted of boiling clarified white wine and honey mixed with rice, ginger powder, pepper, cinnamon, cloves, saffron, sugar, mulberries and sandalwood and "salted [until] it looked stiff." At the same time in Lombardy the residents had a "great love" of ice cream. As eating customs change, so do words and their meanings: "With this great love of sweets came a certain *effeminacy* of manner. The *gay* banqueters sat at the table with their frills and furbelows [pleated hems] completely covered with paper... [while eating] the much relished [ice cream] that they should not dribble on their gewgaws [baubles, trinkets]."

A popular Christmas game was called Snapdragon. A large bowl of brandy was set on fire into which was thrown raisins. Revelers plucked the raisins out of the burning liquor.

A number of popular alcoholic beverages are long gone, such as "egg-hot" made with mixing heated beer, egg yolks, brandy, nutmeg and sugar.

One newspaperman concluded "so pungent and numerous are the condiments required that we are forced to the conclusion that the people of the time [i.e. England's King Richard II] must have had very tough palates and the digestion of the proverbial ostrich…[British soldiers during Queen Victoria's reign] that [inherited and] assimilated these dishes could triumph over anything on earth!" Another writer opined "from an epicurean point of view [medieval cuisine] lacked much in the way of preparation and manner of serving…[but] in succeeding years the manner…changed [a] little by little [and] a certain fondness for dishes a trifle bizarre and grotesque began to be felt."

Wine and the Best Fellow
on the Ship

In 1919 the passenger steamer *Orinoko*, which had originated in Naples, stopped at Gibraltar in route to New York. One of the passengers who boarded was Billy Mickleton. Newspaper accounts advised that he came aboard with a number of crates "which were marked 'machinery.'"

Mickleton, we are told, was "a pleasant spoken, hail-fellow-well-met sort of person." He was an extrovert and "made acquaintance rapidly with the other passengers." A consummate gambler, he "bet freely" and, win or lose, he "opened wine to celebrate his good fortune...[or if he lost] to celebrate the winner's luck." According to newspaperman Fred Young "he soon became known as the best fellow on the ship."

The other passengers made discrete inquiry as to what was in the crates which he had brought aboard. He claimed it was a secret but all his fellow passengers would know the contents of the crates before the end of the voyage. "I'm going to make an experiment that will attract the attention of the world," he said. He went on to explain that he was under contract with a New York newspaper. His experiment was to be kept secret until the ship approached the New York coast and "the newspaper is to have the exclusive rights of publication," he continued.

As the ship passed the Island of Madeira, Mickleton's fellow passengers speculated as to the nature of his mission. One suggested the crates contained "some kind of new boat," while another speculated they held a one-man "light submarine." Yet another guessed Mickleton would be shot out of a mortar which was inside the crates "and come down with a patent parachute."

When the *Orinoko* was five hundred miles out of New York, Mickleton began to unload his crates. "When they had been unpacked [he] set to work and put together an aeroplane." The passengers gathered to watch his work but he "waited until they turned in for the night" to do the assembly. When they congregated on the deck in the morning "they found the aeroplane concealed under a canvas cover."

The captain ordered the crew to remove the ship's stern rails in order "to render a start possible." Mickleton's fellow passengers peppered him with questions: Was he testing a "new power [source]"; was he going to attempt a new speed or height record; was he going to fly into port ahead of the ship or "make a transatlantic flight?" (Charles Lindberg's historic flight wouldn't occur until 1927, some fourteen years in the future).

Mickleton told his fellow passengers it "grieved him not to be able to satisfy them" but his newspaper contract bound him to silence—the newspaper had extended "funds to carry out his experiment...[if his tongue slipped] he would lose a small fortune." When they became too persistent, "Billy opened a bottle of wine."

When Fire Island, parallel to Long Island, was sighted, Mickleton prepared his plane for flight. "The last article he put on his machine was a small box...[the size of which suggested] it might contain food and drink to last a week." The flight, his fellow travelers agreed, would thus be a long one—"Mickleton [they postulated] was intending to make straight across the Atlantic back to Gibraltar...if necessary he would have stopping points at the Azores or Madeira."

As if to demonstrate the veracity of his story, he went to the ship's wireless office and sent a "ciphered" message to a New York newspaper. He then went to the aeroplane, removed the cover and got aboard. "Sailors on a run pushed him along the deck...and he caught the air, hardly striking the water surface, and then rose gradually." Mickleton turned the aircraft towards New York and "gradually passed out of sight."

The *Orinoko* reached New York a few hours later but was delayed by "quarantine"—a mandatory procedure of the time. The ship docked the following morning and "every passenger...[was] eager to read the account of the aeroplane flight...[but] not a single newspaper mentioned it." The incident eventually "passed out of the minds of the passengers...and was forgotten."

A few years' later newspapers reported that Mickleton, "the slickest smuggler working between Europe and America, who had evaded [custom laws] had been caught red handed." Among his "smuggling devices," the article gave an account of, "[was] his getting a million dollars' worth of diamonds...by flying an aeroplane from the deck of a ship."

Wattles and Bottles

In 1891 Kate Field was a nationally known journalist and temperance supporter. Having studied in Europe, she considered herself an above-average cook with a first-hand knowledge of continental cuisine. At the time the majority of Americans lived on farms and even city folk raised chickens and turkeys in their backyards. Field observed that many folks were friendly with the turkey presented at their Thanksgiving dinner and often experienced "a matter of regret" and sorrow.

Fields proposed the wine and walnuts, then a common part of Thanksgiving dinner, be fed instead to the turkeys "for a short time before they were killed." This, she claimed "would give the poor turkey a good time and compensate it somewhat for its cruel fate." It was a popular suggestion among the temperance crowd but not so with the farmers or homeowners because of the cost.

In 1903 an unknown but enterprising burglar in St. Louis worked hard for his turkey and wine. Between 4 and 7 o'clock Christmas morning he broke into a shed and "found an ax, with which he tried to pry open a window in the Edwin Schiele's home." His endeavors proved unsuccessful and "fearing he would awake the family he "sought another basis of attack," according to the *St. Louis Republic*. The "second-story" man then broke a window and entered the basement of Adelaide Newman's home. He ransacked five trunks, stealing gold, silver, ruby and pearl jewelry. He also purloined a blue skirt, two silk handkerchiefs and six linen handkerchiefs. All told he got off with $66 worth of goods.

Hungry by now, the burglar used his stolen ax to break a kitchen window at the home of Mrs. Rose Kendall. There he secured "six bottles of sherry wine, a turkey, a ham and small quantities of other meats and vegetables, all valued at $20…Even though silverware and other valuable property was within easy reach…the burglar centered his attention on the edibles." All of the crimes were committed while the inhabitants were at home asleep. None were ever solved.

A most bizarre turkey and wine story occurred aboard the U. S. Navy's *Carp F1* submarine in San Francisco bay. It was under command of Ensign Simion Smith with an eight man crew on May 7, 1912. They were conducting the sub's "trial plunge, 200 feet below the surface" of the bay. The boat was launched the previous September in San Francisco and was conducting its normal trials and tests in the bay prior to entering service with the Pacific Fleet Flotilla.

The submerged submarine was tied off with two cables to a lighter (i.e. flat bottomed barge). Ensign Smith and the crew were standing in the boat drinking wine and eating turkey sandwiches—not realizing they were about "to face a tragic death," reported the *Chicago Day Book*. At 200 feet the *Carp's* "dive was the deepest that any submarine had taken," according to Ensign Smith. The lighter discovered that its cable had gotten tangled with the submarine's anchor chain. Below the depths the feasting crew was oblivious to the lurking danger. The sub was contacted by an emergency signaling system and advised of the predicament. The crew immediately cut the chain—releasing it from its anchor—but "made no upward progress." Then it was discovered the other "cable had entangled" the craft. The crew emptied the ballast water tanks of "26 tons of water." Once disgorged "the vessel shot upward like a torpedo" gaining speed as it headed to the surface. The *Day Book* reported "as the nose of the submarine appeared above the surface...the eight men inside were thrown helter-skelter...champagne glasses and bottles were dashed against the [interior] sides of the vessel." The *Carp* shot out of the water 80 feet "like a giant whale...slowly [it] righted itself...the engines were started...[and it] glided [safely] to its moorings." The men were badly shaken and bruised but, all survived the harrowing hour and forty-five minute ordeal.

It wouldn't be the last time the *Carp* was to make the news. Later in 1912 she set a new deep diving record of 283 feet. A few weeks later she slipped her moorings in Monterey Bay on the

California coast and ran aground on a nearby beach. Fifteen crewmen survived but two died. In 1917 while maneuvering with another submarine (F-2) developing submarine tactics, the two boats collided off Point Loma near San Diego. The *Carp* sank in ten seconds—killing fifteen of its twenty-man crew.

A Bad Day for Bootleggers

Nineteen year old Albert Addabbo was arrested on September 16, 1922 for selling illegal hooch in his New York City speakeasy. His illicit whiskey had caused the death of three men and another was hospitalized but expected to die. "Hard drinking" Frank Dalley died in his home after drinking the whiskey made from wood alcohol. William Williams, a thirty-five year old cook, was found sightless and unconscious. He later died at Bellevue Hospital. James Slip "clasped his hands over his eyes and cried 'I am blind!'" The forty year old, 5'7", hundred and fifty-pound longshoreman died before an ambulance could arrive to transport him to a hospital. Leslie Skinner, a civil engineer, had just been in town a week as he had been working in Peru. Skinner reported that he was going blind and had been robbed of $700. Before going to the hospital he agreed to cooperate in a sting operation with police by buying the illicit alcohol from Addabbo with "marked money" resulting in the arrest. Skinner was then hospitalized and was expected to die.

The same day the *New York World* reported that Albert Mori was arrested at his restaurant for having liquors, wine and beer stored in a back room. As the police walked through the "dining room with the seized liquor…the waiters appeared as if at a funeral," the article continued. Mori's restaurant "had been famous for its exceptional wines" some of which "were on ice in tubs" indicating "that certain regular customers were disappointed…when they went to dinner," reported the *World*. Outside, a crowd of several hundred and "scores of people leaning" out of their apartment windows "jeered and joshed" the agents.

A few blocks away James Macklin, who had a Second Avenue restaurant, was out $4,750 "for eleven casks" of "good whiskey." The casks were delivered to him from a garage in the Bronx "and rolled into his place after nightfall." When he sampled them "he might as well have been Moses smiting the rock" with his staff. Instead of getting "*Spirits Frumenty*" the contents turned out to be plain tap water. Oscar Porges who had negotiated the deal with Macklin was arrested and charged with grand larceny.

The previous day, two schooners engaged in rum smuggling were captured at sea and towed into New York harbor by the Prohibition cruiser *Hahn*. The seized cargoes included 1,450 cases of whiskey and $40,000 in cash. The captain of one of the boats agreed that his nine-man crew would sail his boat into New York harbor. Newspapers reported that "all the way in he cursed his luck." The other boat was towed in by the *Hahn*. A third boat was scuttled by its crew and was sinking but Prohibition sailors were able to salvage twenty-three cases of liquor. All told, the street value of the unlawful booze was estimated at $145,000 [$2.1 million in current values].

It was a good day, though, for Mary Catherine Campbell who was selected as America's first "Miss America." The sixteen-year-old Columbus school girl was described by the *World's* reporter Marguerite Mooers Marshall as "quite simply, the smiling yet grave-eyed, the dimpled, yet wide-browed, the girlish yet classic, type of beauty which has appeared to many a poet in his dreams." Campbell only had one dimple for which she apologized. "Her complexion," wrote Campbell "is milk and wild roses." The five-foot, four inch girl was described as "straight, shapely [and] slender as a nymph…[with] small feet and hands" and ankles which "made one hope she will never adopt a long skirt."

Campbell holds a unique position in Miss America contest history. She lied about her age, claiming to be seventeen in order to enter the pageant. Additionally she is the only woman to have won the pageant twice by winning the title again the following year. She was the first runner-up during the third pageant. As a result of her successes—she almost won the crown in 1924—The Miss America

Catherine Campbell

Organization changed the rules so that a contestant could only win the title once. She died in 1990 at the age of 85.

A Thanksgiving Gone Wrong

Frank Eggington and John Sparks were a couple of morons. The two Salt Lake City men "did not have a Thanksgiving dinner to their liking" reported the *Deseret Evening News* in 1904. On the night before Thanksgiving they broke into a neighbor's chicken coop and "appropriated unto themselves 25 chickens, male and female." They had planned a marvelous feast for themselves of "boiled chicken and fricassee hen a la Methodist and roast rooster," continued the *News*.

They expected their second theft to add to their holiday joy. They saw a bushel of "fine" apples and a "big" bottle of wine in the buggy of W. R. Boesley. "They not only took the wine and the apples, but the horse and buggy" too. The *News* reported "they drove around town for some time to whet up their appetite" and then tied up the rig in front of their house and "went to their room with the plunder." At one A.M. two Salt Lake City policemen located them and "threw them into jail." They were charged with burglary and grand larceny.

Instead of "eating chicken and applesauce and drinking choice wine" Eggington and Sparks dined on roast pork, black coffee and "home grown spuds" along with the other jail inmates. The city jail population had increased that day as "any old vag [vagrant] that had a

decent excuse for getting run in [to enjoy Thanksgiving dinner] availed himself of it." Forty inmates, including Eggington and Sparks were served that evening.

The county jail's twenty-five "denizens" enjoyed a much better banquet than their city counterparts. They were served up "spring chicken with dressing, mashed potatoes and brown gravy, tea, bread, apple or squash pie and celery."

The Utah State Penitentiary's one hundred and eighty-two inmates had roast pork, mashed potatoes with brown gravy. Their feast also included "new white bread, apple sauce and cranberry sauce," and of course, pumpkin pie. There were fourteen more prisoners in 1904 than the 1903 Thanksgiving Day dinner. Up until 1904 prison inmates regularly feasted on roast goose but that year the prison "had abandoned geese raising on the penitentiary farm."

No wine was served in any of the institutions of incarceration.

Eggington and Sparks would have been better off that Thanksgiving at the Salvation Army dining hall which served 500 poor and homeless. The free dinner was comprised of "roast turkey with cranberry sauce, roast goose with dressing, prime rib and roast mutton." No wine was served the poor or the homeless. A corps of volunteers also filled and gave out 250 baskets to the poorer families and the elderly "with the makings of a Thanksgiving feast"—to which Eggington and Sparks could and should have availed themselves.

About two-hundred and fifty hunters boarded a special "bunny hunter" train at 8 A.M. which took them to nearby Cedar Fort. The hunters would shoot rabbits "at long range." The man who shot the biggest would be awarded the traditional first place marksman certificate. The train would not be "due back at Salt Lake City" until late in the evening.

There was one sentimental wine story in the news this Thanksgiving Day. In Covington, Indiana a bottle of "ancient vintage" would, for the fifty-fifth time, be removed from a bank vault. At the close of the Mexican-American War twenty veterans "who went to the front from Fountain County, Indiana met in reunion" on Thanksgiving Day 1849. At the dinner a bottle of wine "was presented...and in a half joking manner one suggested that the bottle remain uncorked until but one survivor remained...[he] would quaff the wine to the memory of those gone before," reported the *Palestine Daily Herald*. Each year the annual dinner was held on Thanksgiving Day and "each one more closely cemented the ties of comradeship formed on the plains of Mexico." Every year the bottle was brought out and was "the subject of merry jests and predictions as to who would be the last survivor."

By 1904 only three of the group joined together for Thanksgiving dinner—"seventeen had crossed the dark river," explained the *Herald*. The three remaining veterans were all over eighty years in age. The old men wondered "to whom the lot would fall." "The wine," the article concluded "had preserved a pathetic memory of the shadowy past... [but] it would not be long until its mission [would] be fulfilled." It was likely that the wine would be consumed long before the unfortunate bungling turkeys, Eggington and Sparks, would ever get out of prison and taste wine again.

When a "Cup of Joe" Replaced a Glass of Wine

In April 1916 a small article appeared in the national press announcing that the United States Navy was auctioning off "hundreds of wine decanters and glasses from which Uncle Sam's naval officers were wont to drink a toast to their wives and sweethearts at home." Two and a half years earlier Navy Secretary Daniels had issued Rule 99 which ended the dispensing of wine, beer and ale to line and warrant officers of the United States Navy.

Daniels' 1914 order was part of the growing temperance movement which would culminate with the adoption of the Eighteenth Amendment abolishing the manufacture and sale of alcoholic beverages in the United States.

Naval regulations controlling alcoholic beverages served onboard naval ships had a kind of on-again, off-again history. Beginning in 1794, Congress mandated that each sailor was to receive a ½ pint of beer or distilled spirits daily. In 1831 the rule was amended to allow servicemen to relinquish their daily ration and receive a cash payment of 6¢ per day. In 1848 the daily ration was reduced to ¼ pint per day. In 1851 the rule was amended to provide that only officers and their attendants could enjoy the daily ration— effectively eliminating enlisted men's entitlement to the ration. The provision was repealed two years later. In 1862 with the advent of the Civil War, the daily ration of distilled spirits was discontinued aboard Union ships although beer, ale and wine was permitted. The Confederate Navy continued the policy of allowing officers and enlisted men to consume limited amounts of distilled spirits aboard Confederate naval ships, feeling it was a useful recruiting tool.

In 1893 a new regulation was adopted allowing wardroom and steerage officers to form "wine messes." In 1899 President McKinley's Secretary of the Navy, John Long, forbade the issue or sale of any liquor aboard ship, on any naval base, station or marine barracks to any enlisted man.

172

Daniels' order effectively discontinued the issuance or allowance of any liquor aboard any naval ship. In 1917 Daniels' declared it unlawful to sell, distribute or possess alcoholic beverages at any naval post and, further, "declared it unlawful to sell alcoholic beverages...to men in uniform." The following year, Daniels augmented his earlier ruling by establishing booze-free zones—five miles in width around all naval installations.

Daniels was a teetotaler and former North Carolina newspaper publisher and advocate of the temperance movement. According to the U. S. Naval Institute, Daniels was unpopular with naval men and when he issued the order "it was met with derision and mockery." According to one newspaper, the rule did permit

Navy Secretary Josephus Daniels

"the use of [alcoholic] spirits for medical purposes," facetiously adding "...it is expected quite a number of officers will be in immediate need of medical attention."

When Daniels announced the order in April of 2014 to become effective the following July, the *New York Tribune* noted "there will be a struggle aboard some ships to do away with the large stocks of wine which had been laid in to tide over long cruises." The decision came as a total surprise to naval officers. Daniels justified his decision by claiming it equalized officers with enlisted men who were forbidden to drink alcoholic beverages aboard ship. He also claimed it had just been his "painful duty to approve a court martial for dismissal from the service of an officer for intoxication." The officer involved told Daniels "he had never tasted intoxicating drink until he did so in the wine mess on his cruises."

Just as the *New York Tribune* had predicted, Navy ships did scramble to comply with the July 1, 1914 deadline. Despite commanders selling as much booze as possible, naval ships still found large inventories onboard as the deadline approached. According to the Naval Institute many ships opted to "host one last banquet to say farewell and consume the remainder of the alcohol." Many ships simply "piled tables with food and booze...[while] some got more creative and created themes such as Wild West saloons or held "funerals" where "mourners" could watch John Barleycorn's burial at sea." In Veracruz, Mexico the U.S. Navy squadron "invited foreign contingents to join in the festivities...parties from British, German, Spanish and Dutch [naval squadrons traveled by launch] from ship to ship to help eliminate the soon-to-be contraband." Thereafter the strongest drink sailors and officers would be able to enjoy onboard ships would be a cup of coffee—thereafter derisively, but memorably, dubbed "A cup of Joe" after the now-forgotten Navy Secretary Josephus "Joe" Daniels.

Yellowstone's First Champagne Dinner

In 1872 President Ulysses S. Grant signed into law legislation which established Yellowstone as the nation's first national park. At the time, access to the valley and park could only be accomplished on horseback along primitive trails. There were no railroads or roads.

In 1873 the *Key West,* a large stern wheel wooden riverboat [200' X 33' X 5'4" draft] , captained by Grant Marsh "turned her nose up the Yellowstone [River] for the purpose of exploring the channel of [the Powder River]," relates an 1882 article in the *Bismarck Tribune.* Aboard the exploratory foray was General James W. "Sandy" Forsythe

"with a company or two of soldiers [6th Infantry]." The boat had been commandeered by Forsythe as part of the U. S. Army's efforts to survey the Yellowstone River Valley and its tributaries believing "the area was probably filled with hostile Sioux warriors," according to *Yellowstone Riverboat History.* Their mission was to explore the Yellowstone River environs and select army post sites on the Upper Missouri. The total round trip distance of 460 miles took nine days. The first Sioux warriors to see the steamboat called it a "fire canoe."

Forsythe was a famous army officer who served in the Indian Wars after the Civil War. He took part in military campaigns against the Comanche, Cheyenne, Arapaho and Kiowa Indians during the 1860s. He commanded the 1st U.S. Cavalry against the Bannock and Paiute Indians in 1878.

According to the *Bismarck Tribune* article, a couple of days before entering the Powder River "Captain Marsh's [42nd] birthday occurred, and it was celebrated in grand style." The *Key West* was moored to an island "with beautiful woods." A "cloth was spread on the grass beneath the cool shades of the great trees, and as fine a dinner as was ever seen in the wilderness and the first champagne dinner in the Yellowstone valley was enjoyed." The party consisted of Captain Marsh and his riverboat officers along with General Forsythe and the army officers in command of the troops on the boat. The *Key West*'s "store-keeper had a half dozen baskets of Krug's champagne on board...the excellent wine, to the last bottle, was cracked and drank," related the *Tribune*.

Captain Grant Marsh

Captain Marsh is known to Missouri and Yellowstone River historians as "the greatest steamboatman ever." He was legendary for his steamboat skills and served as captain of over twenty-two boats during a career that spanned seventy years. He and Mark Twain (then a riverboat pilot) served together along the Mississippi in 1858-59 and became life-long friends. He spent the bulk of his career along the Missouri and Yellowstone Rivers. At the time a typical voyage from St. Louis to Fort Benton (Montana Territory), a distance of 2,600 miles, along the Missouri River took two months.

In 1876 Marsh, as Captain of the steamer *Far West*, took military supplies up the Yellowstone River for General George Armstrong Custer whose troops marched alongside the riverbank. Marsh was one of the first to receive word of the massacre at Little Big Horn and rushed his boat up to the mouth of the Little Big Horn River. He loaded wounded soldiers and scouts from the battle and then "made the historic and record-setting river run for which he is most famous—the steamboat trip down river to Bismarck in the Dakota Territory, 710 miles in 54 hours." He delivered the first news of Custer's defeat (initially called "the Yellowstone slaughter") and loss of 210 soldiers. Four hundred soldiers and scouts survived a siege on a bluff about four miles from where Custer and his men were annihilated.   One unidentified passenger relayed to the *Benton Record* newspaper that "the Sioux feel confident they have broken the power of the whites… [and] they call the cavalry "squaw soldiers" and laugh at the "wagon guns" as they call the artillery." Another passenger claimed that George A. Custer's wife "fainted at hearing of her husband's death, and it is reported she is now insane." The scout "who is the only known survivor of the ill-fated command" revealed "he made his escape by pulling a blanket over his head and keeping among the Indians."

Grant Marsh died in 1916 in Bismarck at the age of 83—in near poverty.

President Grant:
Wined and Dined in Nagasaki

On September 20, 1879 former President Ulysses S. Grant landed in San Francisco after a world tour. When he "stepped once more upon the shores of his native land" his two-year, four month world tour officially ended. A cheering, "surging crowd pressed forward" to get a glimpse of the former president. As his entourage drove up Market Street to the Palace Hotel "rockets and blue lights" were fired along the route.

The former president and Civil War hero stood upon a chair and gave an impromptu speech to the crowd. He noted that he had been absent from the city for twenty-five years. As a young army Lieutenant, Grant had first visited San Francisco in 1852 in route to his posting at Fort Vancouver in the Oregon Territory. He was not able to support his family on soldiers pay and resigned his commission in the summer of 1854 in order to join his family in New York. In his memoirs Grant noted 'I left the Pacific coast very much attached to it, and with full expectation of making it my future home." He never did return until that eventful day in 1879.

The story of Grant's return to San Francisco in 1854 was revealed in Captain Richard Ogden's diary. Ogden was a clerk in the office of the army quartermaster in San Francisco. He wrote that he was confronted with a "shabbily dressed person [whom he at first] didn't recognize." A draft for a $40 [$1,600 in current values] per diem requisition to pay for his trip back east was presented. The form was improperly drawn and couldn't be rectified until the following day. The penniless and embarrassed Grant was devastated— borrowing $1 [$39 in current values] from Ogden. He asked that he be allowed "to sleep in the [office] lounge [chair]" which would allow him to use the $1 for his "dinner and breakfast," explained Grant.

Ten years later Grant would negotiate General Robert E. Lee's surrender at Appomattox Court House essentially ending the Civil War.   A national hero, Grant would serve two terms as President. Upon his retirement, in 1877 he left the United States on his world tour with his wife which took them to all major European capitals, the Holy Land, India, Burma, Vietnam, Singapore, China and finally Japan.

The last banquet held for Grant was in Nagasaki. Its opulence exemplifies how he was treated by world leaders. America's press described the feast. It was served "in the style of the daimios, the feudal lords of Japan," wrote John Russell Young. Young (a future Librarian of Congress) accompanied the Grants on their tour and acted as the president's *de facto* press secretary. The dinner was served on "small tables, each guest having a table to himself...the bill of fare...embraced over 50 courses...[with] wine served in unglazed porcelain wine-cups, on white wooden stands," continued Young. Some of the courses included dried fish, seaweed, raw fish, rice, bread and potatoes. A number of different soups were served including fish chowder and a kind of cioppino. A variety of fish dishes: snapper, shrimp, powdered fish, raw carp, mashed fish, baked fish and fish boiled with pickled beans. There were various "combinations:...duck, truffles, turnips, dried bonito, melons, pressed salt, aromatic shrubs, snipe, egg-plant, jelly etc.," related Young. Desert consisted of "sweet-meat composed of white and red bean jelly cake and boiled black mushroom" and tea.

Previous to his visit to Nagasaki, Grant had met with Japan's twenty-seven year old Emperor of the Meiji dynasty in Yokahama in July of 1879. At the meeting Grant (then 57) shook hands with

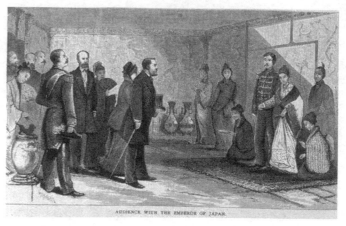

President Grant meeting Japanese Emperor

the emperor. Young wrote, "This seems like a trivial thing to write down, but such a thing was never before known in the history of the Japanese majesty." The emperor held a reception for Grant on July 4th to commemorate American Independence Day. The Emperor also gave Grant a $25,000 ruby ring as a gift [$825,000 in current values]. The ring was inherited by Grant's daughter Nellie who lost it in 1912 when she accidentally dropped it in a hotel sink drain in a New York City hotel. A newspaper article relayed "the entire waste water system of the hotel, and the city's sewer for a block or more…were searched" in vain.

Ulysses S. Grant died in July of 1885 at the age of 63. One and a half million mourners attended his funeral in New York City where his body now lies in the General Grant National Memorial (Grant's Tomb)—the largest mausoleum in North America.

Roast Pig and Wine

In 1913 Yung Chong, a wealthy Chinese man was laid to rest in Philadelphia. Chong had been president of the On Leong Tong Society for a decade prior to his death, according to the Philadelphia press. He was "one of the richest Chinaman in Philadelphia" the reports explained.

As the mourners left the graveyard numerous "scraps of colored papers bearing prayers" fluttered from departing carriages. The "Chinese believe the devils who pursue the spirit of the dead have to stop and read all the prayers, and the mourners of Chong, believe that they [had] scattered enough to keep the devils engaged until he was safely buried," explained the *Bourbon News*. On the casket and around the grave "were left roast duck and pigs, Chinese wine and nuts and other delicacies," related the *News* "to help Chong cross the Styx."

Minutes after the funeral cortege left the graveyard "there was a wild scramble of hoboes of all description... [When the] twenty-five hundred hoboes finished [eating the food] there was little left for Chong," concluded the *News*.

Twenty-five years earlier in Bismarck, the wealthy Griffith brothers entered into a wager. L.N. Griffith bet his "sportive and accomplished brother" Tim "a basket of wine against two [of Tim's prize] pigs that [Tim] would not" bag a deer before New Year's. Tim "penetrated the romantic fastness's of Apple Creek and other game inhabited localities daily." By December 31st he had only killed a jack rabbit. The same day he "started out, wild with excitement and rage, and after tramping for twelve miles through [snow] drifts and woods" he managed to shoot a "yearling steer" which he mistook for a deer. He was chased by a miner who thought he had jumped a claim and wasted ammunition shooting at cloud shadows "which he mistook for a fleeing deer," reported the *Bismarck Weekly Tribune*.

Resigned to his loss, Tim killed and butchered two prize pigs and "served an elegant luncheon on Saturday evening." At the luncheon everyone noticed that Tim "was eating with a relish and laughing heartier than any man in the room." Apparently he had stolen the two pigs from his brother's pen and "had turned the table by arranging for a grand feast at the expense of the brother who had been taunting and jeering him for over a month," concluded the *Tribune*.

A wartime roast pig and wine story was reported in the *Wichita Daily Eagle*. Ernst Rembeck owned a Wichita restaurant which served about 100 people on Christmas Day 1901. Rembeck was a German immigrant to America. Asked by a *Wichita Daily Eagle* reporter what was the merriest Christmas he had ever experienced, he smiled nostalgically. Thirty years earlier he was a cavalryman in the Prussian Army during the Franco-Prussian War. Prussian troops had just taken the French town of Vendome. "We were hungry and made for the butcher shops to get some liverwurst. [The French] never heard of it. Give us some bologna, then. They shook their heads again," he related. The soldiers caught "some pigs" and made their own liverwurst.

Quartered in a "fine chateau" they found wine but couldn't drink it because "it was awful," he continued. Wanting to roast some more pigs, Ernst and another soldier went to fetch some firewood. Walking back with their "arms full of wood" the earth "caved in under" his legs. He put his hand down the hole "and pulled up a fine bottle of wine by the neck," reported the *Eagle*. It turned out the owner of the chateau had buried "his good wine and left the poor wine" for the conquering Prussian soldiers. Ernst reported: "We had a great feast with the wine and roast pig and we danced and sang and had great fun all day...We taught our French prisoners how to make liverwurst and bologna and now you can find them all over France," he told the reporter. The reporter noted it was a remarkable story and the nostalgic Ernst had "dimples [which] chased one another over his face and the light of a guiles soul shone in his eye."

The ancient Greeks and Romans are reported to have also enjoyed roast pig and wine. Historians report that Aesop, the fabulist, once paid out $400,000 [$13.2 million in current values] for a single party. The Roman Emperor Caligula once paid the same amount for a banquet where his guests "drank old wine worth twenty-dollars an ounce [$662 in current values], and [feasted] on roast pig over fires made of nuts and raisins." Cleopatra once drank a glass of wine "in which was dissolved [a crushed] pearl worth $40,000 [$1.32 million in current values].

A Ham Sandwich and Glass of Wine with Mrs. Davis

In April of 1883 a reporter identified only by the initials A.W.C. decided to visit the home of Jefferson Davis in Biloxi, Mississippi. The reporter was a correspondent with the *Wheeling Daily Intelligencer* and on a whim "took a notion...to go up and call on the distinguished gentleman in his retirement" at his 500-acre Beauvoir Estate "and see if he cared to talk."

Varina Davis

Unfortunately the former Confederate president was not at home. However Davis' wife, Varina, and his two daughters Winnie and Margaret were at home. The couple had had six children of whom four died before reaching the age of maturity. Margaret was the only child to marry and raise a family. According to A.W.C. , "by their intelligent conversation and hospitable ways...[they] made me feel quite at home." He wrote that Varina was "a woman of strong individuality...[and] her will and endowments had triumphed over all her misfortunes."

Winnie Davis

Several hours later, A.W.C. excused himself and prepared to leave— explaining he needed to catch a train. To his surprise Varina "begged him to remain and lunch with her in her parlor." She told him she and her daughters were "going out for a ride" and would take him to town. Her servants brought "wine, cheese, ham sandwiches, biscuits and butter...and spread a very palatable collation indeed" wrote A.W.C. During his visit the reporter left us with a glimpse of a compassionate woman. A local "poor woman" interrupted the luncheon to tell Varina "of her misfortune that had just happened"—the death of her family's only horse. The horse had been bought by the "kindliness of [Varina's] heart...she had gathered up the money...that had bought this horse for the poor family." Varina assured the distressed woman she would write to her friends "and see what could be done...in the way of securing another horse." The reporter opined Mrs. Davis kindness evidenced "one of those touches of the good angels of human nature."

They discussed the country and the "the changes wrought by the Civil War" and about Europe. Varina and Winnie had lived in an apartment at Fort Monroe (Virginia) during her husband's imprisonment after the Civil War. Two years later he was finally released and moved to Montreal with Varina and Winnie until he was pardoned by President Andrew Johnson in 1868. In 1869 they moved to Memphis where Jefferson was appointed president of an insurance agency. Title to their Brierfield plantation had been ensnarled in litigation for nearly fifteen years.

In 1877 a prominent society matron who owned the Beauvoir estate invited the Davises to use the plantation. It was at Beauvoir that Davis wrote *The Rise and Fall of the Confederate Government* which was published in 1881. When the owner died, she left the entire estate which fronted on the sea including $50,000 cash [$1.2 million in current values] to the Davises.

A.W.C. left the estate in a buggy seated next to Varina in a carriage to Biloxi. He enjoyed the "further opportunity to hear her intelligent and interesting observations" about the nation. He was "hospitably escorted through a Southern wilderness...with this lady of many vicissitudes—who had borne her fate in reverses heroically," he wrote. She drove him to his beach hotel and introduced him to the "landlady." He concluded his article observing that the Confederate defeat "had but served to bring into prominence a great deal that was attractive and admirable in her character."

Varina Davis was Jefferson Davis' second wife, borne in Natchez Mississippi in 1826. Her grandfather had served several terms as governor of New Jersey. She was educated at a private academy and by private tutors on her family Mississippi plantation. She first met Jefferson (19 years her senior) at his family plantation (1843). Davis was a West Point graduate. They married in 1845. After the marriage, Jefferson rose in prominence—first as a U. S. Congressman, then as an army officer during the Mexican War, a United States Senator, Secretary of War and in 1861 as President of the Confederate States of America, making Varina the Confederacy's First Lady. At war's end the Davises lost most of their fortune and for many years they lived apart—gradually reconciling after Jefferson acquired the Beauvoir estate. After Jefferson's death in 1889 she and Winnie moved to New York City. Both became writers of note— Varina as a columnist for Joseph Pulitzer's *New York World*. Winnie died in 1898 at the age of 34. Varina died in 1906 at the age of 80.

"Diamond" Jim Brady's Stomach

A woman stood flabbergasted as she watched "Diamond" Jim Brady devour one of his meals. She asked him "how he knew he was full," according to H. Paul Jeffers of *The Chef From Hell*. Brady responded that he always left "4 inches between my stomach and the edge of the table...when I feel them rubbin together pretty hard, I know I've had enough."

"Diamond" Jim Brady

A typical breakfast consisted of eggs, pancakes, pork chops, fried potatoes, corn bread, hominy and a 2" steak. This was followed by a lunch of two large lobsters, deviled crabs, oysters, clams, and some beef. Brady's typical dinner consisted of an appetizer of three dozen oysters, six crabs and a number of bowls of turtle soup. The appetizers were followed by an entre of two ducks, seven lobsters, a sirloin steak, slices of turtle meat and mixed vegetables. Dessert consisted of two or three plates of pastries and a two pound box of candy. His drinks of choice were fresh-squeezed orange juice and lemonade by the gallon. From time to time he would partake of a $1 lunch at a local diner to remind himself of his impoverished "old days," reported a 1913 article in the *Colfax Chronicle*.

James Buchanan Brady was born into a poor family in New York City in 1856. As a youngster he worked in his father's saloon. At age eleven he ran away from home, worked as a bellhop and eventually took a job selling railroad equipment. According to *History Spaces* he was "charming, affable and personable." Within a short time his commissions made him extremely wealthy. By his mid-30s he never had to work again. He is believed to be the owner of the first car in New York City (1895).

Brady is probably the greatest American glutton of all time. The *New York Times* David Kamp called him "a serial multigorger whose excesses were endearing rather than vulgar." He adorned himself with diamonds: A diamond imbedded cane, large diamond rings, diamond cuff links, shirt studs, belt buckles, watches and scarf pins—all diamond imbedded. "Tt was estimated when strolling along Broadway...he was wearing 2,500 diamonds," according to *History Spaces*. He tipped waiters and servers with loose diamonds he carried in

Lillian Russell

his pockets. But it was his eating habits that seem to have captured the public's imagination.

In 1912, Brady checked into Johns Hopkins Hospital where doctors, according to era press, extracted his "stomach...[and] said it had been worked to death, gave it such scientific treatment as [they] could and put it back in place again." His stomach "showed signs of being nearly as good as new." He gave the operating surgeon $100,000, three new cars and purchased a new house for him. Shortly after the operation he ordered a dinner of "cantaloupe, cherrystone clams, chicken gumbo, sea bass, broiled squab, turkey, string bean salad, demitasse, cigars, wine and champagne," according to the *Arizona Republic*. In addition he gave Johns Hopkins $220,000 to found the James Buchanan Brady Urological Institute. Newspapers reported that his stomach was six times the size of a normal stomach. Kamp speculates that, in addition to this larger than normal stomach, Brady likely "was one of those fat people who is missing the nerves between the stomach and hypothalamus [brain lobe] to tell him that he's full." Kamp also contradicts the story about Brady's stomach surgery, claiming Brady was unable to urinate and the surgeon actually extracted a portion of his prostrate which relieved the problem.

Brady never married. His long standing girlfriend, however, was the well-known actress and singer Lillian Russell. She never accepted his numerous marriage proposals but they were constant companions. He lavished her with opulent dinners, cash, diamonds and gifts. On one occasion he gave her a gold-plated bicycle with handlebars decorated with diamonds, emeralds, rubies and sapphires. She rode it one time but drew such a crowd that police asked her not to do so again. Brady is also credited as being the inventor of the "bicycle made for two," so that he and Lillian could ride together in Central Park.

"Diamond" Jim Brady died in his sleep of either a stroke or heart attack in 1917. He was 61. At his death his estate was estimated at over ten million—including two million in diamonds [$190 million in current values]. Having no heirs, his estate was distributed to numerous New York City hospitals.

Give Back in Logan, Iowa

On February 3, 1920 three railroad tank cars full of wine enroute from California to Baltimore were set on a siding at the Logan, Iowa railroad yard. National prohibition had become effective just three weeks before and the wine cars were being transported under United States government seal and bond. "One of the cars was leaking and residents of Logan formed lines with buckets and pails to prevent a loss of the wine," reported the *Denison Review*. Logan is the county seat of Harrison County and, at the time, had a population of 1,600.

The county sheriff was notified by a local temperance leader and he "drove the thirsty crowd away...[and] called railroad officials who had the leak fixed and posted a guard at the track to watch the cars," continued the *Review*.

The same evening the Logan post of the American Legion held a dance which attracted a large crowd of visitors from Missouri Valley and "other towns in Harrison County." It was the first American Legion dance in Logan without available alcoholic beverages. Made aware of the wine leak, the partygoers formed a "syndicate and someone notified the wine watchman" that the railroad was refusing to "stand good for the "over-time" of their extra duty," related the *Review* article. Believing the story, the guards "deserted their posts."

The *Review* continued the story: "Buckets, pails, dishpans, washtubs and every conceivable receptacle were drafted into service and lines" of revelers from the dance assembled at the railroad tracks 'around midnight.' The "leak" was reopened and the "celebration waxed hilarious and continued" throughout the night "until after daybreak." The *Review* added: "there was a hurrying of autos from all parts of the county towards Logan as word of the wine orgy spread rapidly." When the sheriff discovered what was going on "and that scores of men and boys were carrying the wine away...he attempted to stop them, but was powerless [to do so]." The sheriff did, however, take the names "of all engaged in the alleged wholesale theft."

Four days later "several United States government secret service men, railroad secret service men and county officials" converged on Logan and were reported to be working "upon the wine stealing case which...[had] turned into a [Harrison] county scandal." The *Review* reported that if it was "proven the [government] seal was broken, as it [was] alleged or that the wine was stolen from the cars a most serious charge will lie against the offenders."

The locals claimed the cars developed a leak and "that the celebrants were merely engaged in saving the liquor from being absorbed by the ground...[a contention that was] denied by authorities." A federal grand jury was convened at Council Bluffs, "investigated the affair and suspended indictments pending a settlement with the railroad company for its loss."

The following April the press reported a settlement had been reached. Authorities, using the Sheriff's list, circulated petitions "among citizens believed to share in the wine distribution and each was requested to donate to a common fund in amounts consistent with individual "shares" of the spoils." In all $2,000 [$23,000 in current values] was raised and paid over to Northwestern Railroad which settled the case.

The story didn't end there, however. Three young men ranging in age between 17 and 22 were indicted "for high-jacking cellars containing some of the stolen liquor." The boys posted $1,000 bonds and were liberated from the local jail pending trial. It was alleged the boys "all scions of prominent families" had not received what they termed "adequate shares of the [stolen] liquor on the riotous night, so they attempted to equalize matters by raiding [wine] cellars where they knew quantities of the liquor had been stored. They were arrested and charged with breaking and entering"—essentially charged with stealing stolen wine. The charges were later dropped.

The King's Gift

Homburg, Germany 1907. Siam's King Chulgalongkorn was in town undergoing treatment at the world famous *Kurhaus Spa* for a kidney ailment. The fifty-four year old monarch was so pleased with his progress that he invited the entire city of 30,000+ residents to celebrate his birthday by giving each citizen "three bottles of wine, one each of champagne, white and red wine." He put up three pavilions on the spa grounds to handle the crowds and, in addition, "free beer was distributed," according to an article in the *San Francisco Call*.

The king "decided the celebration should continue at his expense for three days...and also distributed large sums of money to the poor and benevolent societies." He also held a banquet serving 600 of the wealthier citizens of Homburg. Thankful citizens "joined in the spirit of the King's hospitality" by placing pictures of him in all "the local shops" windows and the houses "were decorated with the Siamese flag," continued the *Call* report. Additionally, the city put on a giant fireworks display to help celebrate the birthday. The only problem was finding enough wine for the give-away. The newspaper reported "The *Kurhaus [Spa]* has been hastily gathering in wine by the [train] carload from neighboring cities."

Father and Son--Mongkut (l) and Chulgalongkorn (r)

It was reported that Chulgalongkorn normally paid out $3,000 [$81,000 in current values] a day for himself and his retinue when traveling. It was estimated that his Homburg birthday celebration would cost $250,000 [$8 million in current values] and that he had spent $1.5 million [$41 million in current values] during his stay in Germany while undergoing treatment.

King Chulgalongkorn is best known to American audiences thru the Oscar and Hammerstein musical *The King and I*. The musical duo introduced a number of still-popular tunes in the play such as: *Hello Young Lovers, I Whistle a Happy Tune, Getting to Know You* and *We Kiss in a Shadow*. As a Broadway play the musical won numerous Tony awards. Later as a movie starring Deborah Kerr and Yule Brynner it received numerous Golden Globe and Oscar nominations. Brynner won an Academy Award for his portrayal of Mongkut and Kerr was nominated for her performance as well. The movie's plot involved the interaction between Siam's King Mongkut (Chulgalongkorn's father) and Anna Leonowens whom he hired to tutor his children. Anna Leonowens' part was played by Deborah Kerr. Patrick Adiarte portrayed the heir apparent Prince Chulgalongkorn in the movie.

King Mongkut died in 1868 and his heir, Prince Chulgalongkorn, acceded to the throne at the age of fifteen under a regency which lasted until 1873.

Yule Brynner (r) and Patrick Adiarte

As a monarch, Chulgalongkorn is considered the greatest king of Siam who ended a feudal system of government controlled by the country's nobility. He oversaw the modernization of the Asian kingdom which involved intense social and government reforms—the Siam government had remained relatively unchanged since the 15th Century.

Chulgalongkorn abolished slavery; modernized the military, and; introduced modern land ownership through a national survey and deeds. As king he oversaw the construction of a national railway and electric energy production plants in his modernization efforts. He accommodated French and British colonial ambitions by ceding territory to them in order to avoid his own kingdom being colonized by ceding Cambodia and Laos to the French and four sultanates of Malay to the British.

Chulgalongkorn had 96 consorts and concubines. He sired thirty-three sons and forty-four daughters. In his efforts to reform his kingdom he sent his sons (royal princes) to Europe to be educated—he himself had visited Europe twice in his lifetime (1897 and 1907). His European-educated sons encouraged him to institute a constitutional monarchy form of government like the ones in Britain and Germany but he resisted democracy throughout his life.

Chulgalongkorn succumbed to his kidney disease in 1910. He was fifty-seven. Siam became a constitutional monarchy in 1932—the result of a *coup d'état*. The nation's name was changed to Thailand in 1933 but changed back to Siam in 1945 through 1949 when it was officially changed back to Thailand. It remains today the Constitutional Monarchy of Thailand.

Wine Orgy on the British Coast

In early January of 1905 the Spanish cargo ship *Ulloa* ran aground "upon one of the many sandbanks in the mouth of the Mersey River" near Liverpool, England. Two weeks later "a heavy storm arose and broke up the front part of the vessel liberating a large part of the cargo," reported the *St. Paul Globe*. The *Ulloa* was a Spanish ship loaded with three hundred crates of oranges and numerous boxes of raisins, lemons, figs, onion and "five 100-gallon casks of port wine." The boxes had broken and most of the fruit was strewn along six miles of shoreline beach near the Village of Wallasey at the mouth of the Mersey River—which empties into the Irish Sea.

According to the *Globe,* the local villagers "turned out to view the debris left on their shore by the receding tide" and watched the sinking sun rays catch "the wet surfaces of the oranges [causing] a spectacle of the most dazzling brightness [which] was the result." As darkness crept over the beach "when nighttime drew on and the fear of detection [by customs officials and the coast guard] was reduced to a minimum [Wallasey villagers] crept out on the dunes, silently appropriating first three hundred cases of oranges." The other fruits and onions were also slowly and methodically expropriated as the night progressed. The villagers "carried or dragged them home...all night long boys labored through the quaint streets under the burden of bags of oranges, laying up stores of enjoyment for weeks to come," continued the report.

The real prize, though, was the port wine. The *Globe* reported "The denouement was reached when the first brave man approached a cask...with a bottle in hand." He was able to puncture the barrel with a gimlet [a small boring tool] and access the port and fill his bottle. "His example was quickly followed by others, and the casks, were pierced with numerous small holes from which spurted streams of tempting liquor," the article continued. But the "method of tapping" was so slow that some were forced to suck at the holes. Finally the "bungs were extracted, and out poured streams of red wine. Buckets, cans, bottles were filled "and men were seen trudging home carrying…buckets…carelessly as if it had been water from the pump."

As the villagers ran out of containers bottles "were soon at a premium…six pence and a schilling each [were paid] for empty whiskey bottles." Another ingenious townsman hit upon using beer bottles. One man was reported to have filled seventy-four bottles. The "wine was consumed in large quantities, many drinking it as if it were beer…and the shore soon became a scene of an orgy." Drunken men "sang loudly and danced around the casks." Many passed out "upon the damp sands" while the "more seasoned topers paraded the streets on unsteady legs." All this, the *Globe* related, lasted into the wee hours of the morning. Many "have drunk the wine unwisely and too well until the scene developed into a drunken orgy."

Did a Glass of Wine Cause the Civil War?

"It is said that a single glass of wine probably wrecked the Democratic Party in 1860," alleged an 1899 article in the *Atlanta Constitution*. The article went on claiming a "little glass of wine…ruined a great party, caused a disastrous war, and besides the loss of life cost the south over $400,000,000 [$13.9 billion in current values]." Acknowledging the story was

Herschel V. Johnson

"speculative [but]…there are many who believed it a generation ago."

The story is about Georgia politics and the tug of war between two factions—to secede or not secede from the Union. While 150 years of history have obscured many of their names, Georgia Senators and Governors debated the great issue of the day.

Henry R. Jackson

In 1860 the national Democratic Party failed to agree on a presidential candidate at its convention in Charleston, South Carolina. The front runner was Illinois Senator Stephen Douglas. Douglas had advanced the doctrine of popular sovereignty which dictated that settlers in the various U. S. Territories should choose whether or not they wished their state to be slavery or anti-slavery. At the convention, militant Southern Democrats (called "Fire Eaters") insisted on the inclusion of an absolute "pro-slavery" plank in the party platform. Northern Democrats opposed the plank. Fifty of the Southern delegates walked out. The two factions agreed to reconvene six weeks later in Baltimore.

In Baltimore further disarray occurred with most of the southern delegates and numerous northern and western delegates withdrawing. Ultimately the convention nominated Stephen Douglas for President and Georgia's former Governor and Senator Herschel V. Johnson for Vice President. In the meantime the southern delegates who bolted the convention met and selected Vice President Breckenridge as their standard-bearer with New York Senator Daniel Dickerson as their Vice Presidential candidate. The Republican Party nominated Abraham Lincoln for President and Maine Senator Hannibal Hamlin as their Vice Presidential candidate.

Shortly after the conventions, Georgia Democrats convened in a Secession Convention. A majority report endorsed secession. Senator Johnson, the Democratic Vice Presidential candidate, rose to speak on behalf of the minority report. Johnson had served in the United States Senate for two years and two terms as Governor. "The leading champion of the minority, and his followers were confident

Howe Cobb

that [Johnson's] eloquence and logic would carry the day," continued the *Constitution*. The *Constitution* went on: "Old men who remember that speech say that it was a powerful argument [and believed] after the recess [Johnson} would demolish his opponents [those favoring secession]." He had begun his long speech shortly before noon and several hours later the session adjourned for dinner. "Johnson felt the strain of the session so much that he was unable to eat anything, and he took a glass of wine upon an empty stomach....[which] was a fatal mistake. The one glass of wine...changed the destiny of the nation," concluded the article.

When Johnson resumed his speech he became nauseated. "He was hazy, verbose and unintelligible...his style and argument lacked vigor, consistency and positiveness," reported the newspaper. The orators who were to follow Johnson in favor of secession "were exulted." Johnson's gubernatorial successor, Howell Cobb (a former

Speaker of the U. S. House of Representatives and Secretary of the Treasury) and Henry R. Jackson, former U.S. Ambassador to Austria-Hungary pleaded the secessionist cause and won the day.

Georgia voted to secede and became the fifth state to do so— "all because of a little glass of wine."

With Abraham Lincoln's election, Herschel Johnson, loyal to his state, served as a Senator in the Second Confederate Congress (1862-1865). After the Civil War he was a strong leader and advocate for reconstruction. Returning to law by serving as a Georgia circuit court judge, he died in 1880 at the age of 68.

Howell Cobb became the first Speaker of the Confederate House of Representatives. In 1862 he was appointed Brigadier General in the Confederate Army and surrendered at Macon, Georgia in 1865. After the war he became a bitter opponent of reconstruction. Cobb died in 1868 in New York City. He was 53.

Henry R. Jackson was appointed Brigadier General in the Confederate Army. He was captured and imprisoned at the Battle of Nashville in 1863. After the war he was pardoned and returned to the practice of law. In 1885 he was appointed U. S. Ambassador to Mexico. He died in Savanah in 1889 at the age of 78.

Hiding out in a Wine Cellar

In August 1917 Patrick O'Brien, a Royal Canadian Air Force pilot, was shot down over Belgium. A German bullet had "gone thru my upper lip, came out the roof of my mouth and lodged in my neck," he wrote in his1918 best seller *Outwitting the Hun*. After recuperating in a field hospital he was put on a train enroute to a prisoner of war camp in Germany. As the train moved across Germany, O'Brien leaped out an open window—landing on rock ballast which "closed my left eye, skinned my hands and shins and strained my ankle…and knocked me out."

"Bleeding profusely from his wounds" he began his seventy-three day trek to freedom. O'Brien hid during the day and walked at night—crossing ditches, rivers, canals and streams. Starving, he subsisted on cabbage, sugar beets and carrots found in farm fields during his nighttime hikes. Crossing through Luxemburg and finally back into Belgium, he visited farmhouses begging for food. The farmers fed him at great risk—if found out they would be executed "for helping escaped prisoners and other fugitives."

Patrick O'Brien

O'Brien was an American who had started flying in 1912—one of the so-called "early birds." For a while he flew for the U.S. Army during the Poncho Villa incursions across the Mexican border. Frustrated by America's reluctance to join Britain during the early days of WWI, he moved to Canada and volunteered for the Royal Canadian Air Force.

After two months he located Belgian insurgents who put him up in an abandoned house. At night he would "steal out quietly to see what I could pick up in the way of food…scouring the streets, alleys and byways for scraps of food." Bored, he found an old copy of the *New York Herald* which he read "and re-read from beginning to end." During the days he would occupy himself by "catching flies [and] putting them in a spider web…[and he then] rescued the fly just as the spider was about to grab him."

One night he heard soldiers marching towards his house and then entering. He hid in the wine cellar "finding a satisfactory hiding place in the extreme rear of the cellar…between two" big wine cases. The cellar contained 1,800 bottles of "choice wine." O'Brien writes that "rats and mice were scurrying across the floor…some of the creatures ran across me…" Standing in the dark with "a bottle of wine in each hand" he prepared to defend himself against the Germans who "were smashing and crashing upstairs" searching for him.

Just as the soldiers were outside the cellar door, he heard "Halt!" and the soldiers "turned right about face" and left. When he finally got the courage to go upstairs he discovered the "water faucets …water pipes…everything brass or copper…torn off, and gas fixtures, cooking utensils…[and anything of metal] the Germans so badly needed [for their war effort]." They hadn't been searching for him after all—just badly needed war supplies.

When O'Brien reached the Dutch border he was confronted by a nine-foot electrified fence. Feeling "like a wild animal in a cage," he contemplated pole vaulting the structure or building a pair of stilts. He settled on two fallen pine trees. Stripping off all the branches, he used the branches as ladder rungs "tying them with grass and strips from my handkerchief and shirt the best I could." Placing the ladder against a wooden fence post he began climbing. The ladder slipped into the wires—"a blue flash…[and I] fell to the ground unconscious."

When he came to, he decided to dig a hole under the fence, a three hour ordeal—all the while ducking and dodging German sentries. Once under the fence he was free in Holland. A week later he was back in London meeting with King George V. His story was broadcast around the world.

In 1918 O'Brien was discharged and returned home to Illinois. That same year he wrote his best seller and went on a national speaking tour. By 1919 he was a wealthy man. In 1919 he moved to Hollywood underwriting a movie in which he starred with Virginia Allen. The same year they married. The movie was financially and critically unsuccessful and his marriage collapsed. Unsuccessful in his reconciliation attempts with Virginia, Pat O'Brien shot himself a week before Christmas 1920. He was 30.

Off With Their Reds:
WINE AND THE GUILLOTINE

It was a macabre story that appeared in the world's newspapers in March of 1870: "A Paris club composed mainly of rich merchants...[which] enabled members to witness executions." The club was located directly opposite the guillotine in a wine shop. Whenever an execution was planned, a circular was sent around which read: *"I am happy to inform you that tomorrow is the execution of* _____. *Do not fail to be present. He is afraid to die and there will be fun."* The article went on to report that the members "assembled [at the wine shop] and pass the night over a bowl of punch" until the "interesting moment."

The entire execution procedure using the guillotine was witnessed by Murat Halstead of the *Cincinnati Commercial* in 1878. He was allowed to witness the execution of two killers—one a medical student and the other a journalist. The two had killed a milk-woman who had saved $3,000 [$82,000 in current values]. The time between the conviction and execution was a "few weeks." It was the French custom to perform the execution "in the public street in front of the prison without making  known the exact time." Also the prisoner was not "notified until" awakened and taken to the guillotine. Only the press was tipped off so that "they may certify that the work had been done." The executions which Halstead witnessed were scheduled for 5 A.M. He and a group of newspapermen met at a local café at 1 A.M. and arrived in front of the prison about 3 A.M. By then "the streets were filled with people...restrained by a strong force of police from crowding upon the prison doors." The police force was backed up by horse cavalry which once during the morning was used "in a clattering charge to drive back the violent multitude [crowd]."

At 3 A.M. two black vans "came up and were recognized as containing the machinery of the executioner." The executioner, in a black silk hat, gave orders which were "swiftly and noiselessly obeyed." The guillotine was assembled by the "light of two gas-lamps in the midst of a curious crowd of reporters...it was not handsome." Within an hour the machine was fully assembled and functioning. "The ugly knife glided to the top of the frame on a trial trip," wrote Halstead. Again the soldiers and gendarme forced back the crowd. A basket "half-filled with sawdust to receive the heads, and the heavy box for the [beheaded bodies]" were in place. "At intervals," Halstead continued "there were lights from matches used by smokers, revealing parts of the dismal [machine]." The two prisoners were awakened at 4:15 A.M. One asked for wine and a cigar, the other wanted nothing. The prisoners arrived one by one, bare chested "with hair cut short...arms pinioned...shoulders covered by a tunic." They kissed a "crucifix" presented them "convulsively." Then Halstead heard the knife drop "the crunching hiss...as it clove through the thick neck...I shall not forget that noise." An assistant held the ears "until the head [dropped] into the basket." The crowd erupted with "a low cry of horror...the spectators murmured for a moment...[then left] in such haste that they seemed to be in flight." Within minutes the heads and body trunks were in the black vans and the guillotine unassembled.

Another reporter gave us a glimpse of the last days and hours of a prisoner destined for the guillotine. Those on death row "have wine, tobacco and playing cards and two [guards]" during the day to amuse themselves. Their nights "are wretched...agitated and feverish" because they never knew when they would be awakened and notified of their execution. When the time arrived "the prisoner may be dozing fitfully" when suddenly confronted by the warden and a priest. "The majority are so dazed...they dress and move about mechanically." Besides having their hair cut short, their shirt collar was cut off to facilitate the guillotine blade.

French humanity—let the "wretch…work up a kind of 'Dutch courage' with unlimited brandy…it aids the victim to walk out in good style." The warden told the reporter about one prisoner who "drank a full goblet of rum while dressing" and then had a lit cigarette placed between his lips. He then asked for another goblet of rum—"it so buoyed him, that he walked firmly…almost gaily…to the guillotine." With enough alcohol "they often stagger stupidly…between the prison and public square," if not they often struggle.

By 1900 the French Chamber of Deputies enacted legislation making executions private. With its passage the "terrible, century-long spectacle of the death machine in France" ended.

The Béchamels and Grand Constance

The Marquis of Béchamel (1630-1703) is remembered for the white sauce named after him. *Béchamel Sauce* is one of the four main sauces of French cooking, the others being: *Sauce Tomat, Sauce Veloute* and *Sauce Espagnole*. A fifth mother sauce, *Sauce Hollandaise*, was added in the 20th Century by Chef Auguste Escoffier.

Early in his life Béchamel married Valentine de Rochemont. He was attracted to her, it was said "purely because she was a wonderful good cook, and had a remarkable appetite." Together, as the Marquis and Marchioness de Béchamel, they became "famous epicures in the days of the old monarchy [Louis XIV] in France," according to an article that made the rounds in both newspapers and books in the 1890s.

Marquis of Béchamel

The story relates how the couple "cooked and ate together for fifty years in perfect accord and perfect health." It was said "they almost passed their lives at the table...when not at the table...they were generally in the kitchen together."

On their golden wedding anniversary they had a wedding feast. The Marquis "had for many years been saving for this occasion a bottle of priceless Constance wine from the Cape of Good Hope; and every guest was to have a drop or two of it," the story continued. As the bottle was brought out for presentation, "the Marchioness…sank to the ground…dead." The bottle of wine was put away unopened.

It wasn't long after his wife's death that the Marquis himself "fell hopelessly ill." The deathbed Marquis asked that the bottle of Constance be brought out and he drank it. He told his deathbed watchers "When I meet my beloved Valentine on the other side…[she will ask] 'What is the perfume I detect upon thy lips?' My answer will be 'It is the Constance wine, my beloved, which we had saved for our golden wedding [anniversary]." He drank the wine and "fell back on his pillow." All believed he was dead but an hour afterward he awakened and asked his nephew to fetch a "wonderful Perigord [game meat] pie, dressed with truffles of Sarlat" from a locked pie locker. The Marquis "ate freely of it, and again sank back upon his pillow." His doctor detected "the fatal rattle in his throat! It will soon be over!," he declared. "But the rattle turned out to be a snore." The story concludes "he lived fifteen years longer, and developed several more famous dishes."

Food historian Linda Stradley, in her *History of Sauces* opines that Béchamel sauce was actually developed in Italy in the 14ᵗʰ Century by de Medici chefs and the French Béchamel sauce version was introduced by Duke Philip de Mornay who also invented *Sauce Mornay*, *Sauce Chasseur*, *Sauce Lyonnais* and *Sauce Porto*. She writes, "there are no historical records to verify that he [Béchamel] was a gourmet, a cook, or the inventor of Béchamel Sauce." History does record that Béchamel was the honorary chief steward to King Louis XIV and claimed to have come up with the sauce "as a new way of serving and eating dried cod," explains Stradley.

The Grand Constance (*Groot Constantia*) wine at the time of the Marquis de Béchamel was indeed an extremely rare vintage. Boela Gerber a present day wine-maker explains it is the oldest commercial wine of South Africa dating back to 1685. Over the years variations of the wine "graced the tables of the nobility in Europe and England…Jane Austin and Charles Dickens wrote about [its] virtues in their classic novels…Napoleon…demanded the sweet wine [30 bottles a month] while in exile on [the Island of] St. Helena," writes Gerber. Another wine historian, Jill Baikoff, relates that Napoleon, insisted on drinking a glass while on his deathbed. He died a few moments later. The vineyards were destroyed by phylloxera (a plant destroying sap-sucking insect related to Aphids) in the 18th Century. Beginning in the 1980s and 90s research was undertaken to recreate the wine which culminated in a successful debut in the mid-2000s. In her article *Vin de Constance*, Jill Baikoff explains that the recreated Constance is believed to be a duplicate of the original based upon detailed research of the original wine. Alas, no one can ever be sure.

A Sodden, Not Solemn Procession

A Congressional funeral train departed Washington's Union Station on March 7, 1891. On board were the remains of United States Senator George Hearst who had died a week earlier. A committee of mourners included nine United States Senators and eight Representatives, some of their wives and relatives and the United States Senate Sergeant of Arms—all told a party of fifty. The train, according to the *Dalles [Oregon] Daily Chronicle* had "a great deal of unpleasant gossip in Washington concerning it." The paper went on to report "funeral parties under congressional direction are more or less of a picnic...the mourners [and] friends of the senators...had not the remotest interest in the [mourning other] than a desire for a free trip to [San Francisco] California with refreshments and wines on tap at the government's expense."

GEORGE HEARST
An unsurpassed mining genius, former U. S. Senator

When Hearst's California colleague, Senator Leland Stanford, arrived at Union Station to join the Hearst funeral train he saw "airily dressed relatives of senators...and a general air of good humor about the affair that indicated expectations of a rousing good time," reported the *Chronicle*. He was so shocked "at the spirit of the alleged mourners and to show his disgust..." he had his personal car uncoupled from the funeral train. "He did not care to go across the continent with poker players and wine drinkers," concluded the article. He attended the funeral in San Francisco but had his personal Pullman [railroad] Car attached to another train.

The Harvard-educated Senator Hearst had made his fortune in gold, silver and copper mining in California, Nevada, South Dakota and Utah. He was a major player in the Virginia City [Nevada] Comstock Lode discovery. It was there in 1859 that he and his partners mined about 40 tons of high grade ore which, after smelting, yielded $91,000 in profit [in current values $3.5 million]—essentially putting the lode on the map. His only son, William Randolph Hearst, parlayed his father's fortune into an international newspaper syndicate.

Helen Gouger

The funeral train cost the taxpayers $100,000 [$3.2 million in current values]. The scandal broke when Helen Gougar, a nationally prominent temperance leader, personally observed the drunken antics aboard the train by mere happenstance. Gougar was in a separate train which caught up with the returning funeral train in El Paso and followed it back to Washington, D.C. Mrs. Gougar related her observations to the nation's press, relaying she "could see tier after tier of wine boxes stacked up in the baggage car." "They were," she reported, "opening bottles every minute, night and day, and at many stopping places invited people into the baggage car to drink." The funeral train was made up of two sleepers, a coach, a dining car, and a baggage car. "Everybody must have been drunk, as the train met with many accidents," she alleged. The baggage car apparently went off the track at Texarkana and the "dignified Senators and honored Congressmen; the highest lawmakers for the American people…[ran around]" unpacking the wine and liquor "comprised of at least 100 cases, with ten barrels of empty barrels, two sacks and several boxes of the same." These were transferred to the dining and sleeping cars…[then] a new baggage car was added…and the porters on [her train] assisted in transferring the wine" to the new baggage car.

The "Senators and Representatives" initially refused to pay for the transfer "whereupon the yardmaster said the train would not leave Texarkana until the bills were paid." The honorable gentlemen relented and paid for the services. Mrs. Gougar went on to claim "The Hearst mourning party did not have a drop of water on the train but they drank wine altogether...the empty bottles were...being carried back to Washington for the purpose of establishing with thoroughness the committee's disgrace by having the sergeant-at-arms make a record of how much they drank on this trip." It was rumored the wine had been given the congressmen as a present "but" claimed Gougar, "the government will doubtless pay for it [again]."

An article in the *San Francisco Call* commenting on the scandal alleged "the stories concerning the funeral train... [were] mostly...absurdly exaggerated." The *Call* did go on to observe "every such funeral excursion train results in some such scandal." The article recalled the assassinated President James Garfield funeral train ten years earlier "was so uproarious and hilarious that they disturbed even the mourners in the adjoining car and were again and again requested to make less noise... [and] to remember that they were in effect attending a funeral...and to have some consideration for the widow."

A Rigorous Stiff

On Columbus Day 1878, Polish Count Max de Bertkowski married Fannie Emmeritz in New York City. After the wedding a reception was held and the guests "had wine and cakes just as at any other wedding," an 1886 article in the *New York Sun* read. There was a slight deviation, though. Max was dead and laid out in a coffin in an adjoining room.

Jonas Stolts, coffin maker, relayed the story to an investigative reporter. "They dressed him in a wedding suit, propped him up in his room, and photographed him for his bride." Afterward Max was laid in the coffin. When they started to screw down the lid, "a little man with gray hair…mustache and old fashioned glasses walked to the head of the casket." He beckoned Fannie with her "blond curls" to the head of the casket and took her hand. The man was Fannie's step-father: "These two loved one another and had it not been for the young man's death they would have been married…in the Catholic Church." He lifted Max's dead hand and asked Fannie: "Will you have this man, in the presence of these witnesses, for your husband?" The girl "sobbingly replied 'I will.'" He bent down and asked Max if he took Fannie. Then he "straightened up and answered "I do" on behalf of the corpse." He placed a ring on Fannie's finger and "pronounced them man and wife." Stolts added it "was the desire of the girl and her parents that she should take the young man's name because there was a [noble] title attached and there was a question of property supposed to be involved."

The property in question was the 1670 painting *The Flagellation of Christ* by Bartolomé Murillo valued at $100,000 [$3.5 million in current values]. The painting was owned by Max's aunt, Countess Marie de Pruschoff, who raised Max after her sister lost her fortune. Pruschoff had a large number of paintings and "was forced to sell a picture now and then" to make ends meet.

As a teenager Max entered a Paris seminary to train for the priesthood. He left the seminary to move to New York City.

According to the Countess because of his religious schooling "Maximillian was utterly ignorant of the world...as innocent of the wickedness of the world as any young girl leaving her convent." After they moved to New York, newspapers commented "[on] the famous picture she had brought with her."

Fannie's mother owned a boarding house. She searched out the Countess then living in a "fine apartment" and invited her to move into her home. Shortly after the invite, the Countess became enraged with her landlady for scolding Max who "interrupted the landlady's children in the occupation of hanging a neighbor's cat." They moved into the Emmeritz boarding house and "an intimacy soon sprung up between Max and Fannie." Max developed a sudden case of tuberculosis and "grew weaker and weaker" until the end came on October 12, 1878.

After the marriage the countess made several unsuccessful attempts to sell the painting. In the process she incurred debts with pledges against the future proceeds from a sale which resulted in litigation. Fannie's mother alleged the countess owed her $8000 and Fannie herself claimed an interest resulting from the marriage. The countess hired several attorneys whose legal fees added to the debt. One attorney asserted she had executed "an absolute and unconditional bill of sale" while another asserted she had given him a "power of attorney." The painting was hung in the Metropolitan Museum of Art at the request of the disputing parties pending the outcome of the litigation.

In 1887, the Countess was living in a 12' X 15' "ill smelling apartment...an old woman whose locks are silvery white...[eking out a living on a] sewing machine she works daily making shirts...stitch, stitch, stitch she hides her head from the world," reported the *Memphis Appeal*. She died penniless. Fannie ultimately married a truck driver.

The Dog in the Wine Cellar

It was one of those sentimental-miracle stories that appeared in the press shortly after the 1906 San Francisco earthquake and fire.

Era newspapers reported the survival of a tiny fox terrier who had somehow survived being locked in the wine cellar of the St. Francis Hotel on San Francisco's Union Square. The prominent landmark hotel had been opened just two years before, patterned after Europe's most luxurious and elite hotels. From its inception, the hotel has "been one of the most prestigious hotels in the [American] west," writes Charles Fracchia in the *Encyclopedia of San Francisco*.

The new hotel included an excellent wine cellar within which boasted the finest wines from around the world. James Hall was in charge of the cellars and routinely locked his fox terrier inside—partly to keep him contained but also to roam the cellars for rat duty for which the breed was suited. On the morning of April 18, 1906 at 5:20 A.M. the earthquake struck, shuddering the multi-story structure—one of the tallest in San Francisco at the time. The dual twelve-story towers withstood the quake itself but, like much of San Francisco, was soon engulfed in flames.

The hotel staff was forced to abandon the structure "during the early hours of Thursday morning, April 19 [1906]…flames were licking up everything inflammable within the walls of the Hotel St. Francis" reported the *Pacific Commercial Advertiser*. The little fox terrier, Francis, "remained locked up in the wine cellar…deserted and forgotten," continued the report.

Francis would remain locked up in the cellar for five days "while the hotel was a seething furnace." Hall was "powerless to rescue [Francis]…for days the…ruins were so hot that all thought of probing about…was out of the question," the *Advertiser* related. Fortunately

St. Francis Hotel after 1906 Earthquake

no one was injured at the hotel. All of the hotel guests were able to vacate the structure, other than the terrified fox terrier. One of the guests, Frank Shipman, described the mayhem: "I could see the hotel stairs crowded...men, women and children—frantically rushing down to the street in their nightclothes...it was the nearest thing to a stampede that I have ever seen." Another guest, S. C. Welling, who fled from the fire reported seeing "over 100 dead bodies" as he passed the neighboring Cosmopolitan Hotel. He also commented on ruthless gougers exploiting the terrified fleeing crowds: "Thirty dollars [$845 in current values] were charged [passengers] by wagons to carry one out of the danger zone...water was selling at $1 [$28 in current values] a glass and bread at fifty cents [$14 in current values] a loaf...several men were shot for looting," Welling concluded.

It would be five days before the heat subsided and Hall could sort through the rubble and locate the cellar door. When he finally managed access "one of the first things to greet his startled gaze was the little fox terrier...crouched beneath some machinery." The report added "The heat in the cellar must have been intense, but the little animal had managed to escape the flames and came out of the ordeal unsinged, although nearly dead from thirst and hunger."

The newspaper went on to report that "Hall nursed the dog[s] health and spirits, and not many days after his rescue he was as cheerful and lively as before the fire." Hall, like many others who survived the earthquake, must have lost his living accommodations. The newspaper, without explanation, noted that the wife of the manager of the hotel, James Wood, had taken over as owner of Francis. Mrs. Wood "declared that henceforth he [Francis] shall be clothed with the dignity of the hotel's mascot."

Like Francis the fox terrier, the luxury hotel's outside structure survived the earthquake. Its gutted interior was rebuilt, renovated and refurbished. The St. Francis Hotel reopened a year and a half later in November of 1907. Mike Gerrard, travel and drinks writer for the *Huffpost* recently ranked the St. Francis as one of the top ten historic hotels in America.

Chariots of Wine

Dorando Pietri was a world-class runner who hydrated himself before, during and after his races with wine. In 1908 he won the Olympic Marathon but was later disqualified. His valiant effort won him the hearts of millions. Irving Berlin, inspired by Pietri, wrote his first commercial song "Dorando" about him and sold it for $25. The author Arthur Conan Doyle, then a journalist with the *London Daily Mail,* witnessed Pietri's finish: "It is horrible, and yet fascinating, this struggle between a set purpose and an utterly exhausted [human] frame." Pietri's success/failure was the result of a Princess' whim.

Dorando Pietro Crossing Finish Line with Help

Shortly after the race the 5' 2" Dorando was quoted as saying: "Give me wine, red wine, because it makes me run fast, and faster and faster. Give me Chianti and give me lots of it for it's life itself, is wine. I love it because it makes me forget that I am tired. I want wine because when I drink it no one can catch me. Ah. Chianti, it means life and victory." After the Marathon, he came to America to compete in a number of highly advertised races. While here he was seen "drinking several bottles of wine each day. He took it while running, while eating, before arising and before retiring," reported a January 1909 edition of the *Deseret Evening News*. He told a *Newport News Daily Press* reporter he drank three quarts of wine each day. He claimed he lost the marathon because someone gave him whiskey and champagne while running the race and "declared he would have won...if he had been given wine."

Pietri was born in Carpi a small village in Northern Italy. As a youth he worked in a bakery. Legend has it he ran his first race in Carpi against the number one Italian long distance runner wearing his work clothes clad in flour and easily outdistanced his opponents. In the 1906 Olympics he competed in the marathon but dropped out with an intestinal illness—at the time he had a five minute lead on the field.

He was the outside favorite for the 1908 Olympic marathon when he arrived in London. Britain's Queen Alexandra "was so excited by the event that she demanded to be involved in both the start and finish," writes Simon Burton of *The Guardian*. The Queen's daughter, the Princess of Wales insisted the finish be inside the gates of Windsor Castle so that her children could see the finish through their nursery window. The change added an extra 385 yards, at the last minute, to the marathon distance—"which remains the official marathon distance to this day," writes Burton. It would be those last 385 yards that disrupted Pietri's pace.

The twenty-two year old Pietri was well out front by the time he entered the stadium track enroute to the finish line. He fell and was quickly attended to by the Chief Medical Officer who held him erect and instructed another to rub his legs. Doyle, who was sitting in a front row seat, observed the spectacle "amid stooping figures and grasping hands I caught a glimpse of the haggard, yellow face, the glazed, expressionless eyes, the long, black hair streaked across the brow. Surely he is done now." Pietri was "bundled over the [finish] line by a posse of brits," wrote Burton. He was followed by Johnny Hayes of the United States. The U.S. Team immediately lodged a protest and won. Pietri was disqualified because he was helped over the finish line. Hayes was declared the winner. Pietri's time was 2h 54min 46s—of which ten minutes were exerted in covering the last 385 yards.

Doyle was distraught over the outcome writing: "The Italian's great performance can never be erased from our record of sport, be the decision of the judges what it may." He started a fund to raise money to help Pietri open a bakery shop in his home town of Carpi. The fund raised $900 [$25,000 in current values].

The following year Pietri came to the U. S. and ran two races against Hayes—beating him both times. He stopped racing in 1911 after running 46 races during his professional career. As a professional he accumulated $300,000 in winnings [$7.5 million in current values]. He purchased a hotel which later went bankrupt. The remainder of his life he managed an auto repair shop in San Remo where he died in 1946 at the age of 56.

Horsemeat with a Fire Chaser

In June of 1846, "a happy-go-lucky chap" named Bill Dean met up with a group of Texas Volunteers in Corpus Christi. Dean was identified in era newspaper articles and books as a Texas Ranger. The Mexican-American War had started just one month earlier. The war started over a boundary dispute between the U. S. and Mexico when a 2,000-strong Mexican Cavalry detachment attacked a 70-man U.S. army patrol—killing sixteen Americans.

Dean met up with the volunteers who were "sitting out on the stoop of [the] Kinney House." Henry Kinney (1814-1862) is considered the founder of Corpus Christi. The Texas Volunteers were military contingents' enroute to the Rio Grande to support U.S. military efforts to establish the river as the Southern border of the United States.

Dean told the Rio Grande-destined Volunteers: "I've been there, myself, and done what a good many of you won't do—I come back." He went on to tell the assembled men of the hardships due them—including the intense prairie temperatures in August which he called "nateral hell." Then he related how he and a group of Rangers had "lived eight days on one poor hawk and three blackberries—couldn't kill a prairie rat on the whole route to save us from starvation." Finally on the ninth day they "struck a small streak of good luck," he continued "a horse give out and broke down, plumb out in the centre of an open prairie."

The horse was dying and they shot it "saving the critter's [meat] by shootin him, and that was all, for in three minutes he'd have died a nateral death [which would have made the meat inedible]." Within minutes they had butchered the horse and "cut off some chunks of meat and stick'em on our ram-rods [i.e. the metal rods used to push bullets inside the gun barrel against powder in era rifles]," Dean continued "but the cookin' was another matter." There was no firewood on the prairie so Dean claimed he "piled up a heap of prairie grass" which was "high and dry" and set it on fire. His tale of woe continued "but it flashed up like [gun] powder and went out as quick."

One of his listeners inquired "but how did you cook the horse meat after that?"

"Why, the fire caught the high grass close by, and the winds carried the flames streakin' across the prairie," explained Dean. Dean claimed he "followed up that fire, holding my chunk of meat directly over the hottest part of the blaze…[the blaze was traveling just] like a locomotive doins." Once in a while he claimed "a little flurry of wind would come along, and the flame would get a few yards start" and he'd speed up to catch the flame "lap her with my chunk [of meat] and there we'd have it again, nip and tuck…You never seed such a tight race—it was beautiful."

Again one of his listeners inquired "but did you cook your meat in the end?"

Dead Horse and Rider
Painting by Frederick Remington

Dean responded "I chased that damn fire a mile and a half, the almightiest hard race you ever heer'd on and never give it up until I run right into a wet marsh" when the fire went out.

"But was it cooked?" inquired a frustrated listener.

"Cooked! No!—just crusted over a little—you don't cook broken horse flesh very easily, no how; but when it comes to chasin' up a prairie fire with a chunk of it, I don't know which is toughest, the meat or the job…you'd have laughed…to see the fire leave me at times, and then see me bumpin' and moven'…," he concluded his story. George Kendall, who relayed the story in his *New Orleans Times-Picayune* column, ended the story wishing he "could make the story as effective on paper as Dean did in the telling…it would draw a laugh from those fond of the ludicrous."

Mormon Dixie Wine

Time often obscures history. Such is the case with our current understanding about alcohol and members of the Church of Jesus Christ of the Latter Day Saints. Most assume that the anti-alcohol dogma of the Mormon Church started with its founding in 1830 by Joseph Smith. The reality is LDS church served sacramental wine and commercially produced and sold wine until 1892 when it was officially banned. According to Dennis Lancaster in his article *Dixie Wine*, the ban came about because "the abuse of the Sacramental wine increased [and was] abandoned in favor of water in sacramental services."

Brigham Young

The Mormon Church operated a profitable wine manufacturing and sales enterprise in Southern Utah in the area around St. George. The area is known as "Dixie" because of its Mohave Desert climate which differs dramatically from the rest of Utah. St. George was founded in 1862 by 309 Mormons. Thirty of the number were Swiss immigrants who "had come from wine-producing areas in Switzerland," relates Lancaster: "They knew how to make good wine." John Naegle, a prominent Mormon, became known as "the best winemaker in Dixie...his product was marketed under the name "Naegle's Best." By 1866 Brigham Young, who succeeded Joseph Smith as head of the church, is quoted as remarking: "I anticipate the day when we [LDS] can have the privilege of using, at our sacraments, pure wine, produced within our borders." Wesley Larson, in his tract entitled *Toquerville* explains that before his death Joseph Smith "had a revelation that they [Mormons] were to use water in the sacrament [of communion], unless they had wine of their own make." Indeed there is some historical evidence that Brigham Young actually enjoyed a glass of Dixie wine himself from time to time. Lancaster writes "one of the better winemakers…a man named Schmutz who lived in Middleton [near St. George]…whenever Brigham Young passed [his] place…would [have] one glass of wine, that's all he would drink…he would sit there and sip that wine just like a cup of tea."

Dixie wine was much more than sacramental wine. It was used socially by the local Mormon population in Saint George as evidenced by an 1878 newspaper advertisement by Thomas Hall who was selling it from his house. An article in the *Salt Lake Herald* relates "its use has become almost universal in the Dixie country." The *Herald* went on to describe an incident "imagining of the brain [hallucination]" experienced by one cowboy known as "Rover"—causing the paper to state "it ought no longer be tolerated." Other stories about its potency abound in Utah newspaper articles through the late 1800s and early 1900s. A 1909 article in the *Salt Lake Tribune* claimed that regular users could not escape from "its baneful influence…[some citizens even moved away because] they were fast becoming devoted slaves of Dixie wine…" The article also alludes to abandoned stills found that reduced the wine into a "whiteeye"…some of which contained eighty percent alcohol." In 1907 an oil prospector who traveled through St. George observed it had only one saloon and noted: "One drink of Dixie wine will make you forget your name, while two drinks will cause you to steal the saddle off your own horse, and after three drinks you can see oil wells immeasurable." Another Salt Lake City newspaper observed there was a "deadly coil that lies concealed in Dixie wine." Continuing the article repeats a "legend" about a dinner that Brigham Young threw for some "distinguished eastern guests" and poured them "some of our pure Dixie wine made from our home-raised grapes." Overcome by the wine the guests, "paid three days' hotel bills and were thankful to finally get out [of town] alive."

The wine was a great commercial success during the 1870s when a "ready market" developed at silver mining camps in Pioche, Nevada and Silver Reef, Utah. Larson observes the miners were "characteristically hard workers and heavy drinkers…[and] were happy to pay cash for rich Dixie wine." In 1873 Dixie Mormons were

222

allowed to pay their tithes in grapes and wine and "the tithing office sold its surplus to the mining camps." The church's commercial exploitation of their wine surpluses ended in the early 1890s when the silver deposits gave out. As the deposits gave out and railroads brought in California wines, the bulk of the grape farmers pulled their crops—essentially ending Dixie wine manufacture—but not the lore.

The Case of "Handsome" Handly's Case of Wine

Halcyon days gone by—a bunch of fumbling Irish cops at the turn of the 20th Century—a dispute over a case of wine. These were the days when a good pair of women's shoes cost $2, ham sold for 13¢ a pound, and a quart of *Eclipse Champagne* went for 50¢. A gallon of *American Club Whiskey* sold for $1.75 while an Irish dentist, Dr. R. L. Walsh, advertised new dentures (upper and lowers) for $5. Bread could only be had at local bakeries and was sold unsliced. Prepackaged sliced bread wouldn't be introduced to the American public until 1928.

These were the days before police cars. The first police cruiser was actually an electric wagon introduced in Akron in 1899 and its "first assignment was to pick up a drunken man." Policemen for the most part were on foot patrol—just a uniform, a badge, a gun and a Billy club to maintain

First Police Car

order. There were no two-way radios. Officers communicated with precinct headquarters by means of a private telephone call-box system spread throughout the city which the officer periodically used as he walked his beat.

One such foot patrolman was Officer T. W. Handly. According to a 1900 edition of the *San Francisco Call,* he was "recognized as being the handsomest [police officer]" in San Francisco. His good looks won him a "gate prize—a case of wine" at a local picnic. He was given a ticket to present to Bendy Hay, a local grocer of Irish descent, who had donated the prize for the event.

Officer Handly was described as a modest, shy, introverted man who was reluctant to claim his prize for his good looks. But a case of wine was a case of wine and the Irishman decided to give "the card calling for the liquid" to his friend Detective Jack Fitzgerald (another man of Irish descent) asking that he claim the prize for him. Fitzgerald, in turn, handed the card off to another police colleague asking that he have the wine sent to Handly's house on Twentieth Street. Bendy "recognized the order and at once dispatched the case of wine to the residence," reported the *Call*. When Bendy's deliveryman arrived at Handly's residence, he found no one at home—Handly was on duty. The deliveryman, in turn, left the case at the corner bakery with instructions to give it to the police officer when he called for it.

Later that day, Officer J. H. Crowley who lived just a few houses from Handly on Twentieth Street stopped by the bakery to pick up "his daily bread and the man who mixes the dough told him there was a case of wine for him." The *Call* reported "this unexpected news filled [Crowley] with joy." He picked up the case and carried it to his home. The Irish cop, acting with great responsibility, "at once…reported to his superiors that he wished to be excused for a week on very important special business," the newspaper related. The article didn't say but it certainly implied that Crowley spent the week pickling himself in his case of good fortune.

Meanwhile "Handsome" Handly wondered what happened to his wine. He looked up his colleague Fitzgerald asking for an explanation. Jack Fitzgerald who was "at all times ready to explain…told the handsome man of what he had done," reported the *Call*. Handly backtracked the skein of events and within short time "Handsome" figured out what had happened and who was the culprit.

Crowley, of course, feigned any knowledge that the case of wine was intended for Handly. All he knew was he was given the case of wine by the baker. Thereafter "Handsome" took a dislike to Crowley and there "was a Klondike chill" when the two cops passed each other. And, we are told, "poor Fitzgerald blushes at his blunder in beating "Handsome" out of the wine and sending it to [Crowley] who took a week off to consume it."

The story offers some credence to the old saying: "God invented liquor to prevent the Irish from conquering the world."

A Sumptuous $15 Demise

An unnamed elderly Italian man living in New York City's "Little Italy" was suffering from tuberculosis [TB] in 1900. TB, at the time, was a lethal disease with no known cure. Fifteen years earlier medical professionals did not realize that tuberculosis was even contagious. Isolated sanatoria were just being set up in Arizona and other desert states, touting dry desert air and warm temperatures to prolong one's life. But sanatoriums cost money—something the "old Italian street vendor" had little of.

In fact the "old Italian street vendor" had exactly $75.00 in his savings bank account [$2,350 in current values]. The story about his intricate deathbed plan was first exposed in New York's *February Century*: "Feeling

New York City's Little Italy circa 1900

that his end was drawing near, [he] prepared a scheme for ending his days in comfort," the magazine related.

He began to draw out $70 from his savings account and then a few days later he would redeposit it. He "continued the operation at brief intervals." Each time the bank would enter the withdrawal and redeposit in his pass-book. Eventually the credit page showed $800 [$26,000 in current values] in deposits and the opposite debit page showed "about $785—balance $15." Next he carefully cut out the debit page "leaving [only] the long line of deposits [in his savings pass book]."

The old Italian then "took to bed…and called his closest friends…they were good fellows and he loved them all," continued the *Century*. Among those assembled in his bedroom were Pedro the banana peddler, Giovani the boot-black and Arturo the wine-seller. In the dark bedroom with curtains drawn he gave them the bad news of his impending demise. Then he told them that "what he had to leave them was not much" and asked Edgardo to find for him his savings book which was between the mattress and box spring of the dying man's bed. Once it was located, he asked Edgardo to take the book to the window and "tell him how much" he had managed to save. "Eight hundred?" the old Italian feigned surprise, "Ah, well, thanks to God that it was so much; but oh that it were more, for such good fellows as you," he said.

He went on to explain that Doctor Bartollo had told him he might have three months to live—maybe until the springtime. He begged his good friends not to cry. He begged that when he died they should take the bank book "draw [out] the amount and divide it between them…and meanwhile, as his loving friends of the present, his heirs in the future, would [they] kindly attend to his little wants?" he asked.

"Would they? Did they? That old fellow was fed on the fat of the land while he" lay in his deathbed. Arturo brought him Chianti by the gallon. "He drank more Chianti in a week than he had swallowed in five years," reported the *Century*. The push-cart banana vendor brought so many unripe green bananas to the sick man that his Italian neighbors along Mulberry Street weren't sure if "he was cheering his friends finale with fruit, or endeavoring to complicate the consumption [i.e. TB] with other ills" and hasten the old Italian's death.

When the old man finally succumbed to his disease, the *Century* relates, "Little Italy made a decent pretense of sorrow, it was really en *fête* [i.e. a celebration]—at last the $800 was to be drawn!" It was destined to be a happy day—at least that's what Arturo, Edgardo,

Pedro, Giovani and the other benefactors thought. One can imagine them licking their lips in anticipation of their soon-to-be reward. The group of friends entered the bank dressed in "their holiday clothes and...with a few chosen friends...stated their case and asked for the amount." The banana vendor was to receive $40 for his fruit and the wine-seller was to receive $100 for his Chianti and "the others various sums invested for the invalid." Even the funeral director advanced his costs against the banked money. After all the deductions there was still $450 "[to be] the dividend."

The article's author wrote he "need not describe the small-sized riot that followed when the subtraction of the pages from the gone side of the book was explained to the swearing mourners." Still the tender of $15 was made to them—"all that the deceased had in the bank," concluded the *Century*.

The Two Cask Getaway

"The amount of inventive genius man develops under the spur of peril is scarcely short of the marvelous, and it is in nothing better illustrated than in the chronicles of escapes," pronounced an 1880 article in the *New Bloomfield Times* [PA].

One of these chronicled escapes involved Alexander Stewart who was made the Scottish Duke of Albany in 1458 by his father King James II. In a leadership and succession dispute with his brother King James III, he was imprisoned in 1479 in Edinburgh Castle. His daring escape "is one of the most dramatic episodes in Scottish history," declared the *Times*.

Alexander Stewart

Besides Alexander, his brother John, the Earl of Mar, had also been imprisoned and executed by King James III by being "bled to death"—a fate the Duke of Albany himself was soon to meet. While in prison he was attended by his faithful and loyal chamberlain who resided with him.

Some of Alexander's confederates "resolved to save him." A small sloop sailed into the port at Reith Roads near the castle with a cargo of Gascony (French) wines. The region today is famous for its Armagnac brandy and Vin de Pays.

Two of the wine casks were presented to the imprisoned Duke. The *Times* reveals "when the Duke came to sip into them, he found in one a ball of wax containing a letter urging him to escape...in the other...a small coil of rope which would enable him to drop from the walls of his prison." He was instructed to drop down on the "water" side of the castle where the sloop would be waiting to spirit him to his freedom.

Thus having the tools, he executed his plan. On the appointed night the Duke invited the captain of the guard to dine with him "under the pretext of wishing to have his judgment on the wine," explains the *Times*. The captain of the guard arrived with three soldiers, all of whom took positions in the room. When the meal was over the two men played *trictrac* [backgammon]. As the evening progressed the Duke plied his guest with wine and his chamberlain did the same with the three guards. "The heat of the great fire, near where they artfully placed [the captain], soon made the officer very drowsy...and [his] men, too, began to nod their heads," continued the article.

The Duke, described as a big powerful man, jumped to his feet and killed the captain of the guard and two of the soldiers while the chamberlain killed the other with his dagger. They threw the bodies on the fire and made their way to "an out of the way corner" of the castle wall. The chamberlain descended first but found the rope too short. Falling from its end he fell and broke his leg. "Uttering no cry of pain... [the faithful chamberlain]...told his master the cause of the disaster." The Duke grabbed his bedding and tying them together lengthened the rope and made his escape. He helped his loyal chamberlain to a remote hut where he would be safe until his recovery. He then "flew to the seashore" where he boarded the sloop and set sail for France.

The *Times* article concludes, "the following morning...[during morning inspection, guards] found nothing of their prisoner but a room full of suffocating smoke and four bodies roasted to coals in the ashes of the fire."

In Paris, Alexander married Anne de la Tour and became friends with French King Louis XI who protected him. The Duke entered into a secret agreement with England's King Edward IV who funded an army which overtook Scotland led by the Duke. Under the agreement Scotland was to come under the suzerainty of England. In the ensuing battle his brother, King James III, was himself imprisoned in Edinburgh Castle and the Duke became "acting" lieutenant general of the [Scottish] realm but the [Scottish] parliament refused to confirm the appointment. The Duke was forced to flee once again when his brother regained the Scottish throne.

Alexander made two more attempts on his brother's throne, neither of which succeeded. In self-exile in Paris the Duke died in a fluke accident. A splinter forcibly entered his eye during a jousting tournament. The year was 1485. The Duke was 31 years old. In the end, the fluke did in the Duke.

Is There Wine in the Afterlife?

Sir Arthur Conan Doyle visited the United States in 1922. With the introduction of his *Sherlock Holmes* series, he is credited with inventing the forensic detective novel genre. The *New York Tribune* opined that he was "one of the greatest story tellers that has ever lived." The Scottish novelist told the *New York Tribune*, "[he] had been accustomed all his life to cocktails before meals and wine with his dinner." But this was Prohibition America and distilled liquors, wines and beer were simply unavailable other than for medicinal and sacramental purposes. He told the *Tribune*, "I can't get it, and I have rather lost my appetite for it." There is also some evidence that Doyle, like his fictional character Sherlock Holmes, used cocaine which at the time was not illegal. He was a physician by education but a writer by vocation.

Besides his literary genius, Doyle was also a well-known spiritualist—an adherent of the popular movement of the day. Millions had been killed during World War I and spiritualists alleged they could converse with the dead. As an outspoken advocate, Doyle promoted the idea that "the life beyond…was one of great happiness…the dead find themselves in an [unseen] world [much] like this one…Everyone there has congenial work…there is no rich or poor." There was no heaven, hell or purgatory. There were

Arthur Conan Doyle

"punitive circles" in which sinners' spirits were treated in a hospital-like setting where "weakly souls where healed by sorrow," Doyle claimed. Adding that when a child died "it grew up in the next world…under better conditions [and] when the old died the symptoms of age rapidly left them [allowing the continuation of] their life [at]…about 35 years in the case of a man and 30 in that of a woman." The spiritual world had no materialism.

Organized religious leaders condemned spiritualism. W. P. Crozier, in an article published in the *Dearborn Independent* in 1920, related that the secretary of the English Church Union condemned spiritualism as an evil thing designed "to satisfy a sentimental and often unholy curiosity." Another church leader claimed spiritualistic messages were "wicked spirits rushing in...to use the medium and communicate our world for our hurt." The movement "is hooted and reviled by Rome [i.e. Catholic Church], by Canterbury [i.e. Anglican Church] and even by Little Bethel [i.e. Baptist Church]" claimed another era article. Doyle was a sincere believer, debunking his critics by claiming "people insist too much upon direct proof...only the ignorant and inexperienced are in total opposition."

Spiritualism purportedly assuaged the fear of death common to all. It also allegedly gave solace to mourners. Doyle portrayed death "as painless and...rather pleasant...the etheric body [i.e. spiritual body] found itself at once in touch with those whom it was most bound by sympathy and love." Doyle wrote a book on the subject: *The Wanderings of a Spiritualist* after an Australian speaking tour in which he touted the cause. In it, he fondly and forcibly quoted President Teddy Roosevelt: "the grandest sport upon earth is to champion an unpopular cause which you know to be true."

But what about cocktails after death? The *Tribune* reporter expressly inquired (probably facetiously) if the dead will be denied "these [alcoholic] balms, or will we want to return to earth, to some wet place, and warm [our] soul with nature's gift [wine and spirits] to man?" Doyle responded by explaining that the spiritual body for a while would be able to get their cocktails. As proof, he recalled Jesus at the last supper telling his apostles "you will drink new wine with me." Doyle asserted, "I am convinced if the etheric [spiritual body] craves wine it will be given him." But salving wine cravings would only occur during the early period of time after death while the spiritual body was in transformation. Spiritualism dictated that there are a number of spheres through which the etheric passes—eventually reaching a point when it "forgets earthly longings," according to Doyle.

The spiritualist movement gradually lost its momentum after numerous prominent spiritualists claiming to be in communication with the spirits through séances, were exposed as frauds. In many highly publicized instances, séance techniques, upon investigation, turned out to be nothing more than mortal sleight of hand trickery— cleverly executed deceptions.

As to wine in the afterlife? Sherlock Holmes was a figment of Doyle's imagination. Hopefully, his enunciation that there is wine after death is not. Hope can only spring eternal for oenophiles. One word of caution, Doyle believed in fairies too.

Bismarck's Drinking Habits

There are aspects of Otto von Bismarck's personality and greatness that are little known—especially his abundant appetite for wine, champagne, beer and tobacco. In 1890 an article in the *Whichita Daily Eagle* claimed "besides an iron will and iron nerve he had an iron stomach." As a college student he was an active sword duelist. At Gottingen University he smoked a porcelain pipe described as "a yard in length...seldom out of his mouth." Brilliant too, he crowded six semesters into one and passed his state bar exam. As a student, the *Eagle*, claimed "he oscillated between the wildest carousels and fits of melancholy."

History knows him as the "Iron Chancellor." Otto von Bismarck was responsible for unifying German duchies, principalities, states and free cities into the modern German state. He fathered the first socialist nation— introducing social security, workman's insurance compensation and disability insurance well before any other nation. His series of alliances and treaties between European powers maintained European peace for twenty years—he was considered the master of European peace.

Otto von Bismarck

An 1890 article published in the *Omaha Daily Bee* recounts his "proverbial ability to consume vast quantities of liquor and tobacco." His drinking ability served him well in political life. It "contributed to...his diplomatic successes." On one occasion while negotiating a treaty between Denmark, Austria and Germany "wine flowed like water...[Bismarck] drank the [other] weak headed [diplomats] under the table...[and] forced them to make all sorts of concessions which they were not authorized to make," relates the *Bee*. The newspaper continued by extolling "Bismarck's capacity for tobacco is fully as wonderful…known as a chain smoker who connects his breakfast and dinner with an endless chain of cigars, each lighted from the stump of the last one."

Six years after his death in 1898, commentators were still discussing his legendary drinking and eating habits. A 1904 article in the *Washington Evening Star* recounted how he "refused to drink German champagne" which he despised. He preferred French champagne. He so coveted the French beverage that during the negotiations between Prussia and France at the end of the war which essentially unified Germany, Bismarck demanded 5,000 empty French champagne barrels "impregnated with the aroma, the bouquet producing ferment," declared an article in a 1910 edition of the *Salt Lake City Broad Ax*. Bismarck apparently thought the aromatic barrels would somehow augment German champagne closer to the French variety. The French agreed to $1 billion cash in war reparations and giving up the provinces of Alsace-Lorraine to Germany. They refused the barrel request—finally agreeing to hand over five barrels. As a German diplomat at the Russian Court in 1857, the forty-two year old Bismarck revealed that by that time in his life he had consumed "5,000 bottles of champagne and smoked 100,000 cigars." He lived another forty-one years and it is generally conceded he at least doubled those numbers by the time of his death.

Beside his gargantuan drinking and smoking habits, Bismarck was seriously superstitious. An 1883 article in Michigan's *Northern Tribune* revealed that "he would take no important step on Friday, believes in astrology, and has predicted the day and hour of his own death." The Friday ban was a result of three German losses during the Franco-Prussian War in 1870—all of which happened on Friday. The number 13 apparently disconcerted him. He refused to sit at a dining table where he would make the thirteenth diner. On one occasion, as Chancellor of Germany, he sent out dinner invitations. When he discovered there would be thirteen diners, "one of the invitations had to be countermanded," claims a 1902 article in the *Washington Evening Star*. Another article disclosed that he refused to drink water from 9 PM until midnight on New Year's Eve. This self-imposed water fast was an "ancient tradition in [his] family that anyone who set the legend at defiance would pass through a serious illness," recounted the *Star*.

A Tough Night for
Saloons and Cops

Three days before Christmas 1901. San Francisco newspapers touted local sales. Katschinkski Shoe Store offered women's patent leather shoes—"The very latest, swellest fad"—Oxford ties...[with] coin toes and tips...[and] Cuban Heels—for just $2.25." Wood Clothing offered men's wool or tweed suits and serge overcoats for $9 each. A local dentist offered a "full set of dentures" for $4. Levi Straus advertised for workers for its "[denim] overall" factory—no experience required. Local hotels advertised for maids at $20 per month and cooks for $30 per month. A seven room flat rented for $35 while a five roomer went for $15.

On the underbelly side of the town, San Francisco Police had their hands full. Otto Wallen, a local cook, broke a plate glass window at Otto Baherman's saloon and crawled through "the aperture [and] proceeded to help himself to a variety of choice wines." When discovered by beat cops, Wallen told them he had been thrown out earlier in the evening. In an effort to get even, he broke in "and helped himself to as much wine as he wanted."

San Francisco Saloon circa 1901

A few blocks away, two men—J. A. Johnson and H. Stone—broke into the Fearless Saloon—rifling the register of $35.50. A beat cop noticed Johnson, the lookout for the caper, "acting suspiciously [and] he was placed under arrest." Stone was found "hiding in a closet [with] a revolver in his pocket." When he was frisked the $35.50 was recovered.

Later that morning the Casino Saloon was broken into and a number of bottles of whiskey stolen. The police had "no clew [sic]" as to the whereabouts or identity of the burglars.

Not far away, two customers of a saloon located "on Eighteenth and Railroad Avenues" were arrested on "the charge of being drunk and disturbing the peace." One of the two dropped his watch on the floor. The police discovered it had been stolen in a burglary of a private residence a few weeks before.

Twelve blocks away, Antone Rengli shot and wounded John Connolly when he caught him and two others attempting to break into his liquor inventory at the rear of his store. Another shooting involved James McNiece who shot John Dunne. The shooting involved one Josie Martin "a notorious woman." McNiece shot Dunne because he [Dunne] "had stolen Josie Martin's affections from him."

Mrs. E. Oels owned a small grocery store on Stevenson Street—in the rear of which was "a little bar room" in which she served wine and beer to customers. While sitting alone in the bar room three men entered the store and one grabbed Oels "by the throat so that she could not speak." Another grabbed $29 from the "till…behind the liquor counter." The aged Mrs. Oels "deprived of the use of her tongue…scraped her feet along the floor…to attract the attention of her daughter and [her daughters gentleman]…who were in the house back of the store." Her shuffling worked. Just as the third thief picked up a chair "as if to strike her on the head," the daughter and her friend opened the door and the robbers fled. At press time the trio had not been apprehended.

Some 100 miles to the northeast in Auburn, California William Rowe who owned a saloon of the same name shot and killed R. Mitchell. Rowe claimed it was self-defense—"[Rowe] got into a fight with two strangers and one…pulled a pistol and shot [Rowe] through the hand." Rowe in turn "drew his gun." One assailant took off running but Mitchell "came toward [Rowe] with a chair." Rowe shot him "through the heart." It was such a clean and exacting shot that Mitchell "fell dead with a lighted cigarette still in his mouth," reported the *San Francisco Call*.

Farther northeast in a local saloon at Alturas, California Edward Conlon was "the victim of a murderous attack" which nearly cost him his life. Granville Mays invited Conlon to have a drink with him which Conlon politely declined. Mays "sprang at Conlon with a knife...[and] cut Conlon's throat almost from ear to ear." Fortunately the "gash was not deep enough to strike the jugular." Still forty stitches were required to dress the wound.

These were times before police cars and two-way communications—local cops and sheriffs either walked beats or rode horses to crime scenes. Intercity transportation was by street car and/or horse drawn carriages and buggies mostly on gravel roads. Automobiles were just emerging—electric, steam, gas and diesel—the market hadn't yet decided which would emerge as the most economic and user friendly— total combined automobile production nationwide was in the low thousands.

Wine as a Tactical Weapon

"Even the wines of France are fighting against the [German] invader," blared a 1915 edition of the *Hartford Herald*. The story recounted a tale told by the well-known American landscape artist Aston Knight aka Louis Aston Knight. Knight was born in France to American parents and was educated in Europe. His father Ridgeway Knight was also a noted artist. Aston lived the bulk of his life in France. His favorite subjects were French cottages and gardens located in the environs of his residence in Beaumont-le-Roger in

northern France. He won numerous awards and honors at the Paris Salon which, during his lifetime, was the greatest annual art event in the Western world. One of his works was purchased by President Warren Harding to hang in the White House.

Louis Aston Knight

Knight recounted a wartime tale about a friend who grew grapes and produced wine at La Fère-Champeniose. The friend was an officer in the French Army "in the zone of operations of the Marne battles," explained the *Herald*. When the Germans invaded, Aston's vintner friend told his steward "he should open all the doors of his establishment to them." He further instructed the steward to "carefully wall up the best vintage of [his] wines [in one corner of the cellar]...then in another corner...place a great number of bottles of very inferior wine and wall that up carelessly." The main part of the cellar was left intact. The idea was to divert the Germans attention

"Summer Afternoon"
by Louis Aston Knight

242

to the shabbily built and obvious hideaway—away from the premium bottles. According to Knight his friend "[hoped] the Germans would think there was valuable wine there and, breaking down the wall, would look no further."

The steward was further instructed to tell his employer "where the Germans go when they have gotten through with the cellar," continued the *Herald*.

Knight related what followed: "[The] Germans came, entered the cellars and began pillaging them." The soldiers confiscated "hundreds of bottles [of the inferior wine] and left. The ploy of hiding the premium wines was successful. The vintner had safely kept his most valuable wines away from the marauding soldiers.

The steward then crept away and "[managed to get] word to the owner [as to the where the soldiers went]." The owner "knowing the [local] country, informed the nearest artillery commander that he would probably get results by shelling a certain patch of woods nearby." The woods according to Knight, "were bombarded for an hour with shrapnel [shells]."

A couple of days later when the French re-took La Fère-Champeniose they "found in the woods the bodies of more than 3,000 Germans surrounded with [the] debris of the wine bottles." The vintner had guessed correctly—the Germans, after seizing his wine, retired to the local woods "for a drinking bout and the French guns had caught them when they were helplessly intoxicated."

After the war Knight returned to France and continued his profession, winning continuous acclaim for his works. He died in 1948 in Paris at the age of 75. His works are still actively traded. His auction record for a painting titled *A Cottage Along the River* sold at Sotheby's in 2005 for $108,000.

Outing a Fire with Wine

In 1906 the population of San Francisco was 410,000—roughly half its present size. The city was made up a number of interconnected neighborhoods, each with its own ethnic village-like characteristics. One was Telegraph Hill—occupied primarily by Italian immigrants. Today the hill is a well-known landmark, boasting Coit Tower—a monument built in 1933 with a donation from the wealthy socialite, Lillian Coit (1845-1929), who delighted in chasing horse drawn fire engines in her carriage. The tower is in the shape of a fire hose nozzle. An avid gambler, Coit often dressed like a man to obtain entrance to the men-only gambling halls then prevalent in the city. Lillian Coit was a real eccentric who enjoyed smoking cigars and wearing men's trousers (well before it was socially acceptable).

A 1903 *San Francisco Call* article poignantly describes a typical scene in a Telegraph Hill wine shop three years before the big quake. A noisy crowd of [Italian] fishermen were sitting with their pint pots of wine. The men "were laughing, chattering,

San Francisco's Telegraph Hill

pounding their tin cups on the stained board [tables]," recounts the story. One "big bearded fellow...was engaged in a highly heated argument...over the relative merits of socialism and democracy." Suddenly the raucous crowd was interrupted by "the entrance of a little bent old graybeard, bearing a heavy golden harp on his shoulders." At first ignored, the old man, we are told, placed "the tarnished golden base...between his feet...bent caressingly over the strings...his cheek laid in tenderness against the dark sounding board...his knotted fingers began to slip over the chords." He played a "wild, uncanny Hungarian rhapsody...[then simulated] heart cries, sighs, breaths of anguish...[then he switched] drop by drop there sounded sweet liquid rain notes—the smiling of a summer shower [and finally] a song far off somewhere, sounding echo-like, as of a spirit voice." As he worked his magic harp the *Call* article recounts how "the half raised wine mugs [were] stayed midway in that dingy wine shop...men sat with mouths agape, forgetting to breathe," so beautiful was the melodious notes coming from the old man and his harp. The "barkeeper stood with arms rested on the bar, his hands covering tightly both of his eyes...[while] the old musician, head bent in reverence, eyes closed, nursed the sounding board with his withered cheek." Suddenly, "with a shuddering sigh of anguish the music halted and ceased...and the old man...rose...shouldered his...harp and slipped into the night." The bartender muttered to the astonished crowd: "He was a maestro once."

An 1893 article noted that "the language and dialect of the land of song [Italy] are talked in the dwellings and streets, the food of Italy is consumed in the homes and restaurants [on Telegraph Hill]." So distinctive was the Italian presence that a 1901 edition of the *San Francisco Call* recounted how an actual duel—"a challenge to mortal combat"—was brewing between two distinguished Italians living on Telegraph Hill. Domenic Rossi a local druggist was upset when Dr. Cavaliere DeLucas attempted to hire Rossi's chief clerk away from him and open a new drugstore next to Rossi's. This caused Rossi to declare in the local Italian newspaper, "I would die fighting rather than let this man get the best of me." Neighbors eventually smoothed over the affair.

It would be these hardy Italian men and their families who would be confronted by the great fire that slowly began to engulf the bottom of their beloved hill after the great earthquake. The nation's press thought it noteworthy to tell the tale of how the neighborhood banded together when "the only available water supply...found in a well dug in the early days...the pump suddenly sucked dry...the water in the well exhausted," recounted the *Leavenworth Echo*. One of the local residents shouted "There's one last chance, boys." Then neighborhood men and boys "crashed their doors with axes [and began] rolling out barrels of red wine...the cellars gave forth barrel after barrel until there was...500 gallons," read the *Echo* article.

Barrel heads were "smashed and...bucket brigades turned from water to wine...Sacks were dipped in the wine and used for beating out the fire. Beds were stripped...blankets...soaked in the wine and hung over the exposed portions of the cottages and men on the roofs drenched the shingles and sides of the house with wine." A *New York Evening World* article augmented the description: "The moist hangings [of bed clothing and mattresses] were draped over roofs until Telegraph Hill was canopied with wine-soaked dry goods."

One newspaper article summed it up best: "All Friday those [Italian] lads on the hill carried on the fight...using wine instead of water...They saved their homes and went thirsty to save the wine to pour on the fire."

The French Laundry Wine Heist Solved

Headlines in many of the nation's newspapers picked up the 2014 Associated Press' story about the recovery of the Christmas Day heist of 76 bottles of fine wine from The French Laundry Restaurant in Yountville (Napa County) California. The bottles were valued at $300,000. The French Laundry is a Michelin three-star restaurant; has been named the best restaurant in the world twice; and, opined "the best restaurant in the world period," by Anthony Bourdain.

The wine heist coincided with the restaurant's closing for six months for remodeling. The French Laundry's wine list is extensive and offers many rare and very expensive wines including a Domaine de la Romanée-Conti which retails for $10,000, a Krug 'Clos D'Ambonnsy' for $6,950 and a Napa Valley Screaming Eagle at $3,500.

The French Laundry

Most of the wines were recovered thirty days later in a private wine cellar in North Carolina bought by an unsuspecting dealer. Details about the recovery were kept secret by police as they investigated the crime. Finally in April of 2016, the press reported the indictment of two California men who, the indictment asserts, had also heisted "$648,000 worth of fine wines" from a Seattle wine dealer in 2013. The duo are also accused of making "off with about 24 bottles of premium wine [including some Domaine de la Romanée-Conti]" also in 2014 from Redd's restaurant—another Yountville, California high-end gourmet restaurant. Press reports indicated that "sophisticated tracking technology" had been utilized. One of the vintners had used "laser and digital technology on corks, capsules and other parts of each bottle to curb counterfeiting and theft," reported Randi Rossman in the *Santa Rosa Press Democrat*.

From a historical perspective, the burglaries were by no means the biggest. In 1912 two employees of New York's Plaza Hotel were convicted of stealing twelve bottles of wine valued at $75,000. The wine would have a present day value of $1.875 million. Eight years later four men were arrested in Wilkes-Barre, Pennsylvania after taking $20,000 in wines and liquor from George Wright, a local millionaire. In current values the wines and liquor would fetch $245,000. Some burglaries went unsolved, such as the 1921 heist at Joseph Leiter's estate near MacLean, Virginia. Thieves, using an acetylene torch, burned through a steel door to take $50,000 worth of "intoxicants, chiefly wine" from Leiter's concrete cellar, reported the *Washington Evening Star*. The wine would be worth $677,000 in today's values.

While modern lasers and digital technology are now being used to find stolen wine and the culprits, detectives of yesteryear could be just as innovative. In 1901, John Bird, superintendent of New York's posh Madison Avenue Sorrento Apartments, engaged a clairvoyant to aid him in finding the perpetrators of numerous petty thefts at the facility. "He called on an old Negro mammy who, her customers say, can tell the future as well as the past," reported the *New York Sun*. The clairvoyant described "One of his employees accurately…and told him to watch the man and he would find the pilferer," continued the report. The following day he "saw a case of Rhine wine" in the corner of the basement. Half an hour later the case disappeared. Bird then called the police who followed two of his employees (one whom the clairvoyant had described) into a saloon and apprehended them with a bag containing "a half a dozen bottles of the wine."

The following year the world's press carried a story about a Parisian detective "who concealed himself in an empty barrel" to find thieves who were stealing wine by the barrel from wine warehouses at Bercy (a neighborhood in Paris). The thieves "as he expected, took

248

him off, in his barrel…to their headquarters…and so enabled him to…secure the arrest of the four thieves."

Sometimes wine thieves can just ensure their own apprehension. Such was the case with Aaron Daley and J. P. Dolan in 1890. Los Angeles police received a number of complaints of burglaries "from the cellars of the Nadeau winery." In July the duo "fell into a trap which they had evidently set for themselves," reported the *Los Angeles Herald*. After helping themselves to "the contents of several bottles of superlative claret…[and putting] a couple of bottles of wine in their pockets" they prepared to leave the cellars. "But," reported the *Herald* "the fumes of the generous wine they drank circulated through their brains and caused them to forget the way out of the cellar…[and] the noise they created in stumbling about [caused their arrest]," concluded the article.

Mark Twain and Booze

Mark Twain was America's greatest humorist and one of its greatest authors.

"Mark Twain," was Samuel Clemens' *nom de plume.* He drank and smoked his way through a life—resplendent with unbelievable personal dramas—things that would have felled the ordinary man. He lost three daughters and his wife to death, millions of dollars in bad investments and even his house to foreclosure.

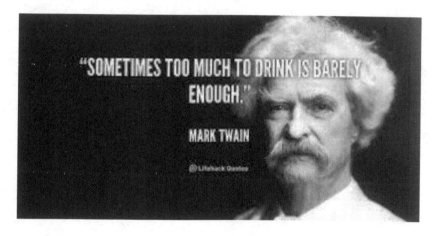

The nation first became aware of his wit and genius with the 1867 publication of *The Celebrated Jumping Frog of Calaveras County*, his retelling of a story he actually overheard in a saloon located in Angels Camp, California, a small gold mining community. He was there ducking the service of a lawsuit against him by the San Francisco Police Department. He had guaranteed a criminal bond and the culprit split town leaving him holding the bag The previous year he had moved to San Francisco from Virginia City, Nevada because there was allegedly a warrant for his arrest in Nevada for dueling—then a criminal offense under the statutes of the Territory of Nevada.

His drinking and smoking were legendary. He spent at least one night in the San Francisco city jail for drunk and disorderly conduct and another in New York City. His San Francisco drinking buddy was—believe it or not—Tom Sawyer, a local saloon keeper—whose name Twain adopted for his bestseller. Sawyer said of Twain: "He could drink more and talk more than any feller I had ever seen…when somebody'd buy him another drink, he keep her up all day…he'd set there till morning telling yarns," according to Robert Graysmith's *Smithsonian Magazine* article, The Adventures of the Real Tom Sawyer. An unidentified Carson City acquaintance of Twain asserted that Twain "could tell a good story and take his liquid potations with the boys and not show it much, even if he would drink all day."

Regarding wine, Twain was opinionated. When in Germany he opined German "Rhine wines were distinguished from vinegar by the label." As his literary career blossomed, he pronounced wine as a "clog to [his] pen, not an inspiration." He did, however appreciate wine symbolically when observing: "My books are like water, those of great geniuses are wine. Fortunately everybody drinks water." His preference in spirits was whiskey which he drank "every night" to prevent toothaches. Apparently it worked well because, he said, "I have never had a toothache and…never intend to have [one]."

In 1908, two years before his death, Twain copyrighted his name, photograph and signature and went into the cigar and whiskey business. He did so to "head off the possibility of electric signs exploiting Mark Twain "Rye" or Mark Twain five for 10 cents Cheroots," asserted an article which appeared in numerous newspapers around the country. In order to prove-up the patent's legality, Twain went into business labeling his own "Mark Twain Whiskey" and a "Mark Twain cigar." He wanted to insure only his heirs would benefit from the future trademark use of his name.

Twain did enjoy champagne very much. Two years after his death, the Chicago Waiters Association purchased a set of Mark Twain's books using champagne corks. The books were for their club room in which they maintained a rather extensive library—all the books were bought with used champagne corks. Chicago waiters collected the corks at work and dropped them in a barrel. Every thousand corks fetched $3.50 and as of 1912 they had 2,000 volumes. A diner noticed a waiter "chasing a cork along the floor...the waiter picked up the cork and deposited it in a barrel." When asked why, the waiter responded they were buying a set of "old Mark Twain." The club members saved the corks wherever they were employed. The waiter told the diner "I guess the library is the most expensive in town...it must have cost several hundred thousand dollars." At least it was other people's money.

Doctored Watermelon

An 1888 article in the *New York Sun* entitled "Doctored Watermelon" was about "an odd little Italian restaurant" in New York City. The story recounts how "one night...a plugged melon was served. No one except one of the diners knew about it. When it was brought on and the party began tasting what appeared to be an extraordinary watermelon, there was instantly noticed a change in the demeanor of everyone. They sniffed the air and looked at each other, and then sniffed again. There was no suspicion then that the watermelon was of more than the ordinary kind. But after two or three mouthfuls someone remarked [about] the peculiarly rich taste and the exquisite aroma, and then the secret was out. There weren't many people in the party, and the melon was a fairly big one, but it was all eaten, every bit of it."

A search of current culinary archives failed to locate anything remotely close to the recipe disclosed in the article:

Put the melon on ice overnight and in the morning wipe dry the surface.

Cut a slit straight into the heart of the melon. Follow this by three other slits so that you can lift out a plug that is one 1 ½" square.

Pour into the hole a pint of *Claret de Bordeaux* which will "spread through the spongy fruit." Then plug up the melon and put it back in the refrigerator.

After an hour, reopen the plug and you will be able to pour in the remainder of the *Claret de Bordeaux* (a total of one quart). "The melon will drink up the wine and every part of the sponge will become saturated and from hour to hour the position of the big egg-shaped fruit will be changed from side to side and from end to end."

Six to eight hours later, take out the plug and taste the fruit. "You will find it surprisingly delicious, and yet perhaps the flavor will be not quite so pronounced as you would like it. In this event pour in from half a pint to a whole pint of brandy." If the brandy is added "see that the melon is closely plugged and wrapped up, and have it turned at least twice and kept on ice for the next hour."

Cantaloupe Wine on the Vine

In 1921 a local column appeared in the *Alliance Herald* [Box-Butte County, Nebraska] commenting on the newly organized Burlington [Colorado] Melon Growers Association. The purpose of the new venture was to grow intoxicating cantaloupes. The general idea was to circumvent the newly enacted Volstead Act which outlawed the manufacture and sale of alcoholic beverages in the United States.

The Burlington Melon Growers planned on "inserting a high dose of yeast" into each cantaloupe while still on the vine. The theory was the yeast would cause the fruit to ferment and become alcoholic while growing and thereby avoid the application of the Volstead law. If it worked, the growers visualized "an era when the cantaloupe will be a  food for the night before instead of the morning after." One press dispatch facetiously described "a husband stumbling up the stairs and making this sort of explanation: 'I can's shee, m'dear, how only two honeydewsh could 'fect me thish way.'"

The publicity generated by the melon growers was premature. "The cantaloupes," claimed the article, "were still growing on the vines" and it would be "a week or two before the growers are ready to insert the yeast." Then it would still be another couple of weeks "before a thirsty world will know whether the kick is there."

The writer went on to express his own thoughts on the enterprise. "We fail to see how a cantaloupe wine would be tasty enough to appeal to the connoisseur in booze...[but so much vile brew] was going around that the average topper [may] welcome a pure drink, no matter how peculiar its taste may be," he wrote. Adding the newspaper thought "the growers would have better success with watermelon…[and] wouldn't it be grand if one could feed yeast and raisins to a blackberry bush or a peach tree."

Some twenty years before, a humorist (either Marsh Milder or Eli Perkins) had prepared a comic sketch in which they grafted a rubber hose into the stream of a watermelon and, "the fruit was allowed to absorb the contents of a pint bottle [of whiskey]."

Nothing ever came of the Burlington Melon Growers Association's plan. Simply stated, the experiment didn't work.

But there really is a cantaloupe wine. Jack Keller's website "The Winemaking Home" publicized a cantaloupe wine recipe offered by Jacksonville, Florida's Jonathan Jones.

Jones notes cantaloupe "makes an unforgiving wine. If you do one thing wrong, the wine quickly heads south. Even if you do nothing wrong, cantaloupes can make a poor wine. Quality fruit makes delicious wine. Inferior fruit are better eaten." Several other cantaloupe wine recipes can be found by googling the subject.

James Parks' Last Glass of Wine

In 1853 the nation's press became transfixed with a sensational murder trial at Cyaaoga [now Cuyahoga] Falls, Ohio—today part of the Akron Metro area. In 1853 the population of the entire United States was only 23 million. Only eight states existed west of the Mississippi (California, Texas, Louisiana, Arkansas, Missouri, Wisconsin, Illinois and Iowa). The remainder of what was to become the lower 48 states was comprised of territories (Utah, New Mexico Minnesota and a large swath called only Unorganized Territory). Hawaii was an independent monarchy ruled by a native king and Alaska was a colony of Czarist Russia.

The nation's press focused on the murder of William Beatson whose "blood and other evidence of foul play were discovered near the upper bridge." Not far away "the coat and other clothing…were found in the canal a short distance." The headless body of a man was found the following day along the Cuyahoga River shoreline; "entirely naked."

James Parks, who had been seen with Beatson, was arrested when strong circumstantial evidence pointed to Parks as the murderer. The two men had been together at the local hotel the night before. Beatson was drunk when he and Parks left to walk to Hudson—a nearby town. "The strange conduct of Parks aroused suspicion of foul play, and the matter was talked about after they left," reported the *Portage Sentinel*.

As the story unfolded, investigators discovered Parks' real name was Dickinson. He had emigrated to the United Sates in 1838 from England. At the time of the murder he was 41. A few years earlier, *The Philadelphia Bulletin* reported Parks along with two others had disguised themselves as Indians and committed an "outrageous robbery [at a Germantown, Pennsylvania residence]…tied up [the inhabitants]…[and] stripped the house of valuables." The trio were later apprehended and convicted. The *Bulletin* disclosed that Parks' real name was Dickinson and that he had operated under several aliases—Lee Bryon, Charles Hill and James Russell. He was sentenced to an undisclosed prison term in Pennsylvania for the crime. It was also learned that he had pulled a similar caper and a highway robbery in Bristol, Rhode Island—for which he was apprehended and convicted and sentenced to four years at the Rhode Island state prison.

Parks was put on trial for the Cuyahoga Falls murder. He admitted to cutting off Beatson's head. He claimed he and Beatson had fallen off the bridge and the latter "was killed by the fall." Since he had a criminal past, he feared "being accused of [the murder] and to escape such an accusation, he cut off the head of the corpse, and endeavored to conceal the body."

Parks' trial lasted four days. The jury convicted him of first degree murder on January 10, 1854. The trial judge pronounced sentence: "you [James Parks shall] be taken hence to jail...till the 26th day of May next...and hanged by the neck until you are dead." *The Ohio Star* reported "The Judge, the prisoner's counsel, and many of the spectators seemed wrung with irrepressible anguish [but Parks] kept his countenance unmoved."

Parks appealed the verdict, seeking a new trial. The Ohio Supreme Court refused the appeal. Four weeks before his hanging, the *Carroll Free Press* related "He talked about his approaching fate, and about the shortness of his time, with as much calmness as if he were speaking of an ordinary affair." He was being held in Cleveland and the day before his execution he attempted suicide.

The night before his execution newspapers reported his Cleveland jail attendants "did everything to make him comfortable, by administering occasional draughts of wine...he resumed his calm and cool demeanor." His breakfast was raw oysters. At eleven in the morning "he took refreshments of wine and water... [put on a] clean white shirt and...a pipe was procured and he took a comfortable

258

smoke." It was raining and "thousands crowded around the jail yard gates." He calmly "gave directions as to the disposition of his body…that he be taken down, decently shaved, dressed and deposited in his coffin, and those who had a curiosity might be allowed to look upon him." He also asked local authorities to refrain from writing "anything to his friends and parents in England which would

Typical Gallows

inform them of his true fate on the scaffold."

At eleven fifty in the morning he was escorted to the scaffold. He took a chair provided for him, drank a portion of another glass of wine "and held the glass in his hand while he prepared to speak." In a clear and calm voice he addressed the witnesses with a rambling statement in which he expressed no remorse, declaring himself innocent of the charge of murder. He told the assemblage he had a child and wife "who has in my long confinement been an angel in her solitude and care of me…after speaking twenty minutes he took a sip of wine [then started speaking again]" He asked the crowd to help out his wife who would be destitute after his death. The *M'Arthur Democrat* newspaper reported "some kind person…[took] up a contribution…and $14.60 [$595 in current values] was taken up…Parks thanked them with considerable emotion."

At one o'clock "he took [his last] glass of wine, his hands and feet were fastened…the rope adjusted…and he stood upon the platform." A cap [hood] was pulled over his head and "about ten minutes after one, with the words "I die an innocent man'...the [trap door] instantaneously fell launching him down about six feet." The *Democrat* reported he was removed forty minutes later with "many persons present...unable to retain their tears at many of the touching remarks [Parks had made]...speaking of his wife and child."

Source Citations

Napoleon and Patsy   Page   12

Books:
Jerome Clark, *Unexplained! And Delusion*, (Canton [MI]: Visible Ink Press, 2013) unpaginated
Articles
Took the Gold Cure, *Jamestown Weekly Alert* [D.T.], January 11, 1894, page 2
Henry "Pety" Bigelow, *The Pacific Commercial Advertiser*, May 27, 1896, page 7
Henry Bigelow Filed His Copy, *San Francisco Call, May* 20, 1896, *Findagrave.com*
Drunken Snakes, *The Abbeville Press and Banner*, February 15, 1888, page 3
James O'Grady's Snake, *The Helena Independent*, February 20, 1891, page 2
Death by Delusion, *Pittsburg Dispatch*, August 26, 1891, page 1

A Risky Bisque or Gazpacho to Dispatch You   Page   15

Books
Francis Clement Kelley, *The Bishop Jots It Down*, (New York: Harper & Brothers Publishers, 1939)
Articles
ANARCHIST POISON'S SCORES AT DINNER TO PRELATE, *San Francisco Examiner*, February 13, 1916.How Chemist Determined Poison and Amount in Soup: QUALITATIVE TESTS. REINSCH TEST, *Chicago Daily Tribune*, February 14, 1916. Mistake Saves Poison Victims, *San Francisco Examiner*, February 14, 1916.CRONES TELLS POISON SECRETS: THIRD LETTER GIVES DETAILS OF HIS CRIME Says Arsenic Was Put in Soup Stock; About to Quit New York. POLICE GUARD AT BALL, *Chicago Daily Tribune*, February 19, 1916. LATEST EPISTLE FROM CRONES, LETTER-WRITER-CHEF-POISONER JEAN CRONES, *Chicago Daily Tribune*, February 19, 1916. CRONES' VICTIMS MISSED CERTAIN DEATH BY A SLIP: Poison Spoiled Soup and Steward Threw Four-Fifths Away, Making New. SCHUETTLER BARES FACTS, *Chicago Daily Tribune*, February 23, 1916.

Oh What Tangled Web We Weave   Page 18
Articles
Bribery and Swindling, *The Laurens Advertiser*, August 13, 1895, page 4
Raising Spiders, *The Wichita Daily Eagle*, September 12, 1895, page 3
Famous Wine Cellars of Some Wealthy Men, *The Washington Morning Times*, August 30, 1896, page 3
Growing Spiders for Market, *The Cape Girardeau Democrat*, March 12, 1898, page 7
A Spider Farm, *Monroe City Democrat*, November 25, 1903, page 5
Trained Spiders, *Hilo Tribune*, March 28, 1905, page 4
Websites
Tom's Inflation Calculator, www.halfhill.com

A Glass of Wine with Daniel Webster

Page 21

Books
Merrill D. Peterson, The Great Triumvirate: Webster, Clay and Calhoun (New York: Oxford University Press, 1987), page 394
Robert Vincent Remini, Daniel Webster: The Man and His Time (New York: W. W. Norton & Company, 1997), page 508
Articles
Sale of Daniel Webster's Wines, *Washington Evening Star*, February 24, 1865, page 2
Daniel Webster and Jenny Lind, *The Conservative* [M'connelsville, OH], January 27, 1868, page 1
An Exalted Position, *The Forest Republican*, May 16, 1877, page 1
Webster's Old Home, *Washington Evening Star*, January 29, 1887, page 2
Daniel Webster's Drinking Habits Again the Subject of Controversy, *Milwaukee Journal*, September 5, 1930 (from Milwaukee Historical Society), page not denoted.
Websites
Daniel Webster, Wikipedia

The Chicken, the Egg and a Good Yolk Too

Page 24

Books:
DeWiit S. Copp, *A Few Great Captains*, (Washington: Air Historical Foundation, 1980), 29
Articles:
Hen Laid an Egg 5,000 Feet High, *Petaluma Daily Courier*, August 21, 1919, page 8
Petaluma Means Eggs and Chickens to the World, *San Francisco Call and Post*, August 29, 1919
Petaluma Hen Has Her Day in the Sun, *San Francisco Call and Post*, August 30, 1919
Oscar Ingalls, $1000 Breakfast Cooked in Speeding Plane 5,000 Feet in Air, *San Francisco Bulletin*, August 30, 1919, page 1
Websites:
Edward "Hap" Arnold, Wikipedia
Victor Hirtzler, Wikipedia
Carl Andrew Spaatz, Wikipedia

Birds Do It, Bees Do It

Page 27

Articles
Inebriate Among Animals, *The Star* (as reported in the *New York Herald*), November 23, 1898, page 7
Just Fun For the Bear, *Colfax Chronicle*, June 16, 1900, page 2
Palm Tree Wine, *The Beaumont Enterprise*, September 20, 1904, page 5
Animals Drunk at Feast, *Le Meschacebe*, March 2, 1912, page 3
News Told in Brief, *Burlington Weekly Free Press*, April 17, 1913, page 14,
Bees Crazy Drunk, *Charlevoix County Herald*, December 13, 1918, page 2

Tipsy Butterfly

Articles
Insects Love Drink, *The Lafayette Gazette*, October 1, 1898, page 3
Alcoholism among Animals, *The Hawaiian Star*, November 9, 1898, page 3
Insects that Get Drunk, *Juniata Sentinel and Republican*, June 13, 1900, page 4
The Dainty Butterfly, *Daily Press*, October 8, 1907, page 5
Inga Piegsa-Quischotte, Flirting with Butterflies in St. Thomas, *Travelandescape.ca*, April 5, 2013
Mathias Mugisha, Flying into the Butterfly World, *NewVision*, undated
How Long Do Butterflies and Moths Live?, Butterflies and Moths of North America, undated
Websites
Phil Torres, I'm A Pretty Butterfly, I Drink My Own Pee (and other disgusting habits), *TheRevScience,* November 3, 2011), unpaginated

Lobster, Crab, Wine and Beer

Articles
Lobster Alienated Wife, He Declares, *The Salt Lake Tribune,* January 29, 1913, page 1
She Received Letters in Ogden, *The Evening Standard*, January 30, 1913, page 4
John Reed Is Awarded Less Tithe of Sum Asked From Man He blames, *The Salt Lake Tribune*, February 6, 1913, page 1
Use Figures to Render Verdict, *The Salt Lake Tribune*, March 8, 1913, page 14
John Reed Granted Divorce, *The Salt Lake Tribune*, May 10, 1913, page 20
Reed Alienation Suit Dismissed, *The Salt Lake Tribune*, May 22, 1913, page 14
Websites
Tom's Inflation Calculator, www.halfhill.com

Drunk Fish

Articles
Fish That Drank Wine, *The Eagle*, June 24, 1896, page 12
Fish Drunks in Trenton, *Washington Evening Star*, September 16, 1904, page 13
Fish Were Drunk, *Shiner Gazette*, June 13, 1906, page 6
Multitudes Are Feasting, *Rock Island Argus*, July 14, 1913, page 2
Made Fish Drunk, *Hopkinsville Kentuckian*, April 28, 1917, page 7
How to Make a Fish Swim Faster, *Daily Mail Online*, May 15, 2014, unpaginated

Wine Confessions

Articles
A Death Bed Revelation, *Green-Mountain Freeman*, February 9, 1854, page 1
Three Times and In, *Northern Tribune*, March 26, 1885, page 10
Died in Hospital, *The Washington Herald*, August 25, 1922, page 1

Earthquake Wine

Articles
Earthquake To Send Wine Prices Soaring, *The Minneapolis Journal*, May 13, 1906, Part II, Editorial Section, page 6
You Can Pull Corks From These Bottles At $1,000 Per, *The Spokane Press*, August 25, 1906
Wine: The Frauds that are Practiced on the Public, *The Salt Lake Herald February*, 11, 1883, page 5
Jack London, The Story of an Eyewitness, *Collier's Magazine*, May 5, 1906
Legal Decisions
California Wine Association, Respondent v Commercial Union Fire Insurance Company of New York before the Supreme Court of California December 28, 1910
Websites
Renee Montagne, *Remembering the 1906 San Francisco Earthquake*, April 11, 2006
Tom's Inflation Calculator, www.halfhill.com
Jack Sullivan, Those Pro Whiskey Men, blog at *Prowhiskey.com*, March 29, 2013, unpaginated

The Wine That Isn't Wine

Articles:
Welch's Grape Juice, Worldly Wisdom, and Wine, *Fundamentally Reformed,* August 3, 2006
John K. Hoyt, Reply to Reverend J. L. White, *Asheville Daily Citizen*, January 11, 1893, Page 1
The Wine of the Lord's Supper, *The Ocala Banner*, September 28, 1906, Page 9
S. F. Cary, Eternal Hostility to the Liquor Traffic, *The Ohio Organ, of the Temperance Reform*, August 12, 1853, page 1
Charles E. Welch, *Thomas B. Welch*
Daniel Benedict, Changing Wine Into Grape Juice, *BGOD*
Welch's Grape Juice, A Home Necessity, *The Bisbee Daily Review*, June 1, 1912, page 3
British Hoot at Sec. Bryan's Wineless Banquet, *Seattle Star*, April 25, 1913, page 7
Websites:
Thomas Bramwell Welch, Wikipedia
Jason Sample, McClurg Mansion and Museum, Biography 101, Dr. Charles Welch, *Bicentennial Biographies*, June 3, 2011, unpaginated

Corn Wine and Virginia Ham

Articles
Frank G. Carpenter, President Tyler, *Lippincott's Magazine*, as reported in the *Wichita Eagle*, February 3, 1887, page 6
Dan Amira, President John Tyler's Grandson, Harrison Tyler, on Still Being Alive, *NYmag.com*, January 27, 2012
Websites
John Tyler, Jr., Arlington *National Cemetery Website*
President John Tyler , Wikipedia
Tom's Inflation Calculator, www.halfhill.com
Interesting Facts about Presidents and First Ladies, *The White House Historical Association*
Email Correspondence
Ed Behr, June 26, 2014

Jefferson, Hamilton, Madison—Dinner Deal

Books:
Charles Cerami, *Dinner at Mr. Jefferson's* (Hoboken: Wiley and Sons, 2008) 129-133, as reported in Craughwell below.
Thomas J. Craughwell, Thomas Jefferson's *Crème Brûlée* (Philadelphia: Quirk Press, 2012), 142-48
Websites
History of Washington, D.C., Wikipedia
Thomas Jefferson, Wikipedia
James Madison, Wikipedia

Venom From the Vine

Articles
A. Batty Shaw, Benjamin Gooch, eighteenth-century Norfolk Surgeon, *Cambridge Journals Medical History*, January 1972
Rattlesnake Wine, *Semi-Weekly Independent* [Plymouth, In], March 28, 1896, page 3
Items and News, Cycle Therapeutics, *The Medical Age*, Volume 13, pg. 725
Zoe Mintz, Wine Snake Bites Woman After Sending 3 Months In The Bottle, *International Business Times*, September 12, 2013
Websites
Snake Wine, Wikipedia
Leprosy, Wikipedia

'Hi' on Cronk @ 102

Articles
A Survivor of 1812, *Anadarko Daily Democrat*, October 26, 1901, page 6
Larger Pension at 103, *The Star*, April 9, 1902, page 7
Four Persons of Mature Age Who Have Done and Seen Things Worth Relating to the Younger Fold, *New York Tribune*, February 22, 1903, page 3
What Hiram Cronk Saw, *The Minneapolis Journal*, May 27, 1905, page 4
The Last of 200,000 Soldiers, *Daily Capital Journal*, May 24, 1905, page 2
The Last Veteran of the War of 1812, *The Post-Standard*, September 2, 2012
Websites:
Sacket's Harbor, War of 1812, Wikipedia
Hiram Cronk, Wikipedia

Carrots and Wine

Books:
Ted Gott, Kathryn Weir, *Gorilla*, (London: Reaktion Books, Ltd., 2013) pages 101-102
Articles
Circus Parade Route, *The Saint Paul Globe*, July 12, 1897, page 2
Johanna Only Gorilla Now in Captivity, *The Wheeling Daily Intelligencer*, May 20, 1895, page 5
Barnum and Bailey Novelties, *The Washington Times,* May 6, 1894, page 6
Chiko, The Giant Gorilla, *The Scranton Tribune*, May 18, 1894, page 5
Some Remarkable Animals, *Butler Citizen,* September 24, 1896, page 3
An Angry Gorilla, *The Breckenridge News*, November 22, 1893, page 1

Freak Dinners

Articles
To Feast On Horseback, *The New York Sun*, March 26, 1903, page 1
Guests to Ride Wooden Horses, *New York Evening World*, March 29, 1903, page 3
An Equestrian Feast, *Jamestown Weekly Alert*, April 9, 1903, page 12
Monkey Feed Outdone, *Minneapolis Journal*, December 29, 1906, page 1
Pigs Are Guests at Novel Banquets, *Barbour County Index*, February 6, 1907, page 3
Another Monkey Dinner, *The Spokane Press*, July 27, 1907, page 2
Society has Turned Into A Circus Says Mrs. Astor, *San Francisco Call*, November 15, 1908, page 4
Websites
C. K. G. Billings, Wikipedia
Tom's Inflation Calculator, www.halfhill.com

A Seafarers Fare

Page 64

Articles
Jack's Bill of Fare, *The Pacific Commercial Advertiser*, April 13, 1886, age 4
The Sailors Got Seclusion, *The Roanoke Times*, July 26, 1893, page 4
Websites
Grog, Wikipedia
Hardtack, Wikipedia
Salt-cured Meat, Wikipedia

Elephant Sausage

Page 67

Articles
Special European Columns, *The New York Tribune*, September 19, 1909, page 5
Makes Elephant Sausage, *Shenandoah Herald*, April 15, 1910, page 1
The Truth About Germany, *Harrisburg Telegraph*, September 24, 1917, page 3
Elephant Steak or Bear Chop Brought Fancy Prices in Famine Time, *Harrisburg Telegraph*, January 31, 1918, page 17
Captain Fritz Duquesne, Hunting Ahead of Roosevelt in East Africa, *Deseret Evening News*, December 7, 1909, page 14
Karl Amman, Elephant Steak: The New Ivory, *KarlAmmann.com,* 2016
New Industry in California, *The Anaconda Standard*, August 31, 1891, page 1

Brut For the Brutes

Page 70

Articles
Trained on Champagne, *The Hawaiian Star*, December 11, 1897, page 7
Champagne and Athletes, *The Hawaiian Gazette,* December 14, 1897, Page 4
A. F. Judd, Jr., No Such Thing as Champagne Training, *The Hawaiian Gazette*, January 28, 1898, Page 3
Websites:
Frank Butterworth, Wikipedia
Walter Camp, Wikipedia
Albert F. Judd, Jr., Wikipedia

Saving Caruso's Chickens

Articles
Caruso Returns, Sad Over Loss of Wines and Cheese, *New York Evening World*, September 3, 1919
Mrs. Caruso's Father Not Yet Reconciled, *New York Evening World*, September 3, 1919, page 12
Death Stills Voice of Enrico Caruso, World's Greatest Singer, *The Washington Times*, August 2, 1921, page 2
Websites
Enrico Caruso. Wikipedia
Dorothy Caruso, IMBd
Villa Caruso Bellosguardo, In Your Tuscany, Wikipedia
Italian Fascism during the Interwar Years (1919-1938), Wikipedia
Tom's Inflation Calculator, www.halfhill.com

Wine Bath and Beyond

Articles
An American Traveler..., *The Penny Press* (Cincinnati), October 20, 1859, page 4
A Hint to Lovers of French Wine, *Public Ledger* (Memphis), July 23, 1870, page 4
Shirley Dare, Methods of Beauty, *The Pittsburg Dispatch*, February 16, 1890, Page 20
Bathing in Wine, *Holbrook (AZ) Argus*, July 20, 1901, page 2
Some Very Queer Baths, *The St. Louis Republic*, January 6, 1902, Magazine Section, Page 36
Wine Bath for Hair, *The Jasper Weekly Courier,* January 24, 1908
Sour Claret Excellent as a Complexion Wash, *The Washington Times*, May 18, 1911, page 9
Susie Leung, Luxuries or Lame: Red Wine Baths, *Absolutely Fabulous*, October 21, 2010,
Five Strange New Ways to use Red Wine, *The Huffington Post*, May 14, 2014
Naomi Coleman, Can Bathing In Wine Make You Younger and Cure Cellulite? *Mail Online*, May 14, 2014
Websites
Malvoisie Flétrie, *Rouvinez Sierre*
How Much Water does a Bathtub Hold, *Ask.com*
Les Sources De Caudalie

The Frenchman and the Sponges

Articles
The Champagne Maker, Why His Face Is Always Decorated By Scars, *Imperial Valley Press* (El Centro, CA)   July 7, 1906, Page 8
Champagne Scars, *Auckland Star,* June 2, Champagne from Sponges, *The Lafayette Advertiser*, December 20, 1907, Page 5
Making Champagne, *The St. Paul Globe*, October 11, 1903, Page 12
Websites:
Sparkling Wine Production, Wikipedia

Whatever Happened to Susie Johnson? Page 80

Articles
"The Girl in the Pie"—Susie Johnson's Introduction to New York's Luxurious Bohemia, *San Francisco Call*, October 19, 1895, Page 7 (a reprint from *The New York World* newspaper)
Girl In The Pie Was a Victim of Stanford White, *The Spokane Press*, July 5, 1906, Page 4
The Pie Girl Is Alive, *Red Cloud Chief*, July 3, 1908, Page 8
Websites:
Harry Kendall Thaw, Wikipedia
Gilded Age, Wikipedia
Pie Girl, Galley—Gallery Sink Robber Baron
Stanford White, Wikipedia
Tom's Inflation Calculator, www.halfhill.com

Teddy Roosevelt's Occasional Nips Page 83

Books
Edmund Morris, *Colonel Roosevelt*. (New York, NY: Random House; 2010)
Articles
XMAS at the White House, *The New York Sun*, December 26, 1907, page 4
Peter and Paul Strom, Rough Rider Clears Name in the U.P., Trials in History
Roosevelt Takes Stand—Gives Detailed Account of His Occasional Nips, *The [Chicago] Daybook*, May 27, 1913, pages 26-28
Daniel J. Demers, 'Toothsome Rex': The President With the Winning Smile, *Dr. BiCuspid.com*, April 13, 2013,
Websites
Tom's Inflation Calculator, www.halfhill.com

Two Bottles of French Wine and a Harmonica Page 86

Articles
Judge Extends Clemency to Mouth-Harp Expert, *The Tomahawk*, September 5, 1918, page 5
Websites
Charles W. Harrison, Ireland Must Be Heaven, For My Mother Came From There, Wikipedia

Wine Controversy in Christening Ships Page 88

Articles
The Battleship Iowa, *The Dalles Daily Chronicle*, March 26, 1896, page 1
Christening the Battleship, *Kansas City Journal*, September 10, 1898, page 4
Christening Ships, *The Coalville Times*, October 18, 1904, page 3
Water Will Replace Wine at a Ship Christening, *San Francisco Call*, March 12, 1905, page 29
It Swears Off, *Day Book*, July 29, 1914, page 31
Hassayampa Thoughts, *Bisbee Daily Review*, June 26, 1915, page 4
Milk May Replace Wine at all Ship Christenings, *New York Tribune*, September 1, 1918, page 6
Pershing Hates Waste of Wine at Ship Christening, *The Evening World*, March 31, 1920, page 3

T. J.'s Gift-French Fries and Mac and Cheese   Page 91

Letters/Articles
James Hemings, *Thomas Jefferson's Monticello*, Research and Collections
Macaroni, *Thomas Jefferson's Monticello*, Research and Collections
Thomas Jefferson's Pasta Machine, *Library of Congress*
Websites
French Fries, Wikipedia

A Barrel of Fine-Bodied Rum   Page 94

Books
Emily Wortis Leider, *California's Daughter, Gertrude Atherton* (Stanford: Stanford University Press, 1991), p-64-65
Articles
Mysterious Affair, *The Daily Dispatch*, March 10, 1854, page 1
Crimes and Casualties, *Iron County Register*, February 7, 1884, page 2
He Wanted the Body, *The Princeton Union*, June 2, 1892, page 6
Liquor and the Coffin, *The Weekly Tribune and the Cape County Herald,* December 10, 1915, page 2
Rum Preserves Hotel Man's Body, *The Evening Herald*, March 19, 1921, page 1
Daniel J. Demers, Gertrude Atherton's Russians, *Russian Life Magazine,* February 2011, page 36
Websites
Horatio Nelson, 1st Viscount Nelson, Wikipedia
How Rum Got Its Name, *The Rumelier and Caribbean Rum*
Rum, Wikipedia

Poisoned Communion Wine   Page 97

Articles
A Clergyman Poisoning the Communion Wine, *The Norfolk Post,* August 4, 1865, page 2
Murder Dogging His Life, *The New York Sun*, January 12, 1890, page 22,
Plot to Poison Wine For Communion, *The Stark County Democrat*, April 22, 1904, page 1
Steal Communion Wine; Are Poisoned, *The Washington Times*, October 29, 1908, page 8
Priest is Poisoned By Communion Wine, *The Washington Times*, December 11, 1908, page 7
Poison Wine in Church, *Los Angeles Herald*, June 13, 1910, page 12
Drink Varnish; 10 Elders May Die, *Dakota County Herald*, January 12, 1922, page 2
Communion Wine Poisoned, *Tuscaloosa News*, April 10, 1979, page 9

Two Glasses of Wine, a Cigar—End of the Line   Page 99

Articles
Criminal Record
Murray Teigh Bloom, The Money Maker, *American Heritage*, August/September 1984,
Counterfeiter Arrested, *San Francisco Call*, April 3, 1896, page 2
Emanuel Ninger Captured, *Vermont Phoenix*, April 10, 1896, page 3
Ninger Had No Witness, *New York Times*, August 21, 1896
First Jim the Penman, *The Saint Paul Globe*, August 5, 1900, page 12
Real Jim the Penman, *Washington Evening Star*, September 10, 1904, page 3
Websites
Emanuel Ninger, Wikipedia

Rush for Food

Books
Dr. George H. Von Langsdorff, *Narrative of the Rezanov Voyage to Nueva California in 1806* (San Francisco: privately published by Thomas C. Russell, 1927)
Websites:
George H. Von Langsdorff, Wikipedia
Nikolai Rezanov, Wikipedia

California's Misión Indians' Diet

Books
Jean-Francoise de la Perouse, *Voyage Around the World in the Years 1785, 1786, 1787, and 1788* (London: Printed for J. Johnson, 1792)
Dr. George H. Von Langsdorff, *Narrative of the Rezanov Voyage to Nueva California in 1806* (San Francisco: privately published by Thomas C. Russell, 1927)
George Vancouver, *A Voyage of Discovery Around the World,* Volume II, Chapter I Arrival of the Discovery at the Port of St. Francis, page 2
Articles
Daniel J. Demers, Missions, Sea Otters and California Indians, *Wild West Magazine*, October 2012
Websites
The California Missions, Wikipedia

A Wine Tart for the Virgin Mary

Articles
A Pair of Dupes, *Mohave County Miner*, October 29, 1898, page 1
Dealings With Spirits, *Los Angeles Herald*, October 23, 1898, page 1
Websites
Kempten, Bavaria, Germany, Wikipedia
Swiss Wine Tart, *FXCuisine.com*

A Bottle of Champagne in Nome, Alaska

Books
Rex Beach, *The Spoilers* (Guttenberg Project Free eBook)
David C. Frederick, *Rugged Justice*, Chapter 4 Intrigue at Anvil Creek, (Berkeley: University of California Press, 1994)   pages 78-83.
Articles
Wealth at Cape Nome, *Essex County Herald*, October 13, 1899, page
Gold at Cape Nome, *St. Paul Globe*, October 2, 1899, page 2
Alaskan District Judge Noyes Awakens Wrath of Mine Owners at Nome by Astonishing Acts, *San Francisco Call*, August 31, 1900, page 2
Websites:
Tom's Inflation Calculator

"Diamondfield" Jack Davis' Wine Spree

Page 112

Articles
Siberia May Try To Break the Record, *The Pacific Commercial Advertiser*, August 14, 1905, page 1
History of Bullfrog, *Los Angeles Herald*, March 17, 1907, page 73
Greets Zion Friends, *Salt Lake Tribune*, July 12, 1913, page 1
Ted Severe, The True Story of Wilson and Cummings Murder, *Master Bias Leaning,* March 30, 2011 transcribed and reprinted from original handwritten document circa 1896
Juan Ignacio Blanco, Jackson Lee Davis, *Murderpedia*, undated
Websites
Jack Davis (prospector), Wikipedia
Rhyolite Nevada, Wikipedia
Tom's Inflation Calculator, www.halfhill.com

The Raines Law Sandwiches

Page 115

Articles
Sunday "Dry" Only in a Few Spots, *New York Tribune*, May 18, 1908, page 10
A "Fake" Raines Hotel, *New York Tribune*, March 30, 1902
A Raines Law Sandwich, *Cook County Herald*, January 16, 1897, page 2
Initial Sunday Under Mayor Low, *The Minneapolis Journal*, January 11, 1902
Café Keepers Anxious, *New York Tribune*, January 13, 1907, page 7
Charged With Grand Larceny, *The New York Sun*, February 15, 1897, page 2
Sandwich Must Be Eaten, *The Bennington Evening Banner*, June 5, 1906, page 3
Websites
Raines Law, Wikipedia

Wine and Outhouses

Page 118

Articles
Charged With Storing Liquor, *Richmond Times-Dispatch*, December 9, 1916, page 7
Peatross Backs Up Bachelors' Ruling, *Richmond-Times Dispatch*, December 14, 1916, page 10
He Skips Bail, *Richmond-Times Dispatch*, May 5, 1917, page 7
Hatcher is Relieved of Serving Jail Time, *Richmond-Times Dispatch*, September 19, 1917, page 10
Protest Against So Many Pardons, *Bismarck Daily Tribune*, December 18, 1911, page 7
James Kelly Is Free Man, *Bismarck Daily Tribune*, May 11, 1912, page 10
No headline bit piece, *Western Liberal*, December 29, 1899, page 2

Pope Leo XIII's Endorsement of Cocaine Wine   Page 120

Articles
Rerum Novarum, *Papal Encyclicals Online*, May 15, 1891
His Holiness Pope Leo XIII Awards Gold Medal, *The Washington Times*, April 17, 1900, page 3
A Day With the Pope, *Washington Evening Star*, September 3, 1900, page 23
Daily Habits of Pope Leo, *The Virginia Enterprise*, September 6, 1901, page 7
Darryl Mason, The Pope Who Loved Cocaine, *Your New Reality,* July 25, 2009
David Pearce, Vintage Wine, *The Hedonistic Imperative*, undated
Websites
University of Buffalo, *Before Prohibition: Images from the Pre-Prohibition era*
VIN Mariani, Wikipedia

Salvaging Wine From the Sea   Page 123

Articles
Forgot the Diver, *Rock Island Argus*, July 6, 1897, page 2
Liquid Treasure Trove, *New York Tribune*, July 26, 1905, page 1
Ship Can't Salvage Wine, *North Platt Tribune*, May 7, 1912, page 7
Wine Cast Up By Sea Will Be Sold By U.S., *Washington Times*, August 25, 1917, page 12
Alasdair Wilkins, World's Oldest Wine and Beer finally Drunk, Archeology of Booze, *109 We Come From the Future*, November 21, 2010
Rebecca Gibbs, 1735 Shipwreck Wine for Sale, *Wine—Searcher*, April 18, 2013

The White House Basement Wine Racks   Page 126

Articles
The White House – The modern White House, undated
Non Public Areas: The Basement, *Mr. Lincoln's White House*, undated
Where the President Lives, *Omaha Daly Bee*, June 5, 1892, page 17
Gossip and Stories About Prominent People, *Omaha Daly Bee*, June 5, 1892, page 17
Mary Brigid Barrett, A Taste of the Past: White House Kitchens, Menus, and Recipes, *Our White House*, undated
Websites
United States Presidential Election, 1888, Wikipedia
United States Presidential Election, 1892, Wikipedia
Tom's Inflation Calculator, www.halfhill.com
The White House—The Modern White House, Presidentprofiles.com, undated

More Presidential Wine Stories

Articles

They Worked for Presidents, *Deseret Evening News*, March 3, 1894, Part 2, page 12

Wine Bottles and Hollywood Props, Bergman and Grant

Books
Francois Truffaut, *Alfred Hitchcock—A Definitive Study* (New York: Simon & Schuster, 1967)
Articles
Janet Maslin, Ingrid Bergman and the Enduring Appeal of 'Notorious,' Film Review, *New York Times*, October 26, 1980
Websites
Nuremberg Trials, Wikipedia
Notorious (1946 film), Wikipedia
Notorious Kiss, Wikipedia
Notorious Script-Dialogue Transcript

Whale and Dog Meat

Articles
Meatless Days? ---What About the Whale, the shark, the Sparrow or the Eel? *Washington Times*, February 10, 1918, page 4
A Whale of a Meal, *The Bismarck Tribune*, April 28, 1919, page 7
Whale Meat From Vancouver Used in German Hamburgers, *Columbia Evening Missourian*, August 19, 1921, page 6
Whale Meat All Right in War Time, Not in Peace, *Richmond Times-Dispatch*, July 11, 1920, page 3
May Establish Whale Herd, *Bemidji Daily Pioneer*, February 5, 1920, page 7

A Glass of Tokay and the Baby's Rattle

Articles
Dying For Its Master, *Northern Pacific Farmer*, November 20, 1884, page 2
Websites
Cattaraugus, New York, Wikipedia

Torrents of Italian Idioms

Articles
One "Oasis" Here U. S. Can't Touch, *Philadelphia Evening Public Ledger*, October 29, 1919, page 2
No Wine For Meals, Latin Sailors Kick, *New York Sun*, January 21, 1920, page 20
Italian Crew Storms When Liquor Runs Out, *Washington Evening Star*, February 21, 1921, page 9
Arthur Brisbane, Today, *Washington Times*, October 14, 1922, page 1
Ritter's Pungents, *St. Joseph Observer*, November 11, 1922, page 6

Vodka and Holy Water

Books
Catherine Gildiner, *Too Close To The Falls* (Toronto: ECW Press, 1999) pp 296-303
Articles
Kevin O'Donoghue, Holy Water in a Vodka Bottle, *Peace Corps*, undated
Websites
Sanctuary of Our Lady of Lourdes, Wikipedia
Lourdes Cures and Miracles, Wikipedia
Catherine Gildiner, Wikipedia

The Wine Brawl

Articles
Crew Fought Hard for Wine, *New York Sun*, November 25, 1902, page 4
Websites
Charles Gounod, Wikipedia
List of Compositions by Charles Gounod, Wikipedia

Chicken and Wine

Articles
Wine Aids Chickens, *Yale Expositor*, November 30, 1911, page 6
Chickens Get Soused on Wine, *The Crittenden Record-Press*, February 11, 1909, page 6
The Cat and Its Adopted Chicken, *St. Paul Daily Globe*, January 31, 1883, page 2

Duel Purpose Wines

Books
Joseph Hamilton, *The Dueling Handbook* (published 1829), pp 62-63
Articles
Terms of Honor, *The Louisiana Democrat*, December 18, 1867, page 1
R. J. and A. W. Bodmer, Can You Tell, *Evening Public Ledger*, July 25, 1922, page 12
As a Measure of Precaution, *The Owosso Times*, October 14, 1921, page 6
A Duel About a Widow, *The Orangeburg News*, September 7, 1872, page 2
The German Student and His Duel, *The Times and Democrat*, September 5, 1911, page 3
Duel With Knives Between Girls, *The Sedalia Weekly Bazoo*, May 28, 1889, page 3

Wine Bricks

Articles
What Really Happened During Prohibition, *WineFolly.com* July 2, 2014
Kelsey Burnham, Prohibition in Wine Country, *Napa Valley Register*, April 18, 2010
Bev Stenehjem, Prohibition-Wine Bricks, *Morgan Hill Times,* undated
Eric Hwang, About the Title, *Bricks of Wine*, undated http://bricksofwine.com/about/about-the-title/
Reid Mitenbuler, Prohibition and Wine's Darkest Hour, *Serious Eats*, May 1, 2013
What Did the Catholic Church Use for Altar Wine during Prohibition, *The Straight Dope*, June 14, 2001,

Daniel Okrent, 'Medicinal' alcohol made mockery of Prohibition, *Los Angeles Times*, May 18, 2010, page 8
Websites
Tom's Inflation Calculator, www.halfhill.com

Roasted Peacock and Carp Tongue Pie   Page 158

Articles
An Old-Time Christmas, *The Abilene Reflector*, December 25, 1884, page 6
Christmas Cheer, *St. Paul Daily Globe*, December 25, 1886, page 10
Roasted Peacock, *The Pacific Commercial Advertiser*, February 2, 1888, page 3
Some Old Time Appetites, *Hartford Republican*, March 0, 1906, page 7
Charles Cristadoro, Birds and Clams Under a Magnifying Glass, *San Francisco Call*, March 3, 1912, page 26
Elizabethan Cooking Recipes, *The Citizen*, July 13, 1916, page 6

Wine and the Best Fellow on the Ship   Page 161

Articles

Fred L. Young, An Aeronaut, *The Hartford Republican*, October 17, 1913, page 3

Wattles and Bottles   Page 164

Articles
Kate Field's Gastronomic Suggestions, *The Anaconda Standard*, January 5, 1891, page 8
Burglar Prefers Edibles to Jewels, *St. Louis Republic*, December 27, 1903, Part II, page 13
Crew Faces Death When Submarine Breaks Record on her Trial Plunge, *Chicago Day Book*, May 8, 1912, page 30
Websites
USS F-1(SS 20), Wikipedia

A Bad Day for Bootleggers   Page 167

Articles
Two Rum Running Vessels Caught by Dry Flotilla, *New York Evening World*, September 15, 1922, page 3
Three More Die of Poison Hooch; Fourth Victim Dying, *New York Evening World*, September 16, 1922, page 3
Booze Is Seized in Dry Raid on Mori Restaurant, *New York Evening World*, September 16, 1922, page 3
His C2H5 at $468 a Cask Dwindles to H2O Worth $0, *New York Evening World*, September 16, 1922, page 3
Margaret Mooers Marshall, Wild Rose's Loveliness Is "Miss America's," Most Beautiful Girl in America, *New York Evening World*, September 16, 1922, page 3
Websites

Tom's Inflation Calculator, www.halfhill.com
Mary Catherine Campbell, Wikipedia

A Thanksgiving Gone Wrong   Page 169

Articles
Enterprising Caterers, *Deseret Evening News*, November 24, 1904, page 2
Feasting and Athletics, *Deseret Evening News*, November 24, 1904, page 2
Wine Against Death, *Palestine Daily Herald*, November 28, 1904, page 5

When a "Cup of Joe" replaced a Glass of Wine   Page 172

Articles
Danielized Glassware of Navy Auctioned Off, *Washington Herald*, November 9, 1916, page 2
A Hundred Years Dry: The U. S. Navy's End of Alcohol at Sea, *USNI News*, July 1, 2014
The Navy is Dry, *The Watchman and Southron*, July 4, 1914, page 6
No More Drinks on U. S. Warships, *New York Tribune*, April 6, 1914, page 1
Navy Department: Wine Mess Abolished, *The Commoner*, April 1, 1914, page 6
Websites
Alcohol in the Navy, 1794-1935, *Naval History and Heritage Command,* March 26, 1996

Yellowstone's First Champagne Dinner   Page 175

Articles
The River, *Bismarck Tribune*, May 5, 1882, page 5
Ken Robison, Captain Grant Marsh: King of Montana River Navigation, *Historical Fort Benton*, August 11, 2008
The Yellowstone Fight, *The Benton Record*, July 21, 1876, page 3
Websites
Yellowstone Riverboat History, 1873, (last revised 2008)
Grant Marsh, Wikipedia
Yellowstone National Park, Wikipedia

President Grant: Wined and Dined in Nagasaki   Page 178

Books
Ulysses S. Grant, *Personal Memoirs* (New York: C. I. Webster, 1885-republished Modern Library, 1999), pp 101-106
Donald Keene, *Emperor of Japan: Meiji and his World 1852-1912* (New York: Columbia University Press, 2002) pp 311-317
Articles
A Japanese Bill of Fare, *Dodge City Times*, September 20, 1879, page 2
General Grant's Arrival in San Francisco, *The True Northerner*, September 26, 1879, page 2
Ten Years From Penury to Fame, *San Francisco Call,* January 10, 1897, page 17
Gen Grant's Ring Lost, *The Hawaiian Gazette*, November 8, 1912, page 3
Websites
Post-presidency of Ulysses S. Grant, Wikipedia
Ulysses S. Grant, Wikipedia
Tom's Inflation Calculator, www.halfhill.com

Roast Pig and Wine

Articles
Hoboes Feast From Grave, *The Bourbon News,* April 29, 1913, page 7
Tim Bought the Pigs, *Bismarck Weekly Tribune*, January 7, 1887, page 6
Ancient and Modern Wealth, *Orleans County Monitor*, August 18, 1879, page 1
Christmas Day in Vendome, *The Wichita Daily Eagle*, December 29, 1901, page 11
Websites
Tom's Inflation Calculator, www.halfhill.com

A Ham Sandwich and Glass of Wine With Mrs. Davis Page 184

Books
Joan E. Cashin, *First Lady of the Confederacy*, (Cambridge: Harvard University Press, 2006)
Articles
A.W.C., Beauvoir, *Wheeling Daily Intelligencer,* May 5, 1883, page 1
Websites
Jefferson Davis, Wikipedia
Varina Davis, Wikipedia

"Diamond" Jim Brady's Stomach Page 187

Articles
H. Paul Jeffers, *The Chef From Hell*, Diamond Jim Brady, October 15, 2013, unpaginated
David Kamp, Whether True or False, A Real Stretch, *New York Times*, December 30, 2008
An Overworked Stomach, *Arizona Republic*, May 14, 1917, page 4
Gives Wealth for Appetite, *Hays Free Press*, September 14, 1912, page 2
Diamond Jim Brady, *History Spaces*, July 19, 2012, unpaginated
Man Has $500,000 Stomach, *Colfax Chronicle*, January 4, 1913, page 2

Websites
Diamond Jim Brady, Wikipedia

Give Back in Logan, Iowa Page 190

Articles
Secret Service Men at Logan, *Denison [Iowa] Review*, February 11, 1920, page 1
Logan People Pay $2,000, *Denison [Iowa] Review*, April 21, 1920, page 5

The King's Gift Page 192

Books
Leslie Smith Dow, *Anna Leonowens: A Life Beyond the King and I* (Nova Scotia: Pottersfield Press, 1991)Anna Leonowens, *Anna and the King of Siam* (London: Trubner & Co., 1870)

Articles
Free Beer Distributed by the King of Siam, *San Francisco Call*, September 22, 1907, page 23
Websites

Bad Homburg vor der Höhe, Wikipedia
Tom's Inflation Calculator
The King and I (1956 movie), Wikipedia
The King and I, Wikipedia
Chulgalongkorn, Wikipedia

Wine Orgy on the British Coast   Page 195

Articles
Wine Strews Shore, Natives Hold Orgy, *Saint Paul Globe*, January 23, 1905, page 8

Did a Glass of Wine Cause the Civil War?   Page 197

Articles
One Glass of Wine, *Atlanta Constitution* (as reported in the *Bourbon News*), April 7, 1899, page 8
Websites
1860 Democratic National Convention, Wikipedia
1860 Republican Convention, Wikipedia
Herschel V. Johnson, Wikipedia
Howell Cobb, Wikipedia
Henry R. Jackson, Wikipedia
Tom's Inflation Calculator, www.halfhill.com

Hiding Out in a Wine Cellar   Page 200

Books
Pat O'Brien, *Outwitting the Hun: My Escape From a German Prison Camp,* (New York: Harper and Brothers, 1918) Gutenberg Free Press
Articles
O'Brien, Patrick Alva MC, *Clickerty Click*, 66 Squadron, RFC and RAF, 1916 to 1919, unpaginated
Pat O'Brien, Outwitting the Hun, Chapter XIII, *Yale Expositor*, September 12, 1918, page 3

Off With Their Reds: Wine and the Guillotine   Page 203

Articles
Europe, *The Charleston Daily News*, March 2, 1870, page 1
Murat Halstead, The Guillotine, *New Ulm Weekly Review*, November 6, 1878, page 2
Horrors of the Guillotine, *Virginian-pilot*, September 22, 1900, page 11

The Béchamels and Grand Constance

Books
Harriet Anne De Salis, *The Art of Cookery, Past and Present* (London: Hutchinson & Co, 1898), 67
Articles
The Inner Man, *Hawaiian Star*, April 18, 1893, page 3
Linda Stradley, Sauces—History of Sauces, Béchamel Sauce, *Whatscookingamerica.net*, 2004
Concerning Eating and Drinking (from the *Pittsburg Bulletin*), The Story of Two Famous Epicures (from the *San Francisco Argonaut*), *Current Literature Magazine*, September-December 1893, Page 68
Jill Baikoff, The *Extended History of Vin de Constance*, December 1990
The Five French Mother Sauces, *Stella Culinary*, undated
Websites
Louis Béchamel, Wikipedia
Boela Gerber, The Story of Grand Constance, *Conca.com.*

A Sodden, Not Solemn Procession

Articles
A National Disgrace, *Dalles Daily Chronicle*, March 12, 1891, page 1
A National Scandal, *The Advocate*, April 22, 1891, page 7
People And Events In Washington, *The Morning Call*, April 11, 1891, page 8
Websites
Tom's Inflation Calculator, www.halfhill.com
George Hearst, Wikipedia

A Rigorous Stiff

Books
George van Skal, *The History of German Immigration in the United States and Successful...*, page 256
Articles
Married in His Coffin, *New York Sun*, January 31, 1886, page 9
Flagellation of Christ, *Memphis Appeal*, May 8, 1887, page 11
A Dead Bridegroom, *The Arizona Champion*, March 14, 1891, page 1
Websites
Bartolomé Esteban Murillo, Wikipedia
Tom's Inflation Calculator, www.halfhill.com
Email correspondence
Kimberly Sissons, Collection Mgr., Krannert Art Museum, Champagne, Ill. August 18, 2014.
Dr. Peter Cherry, Trinity College, August 18 and 22, 2014

The Dog in the Wine Cellar

Articles
St, Francis Hotel a Prey to Fames, *Weekly Arizona Journal-Miner*, April 25, 1906, page 3
S. S. Olympia, St. Francis Hotel Like a Cradle, *The Hawaiian Star*, May 3, 1906, page 7
F. Schnack, When the Hotel Became Stationary, *The Hawaiian Star*, May 5, 1906, page 5
A Little Dog Passes Safely Through the Fire, *Pacific Commercial Advertiser*, June 8, 1906, page 3
Charles A. Fracchia, St. Francis Hotel, *Encyclopedia of San Francisco*, 2003
Mike Gerrard, Ten Historic U.S. Hotels, *Huffpost Lifestyle*, November 5, 2014
Websites
The Westin St. Francisco, Our History
1906 San Francisco Earthquake, Wikipedia

Chariots of Wine

Articles
Dorando's Wine Theory Does Not Hold Good, *Deseret Evening News*, January 23, 1901, page 10
Hayes Defeated, *Newport News Daily Press*, November 27, 1908, page 7
Simon Burton, How Dorando Pietri lost the race but won the hearts of millions, *The Guardian*, February 29, 2012
Websites
Dorando Pietri, Wikipedia
Irving Berlin, Dorando Lyrics (March 1909), Wikipedia

Horsemeat with a Fire Chaser

Books
William Potter Trotter, ed., *A Quarter Race in Kentucky*, Geo W. Kendall, Esq., of the *New Orleans Picayune*, Bill Dean, the Texan Ranger (Philadelphia: T. B. Peterson and Brothers, 1854) pg 122
Articles
The Culinary Art in the Texas Prairies, *Jeffersonian Republican*, July 23, 1846, page 1
Websites
Mexican-American War, Wikipedia
Henry Kinner, Wikipedia

Mormon Dixie Wine

Articles
Dennis Lancaster, *Dixie Wine* undated
Thomas Hall advertisement, *The [St. George] Union*, July 12, 1878, page 4
Was It Jim-Jams, *Salt Lake Herald*, June 23, 1883, page 8
Utah's Dixie and Its Resources, *Salt Lake Tribune*, September 20, 1909, page 3
Ogden Journals, *The Coalville Times*, September 6, 1907, page 4
He Knew, *Goodwin's Weekly*, January 27, 1917, page 1
Wesley P. Larson, Toquerville, *Utah History Encyclopedia*, undated

The Case of "Handsome" Handly's Case of Wine   Page 224

Articles
Officer Crowley Got "Handsome" Handly's Case of Wine, *San Francisco Call*, June 27, 1900, page 12
Websites
Sliced Bread, Wikipedia
Police Car, Wikipedia

A Sumptuous $15.00 Demise   Page 227

Articles
Luxurious Dying for $15.00, *The [Lincoln, NB] Courier*, February 23, 1901, page 8
Websites
Tom's Inflation Calculator, www.halfhill.com
Little Italy, Manhattan, Wikipedia

The Two Cask Getaway   Page 230

Articles
Remarkable Escapes, *The New Bloomfield, PA Times*, November 30, 1880, page 1
Websites
Edinburgh Castle, Wikipedia
Alexander Stewart, Duke of Albany, Wikipedia
Gascony, Wikipedia
Armagnac, Wikipedia
Vin de Pays, Wikipedia
Earl of Mar, Wikipedia

Is There Wine in the Afterlife   Page 233

Books
Arthur Conan Doyle, *The Wanderings of a Spiritualist*, (London: Hodder and Stoughton Ltd, 1921), pages 17, 23
Articles
W.P. Crozier, The Growth of Spiritualism in England, *Dearborn Independent*, September 18, 1920, page 10
Cocktails Aplenty Just Beyond Vales, Says Doyle, *New York Tribune*, May 24, 1922, page 8

Bismarck's Drinking Habits   Page 236

Articles
Bismarck is Superstitious, *Northern [Michigan] Tribune*, October 18, 1883, page 3
Bismarck's Great Capacity, *Omaha Daily Bee*, April 2, 1890, page 5
A Physical and Mental Wonder, *The Wichita Daily Eagle*, April 11, 1890, page 7
Just What Bismarck Drinks, *The Sunday Herald and Weekly National Intelligencer*, June 20, 1890, page 4
Credulity of Great Minds, Washington Evening Star, Dec 6, 1902, page 26
Prince Bismarck's Appetite, *Washington Evening Star,* July 2, 1904, page 3
The Bouquet of Wine, *Salt Lake City Broad Ax*, October 8, 1910, page 3

Bismarck Was Superstitious, *Earlington [KY] Bee, May 23, 1911, page 2*
Bismarck's Wine Thirst, *The Ward County Independent*, September 25, 1919, page 11
Websites
Otto von Bismarck, Wikipedia

A Tough Night For Saloons and Cops   Page 239

Articles
Turns Thief for Revenge, *San Francisco Call*, December 23, 1901, page 10
Young Man Shot By Irate Fruit-Dealer, *San Francisco Call*, December 23, 1901, page 10
Patron of Placer County Man is Shot Down, *San Francisco Call*, December 23, 1901, page 2
Attacks a Man Who Wouldn't Drink, *San Francisco Call*, December 23, 1901, page 2

Wine as a Tactical Weapon   Page 242

Articles
Paris, *New York Tribune*, April 28, 1901, page 4
Paris Notes, *New York Tribune*, October , 1907, page 4
A French Wine Grower Got Best of Germans, *The Hartford Herald*, November 10, 1915, page 2
To Give Dinner Thursday, *Washington Times*, February 26, 1917, page 7
A Picture, *New York Tribune*, February 10, 1918, page 8
Random Impressions in Current Exhibitions, *New York Tribune*, April 13, 1919, page 7
Websites
Louis Aston Knight, Wikipedia
Louis Aston Knight Art, Wikipedia
Fère-Champenoise, Wikipedia

Outing a Fire With Wine   Page 244

Articles
Italian Life at North Beach, *San Francisco Morning Call*, August 13, 1893, page 17
The Maestro, *The San Francisco Call*, December 22, 1903, page 8
Telegraph Hill May Echo With Wail of Duels, *San Francisco Call*, March 13, 1901, page 4
The Great Calamity (continued from page 1), *The Leavenworth Echo*, April 27, 1906, page 4
Fire Divorce Granted, *The New York Evening World*, May 1, 1906, page 11
Websites
Lillian Hitchcock Coit, Wikipedia
Telegraph Hill, San Francisco, Wikipedia

French Laundry Wine Heist Solved Page 247

It Was Red, *Los Angeles Herald*, July 2, 1890, page 5
Caught by Clairvoyance, *New York Sun*, April 4, 1901, page 2
Good Detective Work, *Omaha Alliance Herald*, December 19, 1902, page 5
Stole the Plaza's Wine, *New York Evening World*, May 27, 1912, page 10
$50,000 Theft of Liquor at Leiter Country Home, *Washington Evening Star*, October 10, 1921, page 3
Millionaire Robbed, *Philadelphia Evening Public Ledger,* May 26, 1922, page 1
Paola Luccheci, The French Laundry Victimized by Christmas Day Wine Heist, Inside Scoop, *San Francisco Chronicle*, December 28, 2014, , page 3
Kristen Bender, $300,000 in Fine Wine Stolen from Famed Restaurant Recovered, *Associated Press*, January 23, 2015
Randi Rossman, Stolen Wine Recovered on East Coast, *The Santa Rosa Press Democrat*, January 23, 2015, page 1
Julie Johnson, Stolen Wine Ended up with Unsuspecting Buyer, *The Santa Rosa Press Democrat*, January 24, 2015, page B2
Julie Johnson, Indictment in Wine Heist, *Santa Rosa Press Democrat*, April 30, 2016, page 1
Websites
The French Laundry
French Laundry Wine List
Tom's Inflation Calculator

Mark Twain and Booze Page 250

Books
Mark Twain, *Wit and Wisdom of Mark Twain, a Book of Quotations* (Mineola: Dover Publications, Inc., 1999)
Mark Twain, *Autobiography of Mark Twain*, Volume 2, edited by Benjamin Griffin and Harriet E. Smith (Berkeley: University of Berkeley press, 2013)
Articles
Filler at bottom of page "The original Tom Sawyer…", *Jonesborough Herald and Tribune*, November 24, 1892, page 4
The Drink of Great Men, *The Indiana State Sentinel*, April 19, 1893, page 10
Mark Twain's First Lecture, *The [South Caroline] Anderson Intelligencer*, September 4, 1887, page 4
Drinks of Germans, The Real Cure, *The Washington Evening Star*, October 16, 1902, page 20
Mark Twain's Dream, or, Why He Patented Himself, The Spokane Press, February 15, 1908, page 2
Cork's Buy Books, *The Topeka State Journal*, November 27, 1912, page 1
Robert Graysmith, The Adventures of the Real Tom Sawyer, *The Smithsonian Magazine,* October, 2012

Doctored Watermelon Page 253

Article
As reprinted from the *New York Sun* in the *Seattle Post Intelligencer*, September 19, 1888, page 3

Cantaloupe Wine on the Vine

Article
Comment and Discomment, *The Alliance [Neb] Herald*, July 29, 1921, page 4
Website
The Winemaking Home Page

James Parks' Last Glass of Wine

Articles
Supposed Murder of a Stranger—evidence of foul play, *The Ohio Star*, April 20, 1853, page 2
The Murder at Cyaaoga Falls, *Portage Sentinel*, May 4, 1853, page 2
Chapter From the Life of Parks, *The Ohio Star*, May 11, 1853, page 2
Trial of Murderer Parks, *The Ohio Star*, January 4, 1854, page 2
James Parks, *The Weekly Lancaster Gazette*, January 5, 1854, page 2
Parks Sentenced, *The Ohio Star*, January 18, 1854, page 2
James Parks, *Carroll Free Press*, May 17, 1855, page 3
Execution of James Parks, *M'Arthur Democrat*, June 8, 1855, page 2
Websites
Cuyahoga Falls, Ohio, Wikipedia

Made in the USA
Charleston, SC
18 October 2016